The
Browningtown
Massacre

The Browningtown Massacre

by
Charles Hartley

Dedication

This book is dedicated to the descendants of those whose lives were forever changed by the events described here.

Table of Contents

Preface

This is a true story, at least as true as newspaper accounts and court documents can make it. All of the characters are real, all did the things described within these pages.

I have taken small liberties by inserting what I believe the people to have thought and considered at certain moments, but I believe in each case that I have been true to the person based on the overall evidence.

The trial dialogue is taken from the court transcription prepared by T. G. Chatten, official stenographer for the Bullitt Circuit Court. Other dialogue, where quoted, comes from newspaper accounts, especially those written by Don Glassman and Mary Chenoweth of *The Courier-Journal*, and Elbert Raney and Eugene Mulholland of *The Louisville Times*.

The Browningtown massacre, as it came to be known, was a social aberration, with unintended consequences, against the background of prohibition and the beginnings of depression. It cost the life of one, and changed the lives of many. This is their story.

Mistaken Blame

Lou Browning, her children and grandchildren, and her sister Kate, were staying in Willie Shaw's old barn when Sheriff Frank Monroe and a local farmer named Clarence Crenshaw came by that autumn day in 1927.

Sheriff Monroe would later tell *Louisville Times* reporter Elbert Raney that he believed the trouble in the Browningtown section resulted from county officials taking four children from Mrs. Amanda Jones, Lou Browning's daughter, and placing them in the receiving home of the Kentucky Children's Home Society in November.

According to the reporter, Sheriff Monroe went to the neighborhood with a legal process in a civil case involving a cow, and while in the area he found the Brownings living in a destitute state, huddled around a small stove in an old barn and without provisions.

He returned to Shepherdsville and conferred with County Judge Wigginton and County Attorney T. C. Carroll regarding the four children, ranging in age from eight months to seven years, and they arranged to place them in an institution.

According to the newspaper reporter, Sheriff Monroe said, "Magistrate Bolton went with me when I went for the children. They ran like rabbits, and I had to catch three of them.

"The fact that Clarence Crenshaw was with me when I first went to the place and that Magistrate Bolton was with me when I went for the children caused the Brownings to believe that these persons had been instrumental in the taking of the children, I believe.

1

The Brownings accused me and the County Judge of accepting money to take the children away from them."

Left behind were mother and grandmother, angry, bitter, and vengeful. As poor as they were, these women had at least had children to call their own. Now Amanda didn't even have that.

The Brownings

The Browning family first arrived in this place in the decade prior to the Civil War.

Sam and Mary Browning had reared a large family in rural Washington County, Kentucky in the first half of the nineteenth century. Like many families of that time, the Brownings worked by the sweat of their brows, mostly as farm laborers on the farms around them. They were poor, without land or education, and working for others was all they knew.

By the century's fifth decade many of the children were becoming adults. Of the boys, only Leroy saw fit to do anything more than work on farms. Good with his hands, he learned how to work leather and tried his hand as a shoemaker. He left home and moved westward toward Bardstown where he married Laura Fields in 1845. Meanwhile, the rest of the Brownings pulled up stakes and headed south into Barren County.

Sometime in the 1850s, Mary Browning died, either while they were still in Barren County, or after they moved north into rural Bullitt County. It was there that Sam died in May 1860 of what they then called dropsy. Physicians today would likely have diagnosed his condition as edema due to congestive heart failure.

Of their remaining children, only Elizabeth was already married, having wed a neighbor of Leroy's named John Greenwell in 1851. After their father's death, the remaining four Browning sons married in fairly quick succession.

Robert married Susan Brooks Hibbs, young widow of Solomon Hibbs, in January 1861; Joseph married Eliza Hilton the following December; John married Sarah Ash in February 1862; and William married Adaline Ash, Sarah's sister, the following September.

Of the Browning girls, we know that Martina married Luther Brown in 1868 in Nelson County. It is unclear if the remaining girls, Fanny, Nancy, or Louisa were ever married.

As the various Browning families grew, the little community took on their name, being known as Browningtown. Today, all that is left of Browningtown is a road that bears that name, a rural, twisting road that runs between Deatsville Road and Cedar Grove Road. It does serve to help us understand just where our story takes place, for it was along these roads, and the land surrounding them, that the Brownings and their neighbors lived.

Most of Sam Browning's sons had sons of their own, helping to encourage the name of Browningtown, but one exception was Joe Browning. Joe and Eliza had eight daughters, and of the eight Kate and Louisa are central to our story.

Thus, by the 1920s, there had been three and four generations of Brownings in the area, and most of them, while still relatively poor, were judged as decent, hard-working folk. Some had even managed to acquire patches of land through marriages.

The same couldn't be said of Kate and Louisa Browning. Neither married, for whatever reason, but Louisa, better known as Lou, had mothered four children. Her first was Amanda, born as the old century faded into the new, followed by Ben about five years later, and then Jerry three years later, and finally Susan who was born in October 1911, the only one of Lou's children with a birth certificate.

Amanda was almost always called Mandy, Ben was Bennie, Jerry picked up the nickname "Peachie," and Susan was called Angie for reasons perhaps known only to her mother.

Following the deaths of their parents, Kate and Lou, along with Lou's offspring, stuck together as much as possible. They survived on the odd jobs that neighbors provided, and on the generosity of those neighbors. They lived within whatever shelter they could find until they wore out their welcome and had to move on.

While their illiteracy was fairly commonplace in those days, their inability to read and write closed many doors that might have improved their situation.

And stealing the odd chicken or sneaking fruit from a neighbor's orchard certainly didn't help them in the eyes of their neighbors.

And now Lou's daughter Mandy was following in her mother's footsteps. After having one child, Mandy did marry a widower named Charlie Jones and her remaining children bore his name. However, that marriage seems to have ended in divorce.

The removal of Mandy's children by Sheriff Monroe would lead to consequences affecting the entire neighborhood before long.

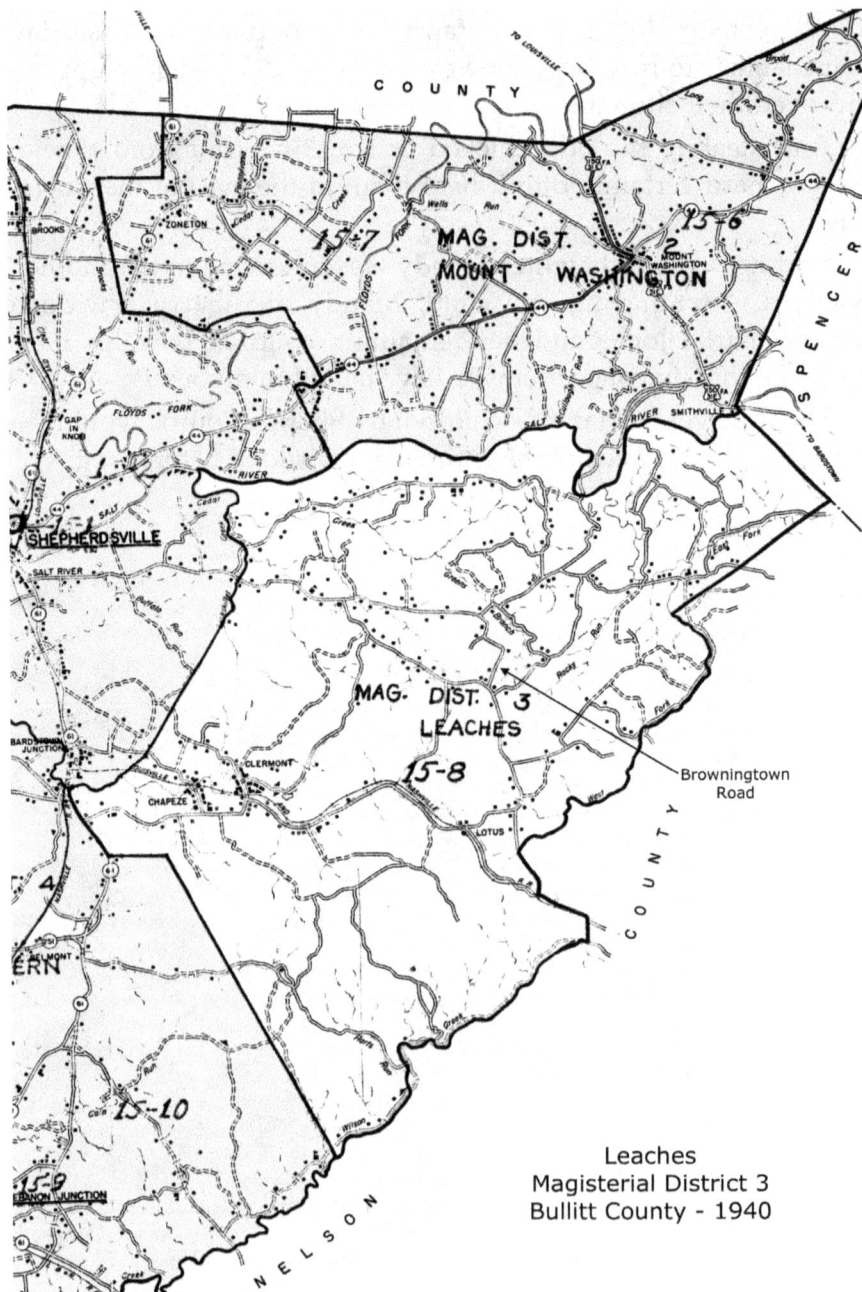

Leaches
Magisterial District 3
Bullitt County - 1940

Figure 1.

Browningtown

Browningtown lay in the northern part of the third magisterial district of Bullitt County, then known as the Leaches District. This district, shown in Figure 1, stretched southward from the Salt River and westward from the Nelson County line, and included the small communities of Clermont, Hobbs, and Lotus along the railroad tracks to Bardstown.

In an unrelated bit of history, in 1849 the Kentucky General Assembly established a voting precinct in Bullitt County at the house of Enoch Leach. Enoch had a mill nearby, making this a useful location for the polling place. Although the voting place was moved to Frank Crist's home in 1856, the name Leach's precinct remained, and was likely attached to the magisterial district as well.

Much of the district was covered with knobs (small rounded hills), and deeply cut hollows, especially in the southern and western sections. While the land encircled by Cedar Grove, Deatsville and Browningtown Roads contained fewer knobs, it was still quite hilly in most places, limiting the space available for farming. You can get an idea of the lay of the land from the section of 1949 topographical map shown in Figure 2.

The 1925 map in Figure 3 comes closest in displaying the area as it was at the time this story took place. You may wish to refer back to it as you read further.

Figure 2.

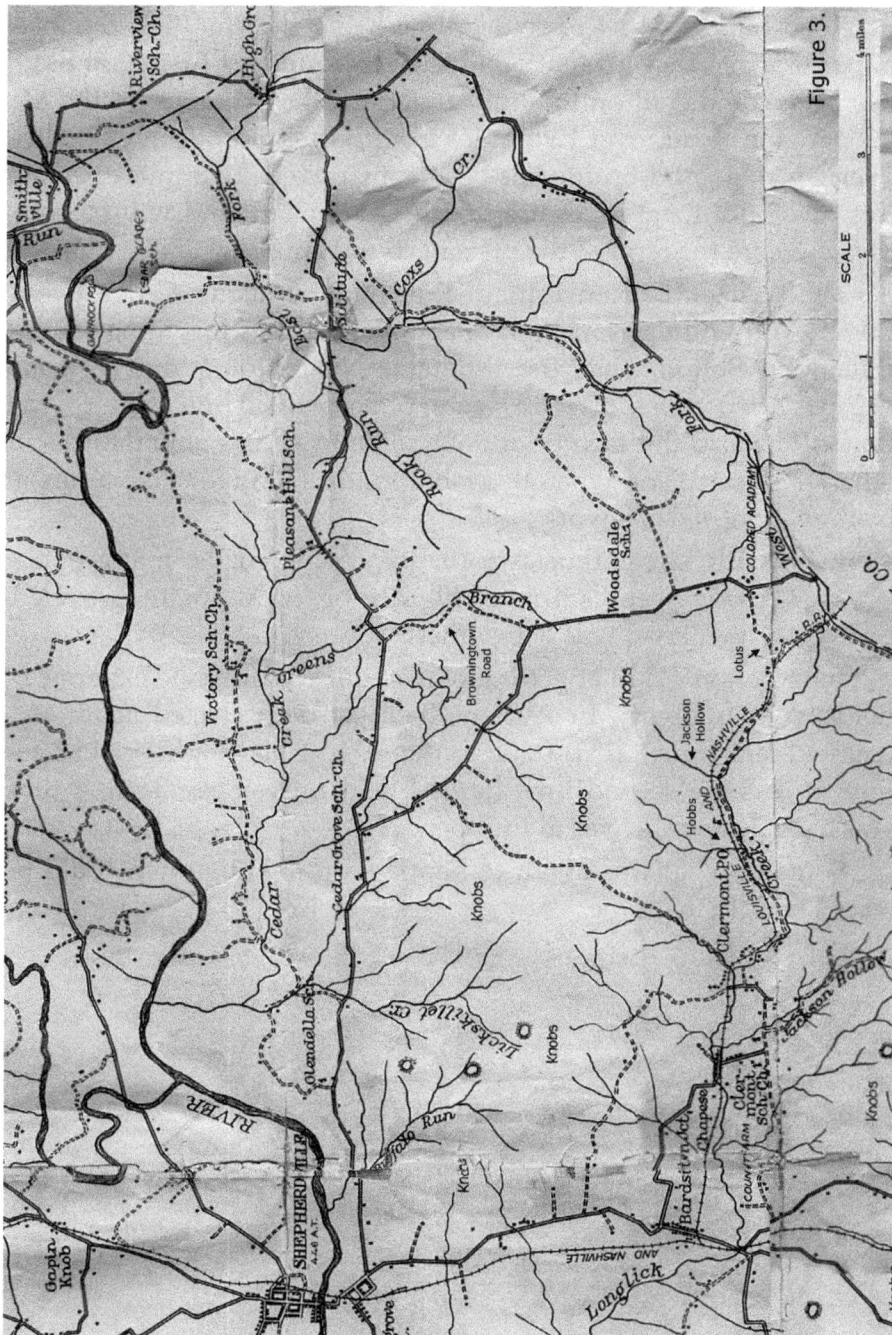

Figure 3.

Road building had perked up following the war, and the local paper bragged in 1925 that "a little over a mile [of first class road] has been completed on the Bullitt Lick Road, two miles on the Mt. Washington Road, over two miles from Buffalo Run to Lick Skillet, over which a good bridge has been constructed. Two miles beyond this, two additional miles are under construction and will be completed before the term of the present court expires."

That last part, from Buffalo Run on, was along Cedar Grove Road. With enthusiasm, the paper reported that incoming magistrate John Bolton, "has the reputation of building the best and cheapest two miles of roads ever put down in this county. Mr. Bolton has also the faculty of being able to secure abundant labor when it is scarce and when this labor follows John for nine hours, it has sure done a day's work."

Even with this enthusiasm for improving roads, many of the county's roads were still mostly dirt or occasionally graveled. Browningtown Road was one of these.

John Bolton's skill at getting roads built was just one example of his leadership ability. In 1925, he had just been elected again as a county magistrate, greatly due to the respect his neighbors had for him. It was the second time he had held this office; the first time was back during the war in Europe.

Some of what was about to happen at Browningtown could be traced back to that time.

The Previous Decade

In 1918, the war in Europe was drawing to a close, and soon European farmers would be back in their long neglected fields, and Europe could begin to feed itself again.

During the war, America had been the Allies' breadbasket, creating a larger demand from American fields, and leading to a higher level of prosperity for American farmers. Now that demand would begin to slowly taper off, eventually leaving a glutted market, and falling prices.

The one area where prices held steady was the distilled spirits industry's demand for grain. And farmers who could obtain the necessary equipment turned their excess grain into whiskey for the local market.

Today we remember 1929 as the year the stock market crashed, but for farmers, the depression started much earlier in the twenties, and their reliance on the whiskey industry was all that kept some of them afloat.

But there was a problem called prohibition.

In January 1920, the doors were locked on the distilleries and the legal sale of alcoholic beverages ceased.

What had been mostly legal during their lifetimes was suddenly illegal. The grain that had helped farmers survive and even prosper was no longer needed by the distillers whose businesses were closed.

While prohibition was popular among large segments of the population, these farmers hated it; and one by one, and in small groups they began to do something about it.

The demand for whiskey and other distilled spirits had not dwindled; if anything, making it illegal had increased the demand, a lesson the nation would eventually learn. But for now, many farmers were eager to supply the grain and even distill the illegal whiskey to survive economically.

John Bolton was one of them, even though getting caught could mean fines and even imprisonment. And caught he was; in August 1921, he was convicted of having a moonshine still in his possession. He was fined $100 and sentenced to a day in jail. The charge of manufacturing spirituous liquors was filed away with right to reinstate charges. He would be more circumspect after that.

And John was not alone. An examination of the Circuit Court docket during those years shows as many as half the cases involved prosecutions for violations of the prohibition laws. Despite the costs of operation and the large fines imposed, farmers like John Bolton and Clarence Crenshaw continued to risk arrest because the whiskey profits were all that kept some of them going.

In 1926, it was Clarence Crenshaw's turn to face moonshining charges. John Bolton was so angry about it that, upon meeting one of the witnesses against Crenshaw in Shepherdsville, he allegedly became very abusive, and was later charged with "intimidating, cursing and threatening a Government witness."

But lawlessness breeds lawlessness. Moonshiners and bootleggers, without the protection of the law, had to protect themselves as best they could, and this meant meeting violence with violence. Men who, in another time, would have respected the law and its protections, now took the law into their own hands to protect themselves.

At the same time that farmers like Bolton and Crenshaw were breaking the law to protect their livelihoods, Lou Browning's little family was having problems of its own.

Lou's two boys, Bennie and Peachie were intellectually challenged to the point that, for a time beginning in 1919, they were sent to an institution in Frankfort called the Feeble Minded Institute. At that time Kentucky had a Pauper Idiot Pension Law. The law, the only one of its kind in the nation, allowed payment of $75 per year to the families of poor feeble-minded individuals in the community. The law was repealed in 1922, ending such payments.

It is questionable how much real benefit the boys received from being there, and it appears that they had returned to Bullitt County sometime in the mid-1920s, perhaps having run away from the institute.

Kentucky birth records show that Mandy Browning had a son in 1919. She then married the widower Charlie Jones in 1922, and would have children by him. They had separated by 1926 when she charged him with desertion, and he countersued, claiming she was mentally unstable. The court sided with him, and Mandy spent a few months at the Lakeland Asylum near Anchorage before being released.

And Lou's family wasn't alone in finding ways to get in trouble. A cousin, Prather Browning was arrested for chicken stealing in 1923, and convicted.

Then the next year, while locked up in the Shepherdsville jail, Prather and a buddy named Albert Warlock sawed away several bars in their cell doors and slipped by the jailer when he brought breakfast. Their escape was short-lived, as Frank Maraman saw them fleeing, and peppered them with birdshot, bringing a halt to the adventure.

And another cousin, Ewing Browning was in more serious trouble when a warrant was sworn out in February 1928, charging him with shooting and wounding his own father.

Indeed, there seemed to be a lot of trouble up in the Leaches District; so much so that when Sheriff Monroe was first advised of a shooting there, his initial response was, "I didn't pay any attention to it because they are always having trouble up there."

But he was soon to learn that this was worse than the usual "trouble."

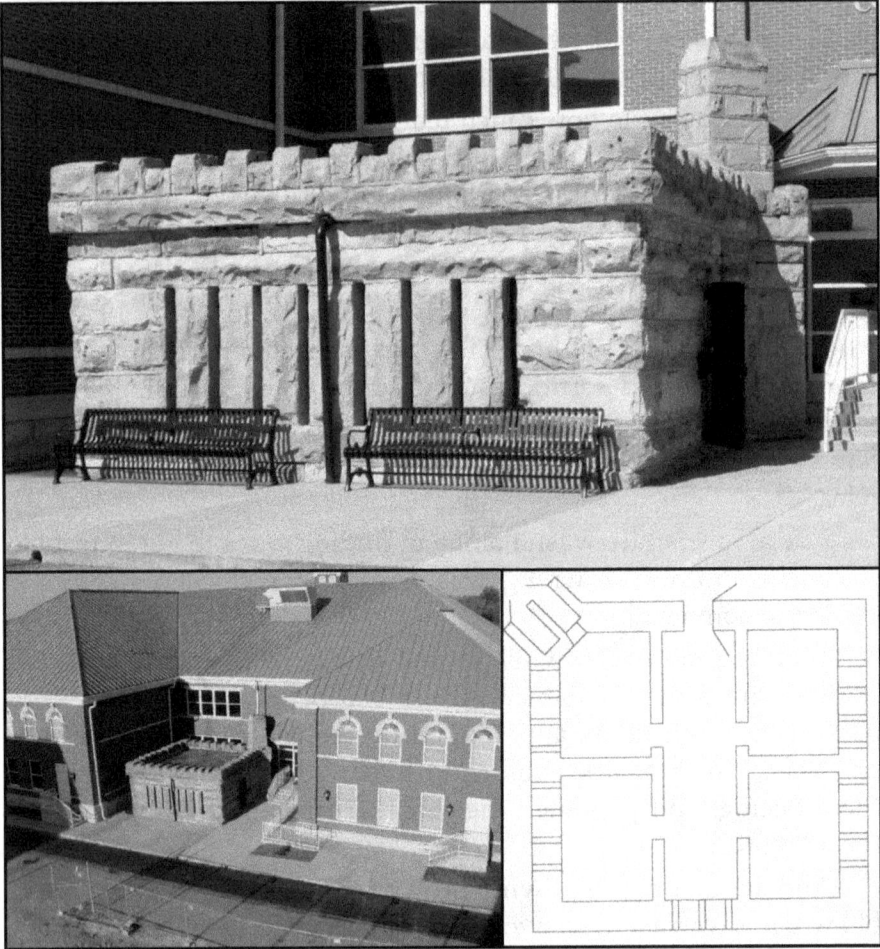

The Shepherdsville jail mentioned on the previous page was constructed in 1891 by the McDonald Brothers of Louisville. This stone structure still stands behind the current courthouse. The top picture shows its current use as a tourist attraction; the picture to the bottom-left gives a view taken from the nearby Judicial Center. Also shown is a line drawing of the basic interior of the jail.

Mandy's Revenge

After the sheriff took Mandy's children, and with winter approaching, John Bolton took pity on Lou's family and offered them a supply of lumber to build themselves shelter. The wood was mostly oak planks and cedar slabs.

Bennie and Peachie set to work constructing a rude shack on the corner of a cousin's land. It was about fifteen feet square with a single door and no windows. The roof was protected by tar paper, likely also provided by Bolton.

Mandy continued to brood over the loss of her children. At one point, as the winter thawed into spring, Lou went to Ainslee Shaw, a nearby neighbor and asked her to write a letter for her to the Children's Home, begging them to send the children home. It was to no avail.

Somehow, they scraped together a bit of money, and decided to try to get legal help in getting the children returned. On Friday morning, April 27th, they left home at the crack of dawn and walked into Shepherdsville. They went first to C. P. Bradbury's law office, seeking his help. From there they visited A. E. Funk's office. Neither lawyer felt they had a case.

Next they went to the county attorney's office and pleaded with Mr. Carroll who was unable to assist them. They even spoke with County Judge Wigginton with no success.

That evening they trudged home, disappointed and bitter.

Most Browning families had always understood that, to survive, they had to defer in most cases to their more affluent neighbors. They understood that you just didn't cause problems for these folks if you expected them to hire you.

But now, Mandy didn't care anymore. She and her mother were convinced that they were never going to see the children again and, in their minds, were sure that John Bolton and Clarence Crenshaw were to blame.

For three days, they fumed, and then they hit on a plan. If Bolton and Crenshaw could hurt them, they could hurt them right back.

The rising sun on Tuesday morning saw Lou Browning set out down the Deatsville Road toward Bardstown. It would take her several hours to reach the office of U.S. Commissioner O. W. Stanley where, after convincing him to see her, she told him about a moonshining still she knew about in Bullitt County.

Prohibition agents had been working in the hills of Nelson County, and were interested in what they might find in neighboring Bullitt. Stanley agreed that agents would come there by the end of the week.

Clarence Crenshaw's son Elmer had his still deep inside a hollow where he produced shine destined mostly for the Louisville market. He had an arrangement with a Louisville man who would take all he produced as long as it met the man's specifications. To that end, another man from Louisville was on the scene, overseeing the production.

Prohibition agents E. A. Larkin, Johnson Walker, and Frank Mather arrived at the Browning place on Friday morning, and collected Lou and Mandy to show them where the still was.

They went as far as the mouth of the hollow, and from there the three agents continued up the hollow about a hundred and fifty yards, following their noses as the smell of the mash grew stronger.

When they first saw the still, there were two men there. One of them saw the agents and escaped into the woods. The other one was Elmer Crenshaw.

They arrested Elmer, and destroyed his still.

The agents had come in two cars, and on the return trip Elmer rode with Frank Mather. On the way, they passed Lou and Mandy, and stopped to give them a ride.

On the way, they stopped by Frank Kinder's so that Elmer could send word to his father to come to Bardstown and make his bail. Then they dropped the women off and returned to Bardstown.

Later that afternoon, around four o'clock, Frank Kinder spoke with Lou about her turning in the still, and asked her if she was turning into a prohibition agent? Defiantly she replied yes, and wanted to know if he wanted to be one too.

Kinder then said, "Lou, as poor as you are, you will be damn sorry you turned this still up." He said this because he knew that the Crenshaws had always helped them, but now that was going to end.

Before nightfall, nearly everyone in the area had heard about it.

The night was partly cloudy, but the moon was full and high in the sky, so no one needed a lantern there in Hilary Hardy's field.

They had picked this location to meet for no reason other than it was convenient. Mr. Hardy was not with them, and likely didn't know they were there. He was new to the community, having just bought his farm from Paul and Margaret Roby.

A jug was passed around, as they decided just what to do about the Brownings.

Some were in favor of running them out of the valley; others suggested more drastic measures.

Jim Harris had been by the Browning home earlier in the evening, about half past seven or so according to him, but later than that according to the Brownings. He'd said that he needed one of the Browning boys to cut some wood for him.

And Frank Hodge had been there earlier in the day, after the still was raided. He said his reason for being there was to search for some meat and other items that had been stolen from Charlie Samuels' store in Deatsville.

Beyond that, there had been little contact with the Brownings until now.

As the jug continued to make the rounds, the voices got louder, and the threats stronger.

It is unclear who made the decision, but off they went down toward the Browning place. When the night was finished, the Browning home was nothing but glowing embers, shotgun shells littered the ground, and Kate Browning lay dying in a nearby thicket.

The Next Day

Lou had barely dozed before a combination of rooster's crow, early sunlight, and Maggie Biven's stirring in the house aroused her again. Suddenly it all came back to her, the fire, the shooting, escaping the burning house, and running for their lives.

Lying beside her were Mandy and Angie, still asleep finally.

The three of them had taken refuge at Charlie and Maggie Biven's home. Maggie was Aunt Bets Greenwell's granddaughter, making her a second-cousin to Lou's children. When the three showed up at their home after midnight, Maggie let them in, without asking questions.

Now it was daylight. Lou had no idea where her sons were, but she was pretty sure where her sister Kate was. She remembered Kate falling behind and then collapsing, unable to continue; and she remembered being too scared to do anything but continue on, to get away from the trouble back there at the house.

She would remember a lot more as the day wore on, but for now they were safe, and something had to be done about Kate. She awakened the girls, and they left Maggie's house without breakfast.

Instead of going to locate Kate, they went to Charlie Browning's house. Charlie was Uncle John's son and Lou's first-cousin; moreover, he was someone that other members of the Browning clan often turned to in times of need.

Charlie went down to the thicket about fifty yards from the burned-out house and found Kate who was still alive, but just barely. Her chest was a bloody mess, as was her face. He sent word back to the house to tell Lou that Kate was dying and she should come there.

By the time that Lou and the girls arrived, others in the neighborhood were already there including Henry Browning's wife and Dena Browning.

It was chilly and it had started raining lightly by the time they arrived.

Lou left and went to Henry Browning's house to find someone to call for help. While she was gone, Kate died.

Word was sent to Shepherdsville and more than an hour later Sheriff Monroe, County Attorney Carroll and Coroner C. A. Masden arrived. By this time a fair size crowd had assembled, perhaps as many as fifteen or twenty according to the sheriff's estimate. Among those he later noted were Clarence Crenshaw, Selby Hodge and Frank Kinder.

A coffin was sent for, and while they were waiting for it to arrive several began digging a grave in the nearby cemetery, while others, including Clarence Crenshaw, worked to clean Kate up and prepare her for burial.

While all this was happening, Peachie Browning showed up at the grave site while the hole was being dug. He said he had spent the night at Jim Campbell's place. Several of the men there would later report that Peachie made some claim of having shot someone the night before.

No one had yet seen Bennie Browning, and some feared that he too was dead.

Sheriff Monroe inquired around, but few had any information to share about what had happened the night before, or were willing to speak up in front of the others except for Lou and her children who said they recognized either the person or voice of ten members of the mob that had attacked them.

Monroe examined the fire site and found some spent shotgun shells in the yard.

Someone connected with the Louisville newspapers was also busy gathering information, and the first report appeared in that evening's *Louisville Times*. While, in their haste to go to press, the newspaper got several facts wrong, the paper did report on the supposed connection between the still's destruction and the events of the night before. The front page article, with the headline of "State Mob Kills Woman, Shoots 3," would be the first of numerous such articles in the weeks to come.

Then Sunday morning's *Courier-Journal* printed a report by Don Glassman, a staff correspondent, which included pictures taken of the scene of the the remaining Browning family members (See next page).

In his second paragraph, Mr. Glassman wrote, "The fire, it is alleged, was started by moonshiners in retaliation for information given by one member of the family to Federal prohibition agents of their activities."

Bennie Browning had finally returned, late on Saturday afternoon, after spending the night in Jim McClure's barn about a mile away.

The newspaper photographer had taken a picture of the family before Bennie returned, and then later inserted a picture of him with the others.

The Sunday paper also reported that C. T. Samuels, the proprietor of a general store at Deatsville, which was about four miles from Browningtown, had come to Shepherdsville seeking aid in searching for robbers who broke into his store on the previous Thursday night, stealing $150 worth of merchandise.

He said the trail of banana skins and candy wrappers led to the Browningtown neighborhood. He also said several boxes of shotgun shells had been stolen, but these were apparently not the same make as the ones Sheriff Monroe had found at the scene.

Trying to get a handle on this attack, County Judge E. J. Wigginton called for a court of inquiry to be held on Tuesday morning at Shepherdsville. Carroll planned to question witnesses already summoned by the sheriff at that time. They were hopeful that arrests would result from that inquiry.

However, things were rapidly swirling out of their hands with the Federal prohibition agents becoming involved and the newspapers eager to publicize what had happened.

And the next day would find the Feds sweeping in with their own charges and arrests.

Pictured above, beginning on the left, are Mandy Jones, Lou Browning, Peachie Browning, and Angie Browning. Bennie Browning is in the insert. They were first pictured in *The Courier-Journal*, 6 May 1928. This later image is taken from *The Austin-American* newspaper, of Austin, Texas, on 12 May 1928.

The Accused

On Sunday, in response to a perceived delay on the part of local officials to act, U.S. Commissioner Osso W. Stanley of Bardstown obtained warrants for nine individuals who he charged with conspiracy to intimidate a Federal witness.

Nine prohibition agents accompanied Sheriff Monroe and his deputies at noon Sunday to the Browningtown community and, between 2 and 5 o'clock, arrested Magistrate John Bolton, Frank Kinder, Clarence Crenshaw, Walter and Elmer Crenshaw (Clarence's sons), Frank Hodge, and James Harris. The men were lodged in the Jefferson County jail that evening.

Ironically, Frank Kinder had been in Shepherdsville on Saturday, and participated in the coroner's jury to determine the cause of Kate Browning's death.

They also sought Arthur and Selby Hodge who escaped into the hills after dropping several bottles of whiskey in their flight.

The next morning's paper reported that Ben Browning said that a man had come to their door shortly before midnight and asked him to cut some wood on Sunday. He said he returned to bed and later was aroused by someone walking on the roof, and found the house afire.

Further he said that with molten tar dripping from the roof the family rushed to the door to find it chained from the outside. He said there were thirty to fifty attackers, all firing at the victims.

Meanwhile, T. C. Carroll said Sunday afternoon that twenty people had been summoned to appear before the examining trial on Tuesday.

Feelings were running high in Shepherdsville, and a number of citizens led by J. F. Combs, Roy Stallings, and Mrs. Pearl Lee arranged a protest meeting at the courthouse, where a resolution condemning the attack on the Brownings was produced.

Others, who perhaps knew the Brownings and/or the alleged attackers, were less certain of what the truth was in this matter.

As the seven prisoners were being transferred from the Louisville jail on Monday, a newspaper photographer managed to get them to pose for the picture shown below, a clear indication that they were being cooperative.

The seven men were arraigned in Federal court, and each denied any complicity or knowledge of the crime for which they were charged. Their lawyers, C. P. Bradbury and A. E. Funk, entered pleas of not guilty before Commissioner Stanley, and bonds were set for each of the men.

Front row, left: Walter Crenshaw, Elmer Crenshaw, Jim Harris; back row: Clarence Crenshaw, Frank Kinder, Patrolman Henry C. Falast, Frank Hodge, John Bolton.

In addition to the conspiracy charge, John Bolton was charged with operating a still on the evidence that his hat was found at Elmer Crenshaw's still site.

Commonwealth's Attorney E. W. Creal of Hodgenville, who would handle the case in Circuit Court, determined that a special grand jury was unnecessary as the court of inquiry scheduled for Tuesday would serve the same purpose.

Mr. Carroll was concerned that the arrests of the seven by Federal agents would prevent him from putting them on the witness stand at the court of inquiry as he had planned in order to obtain a record of their sworn statements.

Tuesday morning's *Courier-Journal* front page headline shouted, "Price Put on Mob Members' Heads," leaving little doubt where the paper's editors stood in this case.

The paper reported that rewards of $300 apiece had been offered by the Bullitt County Fiscal Court for the arrest and conviction of additional members of the so-called mob; and Governor Sampson was urged to increase that amount with state dollars. Again ironically, John Bolton as a member of Fiscal Court voted for the resolution.

The seven already arrested were freed on bond. Walter Crenshaw's bond was guaranteed by H. J. Crenshaw, C. R. Ratliff, and Chester Pace, all of Bullitt County. Crenshaw and Ratliff also covered Elmer Crenshaw's bond. Henry Jones posted Jim Harris' bond, Mr. Funk and Sam Leroy went on Bolton's bond, and Mr. Bradbury on Clarence Crenshaw's bond.

The examining trial on the Federal charges was tentatively set for May 16 in Louisville. But first they would face Tuesday's inquiry.

At the noon recess of the court of inquiry, Commonwealth Attorney Creal announced that he would ask Judge Wigginton to issue state warrants for ten people in connection with the death of Kate Browning and the wounding of her relatives. Nine of the ten would be the nine already charged by the Federal officers, plus one more whom he did not name.

Sheriff Monroe also announced that Arthur and Selby Hodge had sent word that they would be surrendering that afternoon.

Representatives of the public and press had been excluded from the court of inquiry. The newspaper could report that Lou Browning had been the first to testify, and that Peachie Browning had been recalled several times following testimony by his brother Ben and his cousin Ewing Browning.

It also came to light that an attempt had also been made on Friday night to burn the home of Henry Browning a quarter mile away. The paper reported that Browning told Sheriff Monroe how he lay in bed Friday night hearing the shots that killed or wounded his kin, but not daring to venture out. He said the next morning he found that kerosene had been used in efforts to set fire to the home he built 32 years ago. The flames scorched the outside oak boards.

By that evening, the tenth man had been named. He was Leslie Hodge, brother of the other three Hodges.

Courier-Journal reporter Don Glassman later related an exchange between the defendants' lawyer and the prosecutors that evening regarding bail. Mr. Bradbury, who was not present during the secret court of inquiry, stated, "I take it you gentlemen have heard enough evidence to know that this is a bailable case."

After the judge and prosecutors refuted that contention, Bradbury continued, "You have no proof that any one person committed the murder."

He was informed that murder and arson warrants had just been issued for the arrest of his clients. He told Sheriff Monroe it would not be necessary to make the arrests Tuesday night as the men would give themselves up voluntarily. "I'll phone them and they will come in," he said.

Following extensive discussion, an agreement was reached for the ten men to be formally arrested on Wednesday, and remain in custody under an examining trial on Friday.

Following the inquiry on Tuesday, the Brownings voiced a fear of returning to their neighborhood, and W. N. Simmons of Shepherdsville gave them shelter in a house in town.

Early Wednesday morning Sheriff Monroe left Shepherdsville to make his arrests, and met seven of them in two automobiles on their way to town to surrender as their lawyer had indicated. They were allowed to go to Bradbury's office for a consultation until noon before being jailed.

Bradbury refused to discuss the case other than to say that his clients would offer alibis. When Clarence Crenshaw said that he had plenty to tell the newspapers, Bradbury admonished him, "Not now." The lawyer then directed his clients to make no statements.

The arrest warrants had been issued based on affidavits made by Lou, Mandy, Ben, and Peachie Browning who had all testified at the court of inquiry that they recognized either the voices or faces of the ten men named in the warrants.

On Thursday morning, Arthur and Selby Hodge surrendered to Sheriff Monroe, They claimed they had been at home asleep at the time of the attack. Also, Arthur Hodge denied he was one of the men who escaped from Federal agents on Sunday.

Leslie Hodge remained a fugitive.

The Examining Trial

Early Friday morning, Leslie Hodge came to town and surrendered to the sheriff. He walked twelve miles from his home in Jackson Hollow to surrender. When questioned by the prosecuting attorneys he denied being a part of any mob violence against the Brownings. He did admit running from the Federal officers earlier in the week because he was carrying jugs of whiskey and thought that was why they were chasing him.

Two hours after his arrest, at 9:45, Judge Wigginton called the court to order and the process of swearing in witnesses began which took about 40 minutes. Then the County Attorney called Lou Browning as his first witness.

According to Elbert Raney's column in *The Louisville Times*, "Mrs. Browning said that she went to Bardstown and reported to United States Commissioner Osso W. Stanley the still where Elmer Crenshaw was arrested a week ago. She said she accompanied the Government agents to the vicinity of the still and went with them in the automobile when Crenshaw was taken to Bardstown."

According to Raney, she said that Friday afternoon Frank Kinder stopped her on the road and asked her if she had joined the prohibition men.

Her reply was "Yes, have you?"

She said that his response was "You'll be damned sorry of it."

She said that her family was warned by a boy that a mob was coming after them, and they went to bed dressed and awake.

She continued, "About 11 o'clock Harris came to the house and called for Ben. When Ben asked who it was the visitor answered 'You know who I am.'"

According to her testimony, Harris was asked to come in, but refused, and requested that Ben cut some wood for him.

Lou continued, "I told Ben to follow Harris when he left. About thirty minutes later, it must have been, we discovered the floor and roof afire. We tried to get out and the door was fastened.

"Ben chopped the door with an axe and was shot. There were about six shots fired through the door from shotguns. Peachie used the axe and was shot. Kate said 'Give me the axe.' and then she was shot in the face.

"We finally pulled the door open. Ben was the first out. The house was burning fast. We aimed to go to Henry Browning's. We had no gun and had not had one for a year and so we couldn't do any shooting.

"I saw Bolton and heard him ask Clarence Crenshaw, 'Have you shot yet?' Crenshaw said 'no, but I am getting ready.'

"I had known them a long time and knew their voices. I heard Kinder's voice but did not understand what he said. There was a big crowd. I think not all had guns, but Bolton did. The firing was rapid."

Raney continued to describe her testimony, likely condensing separate statements into a continuous dialogue.

"We went to the county road a half mile away. I heard the Hodge boys whistling for us to stop but we kept on going. Then one of them hollered, saying 'Stop, or we'll kill every one of you!'

"Frank Hodge came up and talked to Peachie. They shot at our feet with pistols. Selby Hodge was there too.

"Kate was shot once in the face in the house and once in the chest when she ran out. We got to Charlie Biven's house at 12 o'clock. Me and my girls, Amanda and Angie, stayed there. We didn't know where Kate was. The next morning Charlie Browning found her near the house where she died."

The courtroom was crowded and very quiet as Lou Browning testified.

Mr. Bradbury began his cross-examination by asking Lou if she bore ill feeling toward John Bolton, Clarence Crenshaw, Judge Wigginton, and Sheriff Monroe before this incident had occurred.

Mr. Creal objected to the question, and Judge Wigginton ruled that she could not answer as it pertained to him and the sheriff.

Bradbury then asked her if she had visited his office, along with her daughters, a week before the tragedy and told him that Crenshaw and Bolton had paid the Sheriff and Judge to get rid of Mandy's children. She said yes, but later said that money had been collected to send the children away and did not mean that there had been any corruption.

In response to Bradbury's questions, she denied she had told him she was going to get even with Bolton and Crenshaw, and denied that she had told him the day after the event that she did not recognize anyone in the mob.

She further denied that she had told five different people that she was angry with Kate Browning, and that "Kate was a mean woman and that she had to get rid of her." She also denied saying that Kate was jealous of the boys and was "making a fool of Ben."

Bradbury asked "Were you mad at Kate?"

She responded, "That's a family affair. It don't look like we would shoot ourselves and burn our own home, does it?"

When asked where they got the wood to build their house, Lou admitted that Bolton had supplied it, but insisted that he had owed her for work she had done for him years before.

Bradbury closed his cross-examination by pleading with her to tell what really happened at the house that night.

Her response was, "I told the truth."

The prosecution's witnesses continued to testify during the rest of the afternoon and into the Saturday morning session.

Lou's children each testified, collectively and individually naming alleged members of the mob from the names of the accused.

Additionally, during his testimony, Ben Browning added the name of Golden Hodge to the list.

Among the remaining prosecution witnesses on Saturday was Charlie Biven who testified that the wounded women came to his home, three-quarters of a mile from their cabin, at midnight Friday, May 4th. He said he helped dig the grave for Kate Browning.

Under cross-examination, Biven testified that Peachie Browning, in the presence of others, told him that when he came out of the burning house he had a shotgun with one shell and fired at a man who looked like Frank Kinder, who fell and called out "Oh Lordy!"

Biven also testified that Peachie said he had been to Mt. Washington and organized a mob that was going to get Frank Hodge that night.

However, when Bradbury attempted to suggest that Kate Browning and Frank Kinder were about the same size, and that Peachie might have shot his aunt, Biven said that Kate was of small stature while Kinder was a man of large build.

At the conclusion of the prosecution's case at 10:30, Saturday morning, Bradbury moved for bail to be set for the defendants, declaring that the testimony of the Browning family "was a pack of lies and there was not a word of truth to it."

He declared that there was no mob and the killing of Kate Browning was a family affair, and that Peachie Browning was the only one who fired a shot that killed anyone.

In opposition, Commonwealth's Attorney E. W. Creal declared that the crime was the worst he had seen in twenty-five years of courtroom service.

He said the evidence produced by the State was undisputed, and argued that if the Brownings were persons without funds or means to protect themselves it was all the more reason why the defendants should not be granted bail.

After listening to arguments, Judge Wigginton refused to grant bail to any of the defendants.

At noon, the defense began by attempting to establish alibis for each of the defendants.

John Bolton was the first to take the stand. He denied having anything to do with the incident, and specifically denied Mandy Jones' charge that he had shot at her, or that he had seen any of the State's witnesses who claimed he was seen at the fire.

During cross-examination, he declared that the Brownings had been making threats against him since last November when he was hired by the county to take Mandy's four children to Shepherdsville where they were sent to the Kentucky Children's Home at Louisville. He said that all the members of the Browning family had quit speaking to him since he furnished lumber with which to build their one-room home.

Clarence Crenshaw was next, and he told of traveling to Bardstown with Ewing Crenshaw to be bail for his son Elmer, and then returning home to stay that evening. He said he retired for the evening at about 8:30 and knew nothing about the fire and attack.

On cross-examination, when asked if the Brownings had been "telling things" about him for two or three weeks, answered, "For two or three years."

Next was his son Walter Crenshaw who testified that he had plowed with Jim Harris Friday afternoon and then attended a show in Shepherdsville that evening with a girlfriend. He said he later visited the local poolroom where he stayed until after 11:30. He said he stopped at Elmer Crenshaw's place on the way home to pick up a plow, and then spoke with his father before he retired about midnight.

One by one the remaining defendants took the stand and denied any involvement in the incident, and each offered testimony on where they were and what they were doing at the time it occurred.

The examining trial was adjourned until Monday, but not before Bradbury again pleaded for a bond to be set for Clarence Crenshaw whom he said had thousands of dollars worth of perishable property that needed his attention including a large number of chickens and other livestock. The prosecution objected, and Judge Wigginton denied the request.

On Monday, Bradbury called numerous character witnesses, using their testimony to support the defendants' alibis. Many of the same people would testify again when the case came to trial.

After closing arguments were heard, Mr. Creal moved that Walter Crenshaw and Arthur Hodge be released without bond and recognized to be witnesses at the upcoming trial. Jim Harris and Leslie Hodge were granted bonds of $500 each, but Hodge could not raise his, and remained in jail.

The remaining six, John Bolton, Frank Kinder, Clarence Crenshaw, Selby Hodge, Elmer Crenshaw, and Frank Hodge were remanded to jail without bond.

Meanwhile, Circuit Judge Basil Richardson of Glasgow called a special term of the Bullitt Circuit Court to convene in Shepherdsville beginning May 28 to deal with this case.

Judges & Lawyers

Judge E. Z. Wigginton

Ernest Z. Wigginton, better known as E. Z., was a native of Spencer County, born in 1874. He married Amanda Elizabeth Shanklin (called Bessie) in 1895 in Bullitt County, and they first seemed to have made their home in the Waterford district of Spencer County where we find them in the 1900 census. They later moved to the Bells Mill area of Bullitt County by 1910, where they reared their family of four boys and four girls.

E. Z., who spent most of his life as a farmer, was civic-minded, and served on the County School Board for nearly a decade before running for County Judge in 1925.

In those days, the county judge was both a judge in the courtroom and the head of county government. E. Z. was qualified to administer the government, but when he offered himself as a candidate for the judgeship, his legal knowledge was limited.

There are indications that he took at least one law course in Louisville before or just after he assumed office. And he could always count on the lawyers to see that he didn't stray too far afield on the bench.

Nevertheless, he was unlikely to have felt prepared to preside over such a case as this, even in just its preliminary steps. He was likely thankful when the examining trial was finished, and the burden of presiding over the upcoming trial was passed to Judge Richardson.

Judge Basil Richardson

Judge Basil Richardson was a native of Monroe County who had practiced law there and later in Glasgow, before being elected to the Kentucky Senate. He was then elected Circuit Judge in 1923. He was eminently qualified, having graduated from the University of Louisville Law School. His ability as a jurist was soon recognized throughout the State and beyond its borders.

His skill and qualifications would be rewarded in 1930 when he was elected to the State Court of Appeals. But for now he was tasked with overseeing an emotionally-charged case and applying the law fairly to both alleged victims and defendants.

Commonwealth Attorney E. W. Creal

Edward Wester Creal was a native of LaRue County. A former school teacher, he graduated from the law department of Centre College in Danville, Kentucky, in 1906. While practicing law, he also served as superintendent of schools of LaRue County from 1910 to 1918. He was elected LaRue County Attorney in 1918 and served under his election as Commonwealth Attorney. He was also owner and publisher of a weekly newspaper in Hodgenville.

Creal would later be elected as a United States Representative in 1935, and serve in that capacity until his death in 1943. But for now, he was involved in the biggest case of his career.

Bullitt County Attorney T. C. Carroll

Tarlton Combs Carroll, better known locally as Tot Carroll, had been Bullitt County Attorney for ten years. Born in Shepherdsville in 1889, he graduated from the University of Kentucky in 1909 and promptly entered the law school there. A year later he was a part of its first set of law graduates.

Carroll would continue as County Attorney until 1930. Then from 1941-45 he would be a member of the Kentucky Senate, as had been his father before him. He would also serve on the Kentucky State Fair Board, and serve on occasion as a special circuit judge in several other counties.

But for now, his task was to support Mr. Creal, who would lead the prosecution, and who would need Carroll's local expertise and knowledge of people.

C. P. Bradbury, Defense Attorney

Charles Preston Bradbury grew up in Leaches, a near neighbor to the Bolton family; so it was natural that John Bolton would turn to Bradbury in his time of need.

But it was more than that; Bradbury was considered, if not the best, one of the best lawyers in the county.

He had originally set out to be a teacher, graduating from a teacher's college in Ohio. By 1902 he was superintendent of the local schools here.

However, he wasn't finished with his formal schooling. Deciding to study law, he took a two year course at the University of Louisville in just one year.

Leaving the school system, he ran for county attorney in 1905 and won. He served three terms in that capacity. Then in 1917 he was elected Bullitt County Judge, and completed one term in that office before returning to private practice.

Bradbury would later serve as Bullitt County Judge twice more, with a term in the Kentucky legislature in between; but for now all his efforts and energy were focused on the trial that lay ahead.

A. E. Funk, Defense Attorney

Alverado Erwin Funk, who was best know by his middle name, had graduated from the Louisville law school in 1917. After serving in the army, he returned to the family farm for a spell before formally beginning his law practice in 1923 when he associated himself with the law office of C. P. Bradbury.

Funk ran for county attorney in 1925, but lost to Mr. Carroll. Not deterred, he would run again in 1929 and win the office.

Much later Funk would find himself involved in state government, and in 1947 he was elected Kentucky Attorney General.

Funk's dry, raspy voice and his ability to simplify the complex impressed juries; and Bradbury would count on him to question many of the witnesses in the upcoming trial.

H. L. James, Defense Attorney

Hobson L. James practiced law in Hardin County. He was well known there, especially in Cecilia where he was vice-president of a milling company. He was also a large stockholder in a local bank there.

He was asked to join the defense team partly because of his skills as a lawyer, and partly because the jury for this trial would be made up of men from Hardin County, men he likely knew well.

These then were the men who would judge, prosecute, and defend in this case. Attention would be focused almost as much on them as it was on the alleged victims and those charged in the attack.

Indictment & Jury Selection

Monday morning, May 28th, Judge Basil Richardson called the Circuit Court to order in the upstairs courtroom of the Bullitt County courthouse, and a special grand jury was selected to hear the charges against these men.

Members of the grand jury were G. A. Branham, 43, a farmer living in the Waterford area; Robert L. Bridwell, 47, a farmer on the Mt. Washington Road; Joseph R. Burchell, 55, who farmed in the Wilson Creek area; Walter C. Coakley, 34, a Lebanon Junction farmer; William B. Crenshaw, 44, another farmer from the Mt. Washington Road area; James C. Gentry, 58, a Mt. Washington merchant; Frank T. Harned, 57, who farmed near Belmont; Palmer H. Hedges, 38, whose farm was in the Zoneton precinct; Emmett F. Hornbeck, 32, whose farm was on the Lebanon Junction Road; Jesse Ridgway, 48, a third Mt. Washington Road farmer; J. E. O'Bryan, 66, whose farm was near Smithville; and Samuel B. Stephens, 59, a telephone operator in Shepherdsville.

As the grand jury's job was to determine if there was probable cause to bring indictments, they heard only from the Browning family members and Sheriff Monroe before bringing murder charges against nine men.

Charged were John Bolton, Frank Kinder, Clarence Crenshaw, Elmer Crenshaw, Frank Hodge, Selby Hodge, James Harris, Leslie Hodge, and Golden Hodge, a new defendant in the case.

Judge Richardson announced that the trial of these nine men would begin on Tuesday, at one o'clock.

Then, Tuesday morning, he called the attorneys together to examine the twenty-six members of the regular jury panel to determine if they would be qualified to serve. He was concerned that the sheriff might need to summon a larger pool of jurors.

His concern was warranted, as three of the prospective jurors were related to the defendants, and twenty others indicated that they had formed and expressed opinions in the case.

Also, because of mistakes made in the writing of the indictments, the prosecutors were required to re-write and re-submit them to the grand jury. This appeared to be a mere formality, as the grand jurors quickly re-indicted the nine men.

When the court session began at one o'clock, Mr. Bradbury informed the court that three of their witnesses had not answered witness summons, and additional time was needed to procure them. They included Tom Watts, Charles Samuels, and Mrs. Minnie McGruder.

To accommodate the defense, as well as gain time to add to the jury pool, Judge Richardson continued the case until Monday, June 4. However, the questioning of prospective jurors would continue.

Sheriff Monroe gathered sixty additional Bullitt County men to serve as the jury pool.

As questioning began, the Commonwealth indicated that they would be asking the death penalty for some of the nine defendants, and this quickly narrowed the jury pool. Juror after juror either objected to the death penalty or had already formed and expressed opinions about the case.

After the final prospective juror had been eliminated, Judge Richardson ordered the sheriff to seek potential jurors from neighboring Hardin County.

Hardin County Sheriff Richard Wilson and his deputies assisted Monroe and his deputies in summoning one hundred Hardin County men, completing the task at three o'clock Saturday morning.

Court resumed that morning and by noon only five of forty examined jurors had been accepted by both sides. They included Ben Bowles, a farmer of Cecilia; T. H. Tilford, C. C. Jeffries and Charles Morrison, farmers of Stephensburg; and John Jeffries, a stone quarry worker of Stephensburg.

Jury selection continued into the afternoon, and by evening the last juror had been selected. The additional jurors included mostly farmers with one merchant.

They were Clarence Payne, a farmer in northwestern Hardin County; Jasper Parr, of Stephensburg; Frank Tabb, a farmer from along White Mill Road; Maxie B. Payton, Hardin County farmer; James Charlton, Hardin County farmer; Ben Ailes, an automobile salesman in Elizabethtown; and Robert Skees, a Glendale farmer.

By this time, the defense lawyers had decided it was in the best interest of their clients to have all nine tried together rather than separately.

The stage was now set for the trial to begin.

Bullitt County Courthouse, circa 1909

The Trial Begins

Following their selection on Saturday, the jury members spent the night in a local hotel. They were taken to Frankfort on a sightseeing tour Sunday, and then Sheriff Monroe escorted them to the courthouse Monday morning.

In his opening statement, Mr. Carroll read the indictment to the jury, and then outlined the Commonwealth's case against the defendants. He indicated that each of the Brownings, the victims in this case, would tell in their own words the violence that had been perpetrated on them, and what they knew of Kate Browning's murder.

Mr. Bradbury spoke for the defense, indicating that his clients were innocent victims of a conspiracy, and that they would depend on alibis for their defense.

Judge Richardson then told the Commonwealth's lawyers, "Call your first witness."

Lou Browning was called to the stand and sworn in.

Mr. Creal approached the witness, and asked, "What is your name?""

"Lou Browning."

"You are a sister of Kate Browning?"

"Yes sir." Lou remembered Mr. Carroll's instruction to be polite; that is after he explained that she should always say "sir" when answering a lawyer's question.

"Were you at home the night of the fire out at your house?" Creal continued.

"Yes sir."

"Who were the persons that made up your family?"

"My son Bennie Browning, and my son Peachie and my two daughters Mandy Jones and Angie Browning and my sister Kate." she responded, counting them off on her fingers.

"Are these four, Mandy, Angie, Peachie and Bennie your children?"

"Yes ... sir." she answered, belatedly remembering the "sir."

Carefully guiding her, Creal asked, "Kate was your sister?"

"Yes sir."

"These two boys are your sons?"

"Yes sir."

"Now Aunt Lou go ahead and tell the jury just what was the first thing that you saw or heard there that night?"

Lou took a breathe, and launched into the description she had practiced several times.

"Jim Harris come to the door and called my oldest son Bennie and Bennie says 'who is that,' and he says 'you know who I am,' and Bennie says 'is that you Jim,' and he says 'yes' and then he let on like he wanted some wood cut and I told the boy to ask him how much he wanted cut and he said about a couple of cords and then he stood there a minute and says 'well I could do on one cord,' and Bennie told him that he couldn't cut it for him but that he would see Peachie and Ewing Browning and maybe he could get them to cut it for him."

She needed another breathe after saying all that, and Creal paused before continuing.

"Where was Peachie?"

"He said he was up to Bud Pugh's."

Bud was Lou's brother-in-law. He married her sister Nancy Jane who died about four years earlier.

Creal inquired, "Had your folks all gone to bed?"

"All but the boy."

"That was Peachie?"

"Yes sir."

"All the rest of you were in the bed?"

"Yes sir."

"Had you been asleep that night?"

"No sir."

To establish the time the attack occurred, Creal asked, "Did you have a watch or clock in the house?"

"No sir."

"Just what time in your best judgment was it when this fire occurred?"

"It was about twelve o'clock."

"What time was it that Jim Harris was there?"

Lou thought for a bit, and then said, "Ewing Browning and Peachie came in just a little while after that and Ewing said that it was eleven o'clock by his watch then."

Jim had already been there and gone when they were there?

Yes sir.

"How long had it been since Jim was there?"

"He hadn't left the door but just a few minutes."

"When these boys came in, did any of you people tell them that Jim had been there and wanted some wood cut?"

"Yes sir, I told Peachie about it."

Coming back around to the question of her being awake at the time of the fire, Creal inquired again, "You say you hadn't been asleep that night?"

"No sir, I don't sleep good at night like nobody else."

"Your son Bennie, had he been at home all night?"

"Yes sir."

"Was he in bed?"

"Yes sir."

"After Jim Harris left, state what your son Bennie did."

"I told him ..."

Interrupting her, Creal cautioned, "Don't tell what you told him; what did he do?"

"Got up and went out to see about Jim; we suspicioned that something was wrong."

Bradbury was quickly on his feet. "We object, your honor. What she 'suspicioned' is not relevant."

Judge Richardson agreed, and sustained the objection. "Members of the jury, you will not consider the witness's statement about what she thought."

As would be the case throughout the trial, the opposing lawyer voiced an exception to the judge's ruling. The purpose of these exceptions was to place in the court record their disagreement for the purposes of appeal.

"Did Bennie have his clothes on?" was Mr. Creal's next question.

"He laid down with his pants and shirt on because we heard this mob was coming."

Mr. Bradbury was on his feet again. "Objection, your honor! This is hear-say, and irrelevant."

"Objection sustained. The jury will disregard the last statement by the witness."

Mr. Creal was satisfied. The jury would remember the word "mob" despite the judge's ruling.

He continued, "After Jim Harris left, how long do you think it was until Peachie and Ewing came in?"

"Not very long, I can't say exactly."

"How long did Ewing stay?"

"He didn't sit down, him and Peachie come in and got the can and went to the spring and then he went home."

"What did Peachie do?"

"He went to bed."

Lou looked at him expectedly, more comfortable in front of the packed courtroom than she had been, but still fearful of saying the wrong thing.

"How long had Peachie been in bed?"

"Not but a few minutes."

"How long had Peachie been in bed before the fire?"

"Not but a few minutes." she repeated.

"Who was the first to discover the fire?"

"Me."

"What was the first that you noticed of it?"

She leaned forward on the edge of her seat, and almost shouted, "I heard a roaring and I looked up and seed the roof on fire and I hollered for Peachie and I says get up, I says the house is on fire."

Creal paused to let her words sink in with the jury before asking, "Were all the rest of the folks in the house at that time?"

"Yes sir."

"All in bed?"

"Yes sir."

You were the first one up, who was next?

Kate I think, not but a few minutes till they was all up.

Creal then asked a series of questions to established that they had gone to bed with their clothes on, all except their shoes, and that they had all left the house barefooted. Then he asked, "After you discovered the fire, what did you all do?"

"We went to the door and turned the button and tried to open it and found that it was fastened on the outside and Bennie got the ax and started chopping on the door and he got shot and Peachie says 'give me that ax' and he took the ax and begin to chop and he got shot and fell back between the beds and then Angie took the ax and chopped the door open and we all run out."

Again Lou was almost out of breathe when she finished saying all that.

"What kind of material was that door made of?" Creal asked.

"Little old oak planks and cedar slabs nailed on the outside."

Creal then turned to the question of the shooting. "The shots that were fired, where did they come from?"

"Outside."

"Shot through the door?"

"Yes sir."

"Was the door open?"

"No sir."

"How many tried the ax before you finally succeeded in getting the door open?"

"Peachie, Bennie and Angie." was the response.

Creal next asked, "Why didn't Peachie and Bennie finish?"

This time it was Mr. Funk who spoke out. "Objection, your honor. Calls for a conclusion by the witness."

Judge Richardson responded, "Objection sustained. Rephrase your question, Mr. Creal."

Creal thought for a moment, and then asked, "Angie in her chopping, I will ask you whether or not she got wounded?"

"Yes sir, they shot her here in the face when she was chopping on the door and in the back when she run out of the house."

"Were there any windows in that house?"

"No sir."

"How many rooms?"

"One."

"During the time all these people were chopping there on the door, what were the rest of you doing?"

"Just standing there in the house."

"How close were you all together?"

"Pretty close for the room wasn't very big."

"How did you finally get the door open?"

"The child kept chopping and finally split the piece off."

"How many shots in your judgment were fired during the time you people were trying to get out of the house?"

"Six." she said positively.

There were murmurs throughout the crowded courtroom, and the judge rapped for order.

"Did they sound like pistol shots?"

"No sir, they were shotguns."

As with most of her testimony, Mr. Creal already knew what her answer would be when he asked, "Did you hear anybody talking?"

"Yes sir." came the answer, boldly. Lou had gone over this testimony repeatedly with both Mr. Carroll and Mr. Creal before the trial began, and she was feeling pretty confident.

Everyone in the courtroom, including the defense attorneys, expected Creal's next question to be about those voices; but instead he inquired, "How much had the fire burned when you got out?"

Lou hesitated too, before answering, "A right smart up on the roof."

"Before you went out of the house, did you see fire any place else besides up on the roof?"

"Under the floor," she answered, looking down at the courtroom floor as she spoke; perhaps remembering the flames.

"How high was that floor off of the ground?"

There were a few chuckles when she responded, "It was high enough for a dog or a chicken to walk under there."

"How could you see the fire under the floor?"

"Through the cracks of the floor."

"How long had that house been built?"

"Not so very long, about six months."

"Who built it?"

"My two boys."

"Were the logs in the house green or seasoned?"

"They were green."

"What kind of roof did the house have?"

"Paper."

By these questions, Mr. Creal helped the jurors visualize the scene, and understand just how poor these folks were.

"What did you see when you got on the outside?"

"I saw three men standing in the corner of the yard."

"Could you see them very well?"

"I could see that they were men but I couldn't see their faces."

Returning to the anticipated topic, Creal asked, "Did you hear anyone talking?"

"Yes sir."

This time he continued with that line of questioning. "Did you recognize anybody's voice?"

The men in the jury box, leaned a bit forward, waiting for the answer.

"Yes sir, I recognized John Bolton and Clarence Crenshaw both by their talk."

Several voices were heard in different parts of the room, at least one audibly hissing "Liar!" Again, Judge Richardson rapped for order. Mr. Creal waited for the murmuring to cease before continuing.

"Did you hear what they said?"

"I heard John ask Clarence, says 'have you shot yet Clarence,' and he says 'no but I am getting ready to.'"

This awkward statement puzzled some in the room; but before they could dwell on it too long, Creal asked, "After they made that remark, I will ask you whether or not there were any more shots fired?"

"Yes sir."

"How many shots in your best judgment were fired after you got outside?"

"Two there and when we got on up there further there were more."

"Which direction did you all go from the house?"

"The oldest boy went straight and Kate and me and my two daughters and Peachie all went up by Henry Browning's barn."

"All five of you all went that way?"

"Yes sir."

"As you all went toward Henry Browning's barn, who was in front?"

"I believe Mandy was."

"If you know, who was behind?"

"I was."

"Where was Kate?"

"Walking right along there with us."

Creal could sense that the crowd anticipated his next question.

"Did you see Kate at the time she got shot?"

"Yes sir, she was shot there in the house?"

"Where was she shot?"

"Right in the face."

"After she had gotten out of the house, could you say whether she got shot any more or not?"

Lou hesitated. "I couldn't say about that, I don't know whether she did or not."

"Where did you miss Kate from your bunch?"

"Right up above the house apiece. After we got up there apiece she says 'I can't do no further, I am bound to fall.'"

Creal's questioning had slowed, allowing each answer to have its affect.

Judging that Lou's answer had its desired effect, he asked, "What did the rest of you do?"

"We kept going." She paused, then continued, "We were afraid to go back."

Seeking to insure that Lou's fear was truly felt by the jurors, he said, "I will ask you why you didn't go back to see about Kate when she said that?"

"My youngest daughter was crying and taking on and saying that she was shot all to pieces and was bleeding to death and I was scared about her and afraid to go back too."

"Where was she shot?"

"In the face and back."

"Where did you all go to?"

"Us four went on up the big road."

"What four?"

"Mandy, Angie, Peachie and myself."

"Peachie, is that the boy's name?" inquired Creal, making sure the jurors didn't get lost in the names.

"Yes sir, and somebody got to whistling to us to stop." Lou volunteered.

"At that time how far were you from the house that was burned?"

"I don't know, something like a half a mile."

"Had you passed anybody's house?"

"Yes sir, Henry Browning's."

"How far is Henry Browning's from your house."

"Right there in sight, and Dena Browning was living down there in Mr. Henry Browning's corn crib, we passed right by there too," Lou said, again volunteering more information than Creal sought.

The mention of the corn crib raised a few eyebrows. A few folks knew that Dena was Henry Browning's daughter-in-law, widow of his son Jesse who died two years earlier of pneumonia. Dena had next married Henry's son Wayne who seemed to be in and out of jail with some frequency.

Creal hurried on, asking "Say you went on past Mr. Browning's house?"

"Yes sir."

"Just go ahead and tell about somebody whistling and what happened there."

Mr. Bradbury arose to object that the question was irrelevant and immaterial to the case, but his objection was overruled.

Lou took a visible breathe, and launched into her answer.

"Selby Hodge got to whistling at us and Mandy says 'what is the matter Selby' and Frank Hodge says 'who is that' and Peachie says 'it's me Frank; I ain't going to hurt nobody; I am just looking for a place to stay all night,' and then he says 'stop there or I will kill every damn one of you right there in a pile.'"

Clarifying who said what, Creal asked, "Who was it said that?"

"Frank Hodge, he was right over the wire fence talking to the boy."

"What did he do then?"

"He began shooting across the road and then he got over the fence and he was talking to Peachie and we run."

"That was a pistol he was shooting?"

"Yes sir."

At this point the judge interrupted the questioning, and announced, "Gentlemen of the jury, the testimony of this witness relative to what occurred up there on the road is not competent; you may consider it if, in your judgment, it tends to show the motive of the defendants charged in this case. Do not regard it for any other purpose."

Continuing with his examination, Creal inquired, "After those shots were fired, where did you all go?"

"Me and Angie and Mandy went back to Mr. Charlie Biven's house and stayed the rest of the night."

"What became of Peachie, did he go back with the rest of you?"

"No sir, we never saw him anymore until the next morning."

"When you went back to Charlie Biven's, where did you leave Peachie?"

"Standing up there in the road talking to Frank Hodge, up there in the County Road."

"Then what did you all do?"

"Went and knocked on the door and called Mrs. Biven, she must have been in the bed, it took her a little while to get to the door."

"Where did you spend the rest of the night?"

"There at Charle Biven's."

Returning to Kate's murder, Creal asked, "When did you learn that Kate was dead?"

"She wasn't quite dead when we got over there next morning."

"Did you see her before she died?"

"Yes sir."

"Where was she?"

"Laying up above the house there."

"Did you see her when she said she couldn't go any further?"

"Yes sir."

"Was she at the same place, or had she been moved?"

Lou thought for a bit and then replied, "Looked to me like she was further over."

"Did she know anybody?"

"She was speechless." Lou said, meaning to say that Kate was beyond even the ability to speak.

To clarify that, Creal asked, "Did she make any statements?"

"No sir."

"Did you see whether or not she had been wounded?"

"Her eye was shot out and her breast was all shot up."

Creal paused to let that sink in among the jurors, and then said, "Who was along with you at the time she was killed?"

"Mandy and Angie and Peachie and Kate of course, that was all."

"Who was the first one down there next morning?"

"Charlie Browning was the first one that found her and Dena Browning and Henry Browning's wife had got there before I did."

Changing direction, Creal inquired, "Do you know what day of the week this fire occurred?"

"It was on Friday."

"Had you been at home all the day that the fire occurred?"

"I had went away in the evening."

"Where were you on the day before?"

Lou hesitated, obviously unsure of how to reply. In a low voice she said, "I couldn't hardly say where I was the day before."

Creal paused, and offered "On Thursday?"

"I don't know."

"You mean to say that you don't remember?"

Lou hesitated again, and then suggested "I know where I was at on Friday."

Attempting to get her back on track, Creal said, "I will ask you whether or not you made a trip to Bardstown that week?"

"Yes sir."

"Do you remember what day it was?"

"The best I remember it was Tuesday."

"What did you go to Bardstown for?"

"To tell them about that still."

"You went to make a report about a still?"

"Yes sir."

Mr. Funk half rose from his seat as he objected, saying "You honor, we object to this line of questioning. It is immaterial to this case."

Judge Richardson disagreed, and overrode the objection.

Continuing along this line, Creal asked, "Who did you make this report to?"

"I went up there and told Mr. Stanley about it."

"After you went up there and told Mr. Stanley about the still, then what did you do?"

"The man come down there and got me and Mandy and we went with them over there to the still."

"Tell what they did?"

"We went over there to the branch with them until they could trace the mash and stuff to the still and then the three men went on up there and got it."

"Do you know who they found at the still?"

Mr. Bradbury rose to object on the grounds that this really was immaterial to the case at hand. His objection was sustained.

Creal then asked, "Did you see the officers any more after they had been to the still?"

"Yes sir, we rode part of the way home with one of them."

"Was there anybody with them?"

"Elmer Crenshaw."

Was there anybody else?

"No sir."

"How come you to ride with them?"

"Come along and ask me if I wanted to ride."

Bradbury moved that the court exclude this statement from the record, and the court ruled that the jury would disregard it completely.

Coming at it from another angle, Creal asked, "Who was in the machine?"

"Mr. Frank and I don't know his other name, and Elmer Crenshaw, and Mandy was in there with me."

"Is that your daughter?"

"Yes sir."

"On your way coming and going to and from this place, did you see anybody on the road?"

"John Bolton."

Bradbury quickly declared, "Your honor, I must object! What relevance does this have to the case at hand? Move to strike both question and answer."

To which Creal responded, "It goes to motive, your honor."

Judge Richardson agreed and overrode the objection.

Creal continued to question Lou, asking "What was he doing?"

"He was up there in the field plowing."

"Did you see him going to and coming from the still?"

"Yes sir."

"Did you see anybody else?"

"Saw Frank Kinder."

"Where did you see him?"

"Up there in his field."

"Did you have any conversation with him that day?"

"Yes sir."

Mr. Funk stood up, saying "Objection your honor ..."

Before he could continue, Judge Richardson held up his hand and said, "You may be right, but I want to see where this is going before I rule on any objection."

Creal continued, "What did Frank Kinder say to you?"

"He ask me if I had joined the prohibition men and I told him yes, didn't he want to join them."

Funk again objected to the question and answer unsuccessfully.

Creal went on, "Was that the same day they caught the still?"

"Yes sir."

"What time of the day was it?"

"That afternoon about four o'clock."

"Who was there with you?"

"Mandy and Kate."

"Was there anybody else there?"

"No sir."

To clarify, Creal asked, "Any of his people?"

"His boy was there."

Nailing down the time, Creal asked again, "Do you know what time of the afternoon it was?"

"About four."

When Mr. Creal wanted to know when Lou saw Elmer Crenshaw after he was arrested at the still, she replied, "About ten the best I can remember, it wasn't dinner time."

"Did you see him anymore that day?"

"Yes sir, I saw him that evening with his daddy."

"What time was that?"

"Way late in the afternoon."

"What road were they on?"

"The Bardstown road." she said, indicating the present-day Deatsville Road.

Returning to the night of the fire, Creal wanted to know who she had seen or recognized as they escaped the house. She again mentioned the two Hodges, Clarence Crenshaw and John Bolton.

He then asked, "Where did you see the Hodge boys?"

"Up on the road."

"About how many minutes in your best judgment had it been from the time you left your home until you were held up by these two fellows up there on the road?"

"About twenty minutes I guess."

"In traveling up there could you tell us how you traveled, fast, slow or medium?"

An objection to the question by the defense was quickly overruled, and Lou answered, "Walked off from the house."

Creal next inquired, "Did anybody in your home own a shotgun?"

"There ain't been a gun there in over a year."

Pursuing the topic, he wanted to know if they had borrowed any guns, or if anyone in the house had done any shooting, to which she repeatedly answered "No sir."

Then he asked, "Anybody have anything to shoot with?"

Mr. Bradbury had had enough. "Your honor, I have to object! The question has been asked and answered."

Judge Richardson agreed, and sustained the objection.

Creal then returned to the question of who was present at the fire.

"Do you know whether there were any others there except the ones that you have named or not?"

Bradbury objected again, but this time he was over-ruled.

Lou answered, "Yes sir, there was a big crowd there, I don't know who they was."

"Did you hear anybody anywhere else?"

"Yes sir, up there on the road."

Seeing that Lou wasn't able to name any additional people, he asked, "Do you know who was the first one out when your door was opened?"

She thought for a moment, and then replied, "Bennie."

He then wanted to know, "What was the state of your feelings toward Clarence Crenshaw and John Bolton and your family, good or bad?"

"I didn't like them so well, of course I worked for both of them, but they swore false and everything to send Mandy's children off."

"I will ask you with the exception of these men that were standing out there that night if you saw anything else out there?"

Lou understood what he was talking about; they had discussed it before the trial.

"Yes sir, there was a jug out there."

"What kind of jug was it?"

"A gallon jug."

"Was it glass or stone?"

"It was a stone jug."

He asked where the jug was, and she said it was right at the end of the house. He then asked, "Did any of your family have a jug of that kind?"

"Didn't have none of no kind."

Defendants' counsel objected to the question, insisting that it was immaterial; but they were over-ruled.

Changing directions and inquiring about the house's door, he asked, "This door, how was it fastened that night?"

"It was fastened inside and out. We fastened it with a button inside and then we had a chain on the outside to pull it to and lock it when we left and they had taken this chain and tied a piece of wire in it and wired the door to so we couldn't get out."

"How do you know?"

"Because I seen the chain there the next morning with the wire tied in it."

"What time in the morning did you see it?"

"About seven."

"What was the condition of the house next morning when you got there, had it already burned down?"

"There were just a few pieces of logs left there."

"Where was the chain?"

"Right there at the door."

"What did you say that you saw on the chain?"

"A piece of wire."

"The next morning when you found this piece of wire in that chain, I will ask you whether or not that was fresh wire or had been burned?"

"It had been burned."

"Before that time, before the night of the fire, at any time did you have any wire tied in that chain?"

"No sir."

"Was there any wire of that kind on the door?"

"No sir, there wasn't any wire on the door."

"Show us about how long that piece of wire was."

Lou held her hands about eight inches apart, and said, "About that long."

"Did you see anymore of the jug next morning around there?"

"Yes sir, there was one there where the house had burned."

"What kind of a jug was it?"

"A white looking jug, stone."

"Did you have any jug at your place at all?"

"No sir."

Working to wrap up his questioning, Creal asked, "Was there any loft in your house?"

"No sir."

"What part of the roof was burning?"

"Right about middle ways of the house."

"Did you have a flue?"

"No sir, we just had to run the stove pipe straight up through the roof."

"Where else did you say that the house was afire except on the roof?"

"Under the floor, we could see the fire through the cracks of the floor."

"Was the fire burning pretty big when you got out of the house?"

"A piece of sheeting had already burned up and fell down on the boys' bed before we could get out."

"When you got out of the house, was the fire burning enough to make a light?"

"Yes sir, pretty good."

"What age woman was Kate?"

"Sixty."

"What age are you?"

"fifty-eight."

Creal knew she was about to face a serious cross-examination, but her composure had been impressive thus far.

Turning to return to his seat, he looked toward Mr. Bradbury and said, "Your witness, sir."

Cross-Examination Begins

C. P. Bradbury rose from his chair, approached the witness, and inquired, "Lou, you say you are fifty-eight years old, I believe?"

Wary of him, Lou almost whispered, "Yes sir."

"Where have you lived most of your life?"

"Up there in Leaches."

"Whereabouts up there?"

"Around close to where the house was burned most of my life."

"The children lived with you most of the time?"

"All but Mandy, she was married awhile."

His next line of questions were about her boys and put her on the defensive.

"Did Bennie and Peachie live there with you all the time?"

"They was sent away when they was children for awhile."

"How long were they away?"

"I couldn't say for I don't know."

"Where were they?"

She didn't want to say, but finally blurted out "Up there at the feeble minded institution."

"About how long were they up there in your best judgment?"

Lou leaned back and folded her arms about her before answering, "I don't know, about four or five years."

"How long since they came back?"

"I don't know."

"Say Mandy is married?"

"Yes sir." Lou was glad to stop talking about her boys.

"How many children does she have?"

"Four."

Bradbury paused, and Lou thought he was going to ask more about Mandy's kids, but instead he said, "Lou, you said on direction examination that you didn't like Squire Bolton and Clarence Crenshaw I believe."

"I have worked for them just the same," she answered gruffly.

"You said you didn't like them, didn't you?"

"Yes sir, I said it," she almost spat.

Quietly he inquired, "Why didn't you like them?"

"Just look how they done Mandy's children, you wouldn't like them either would you?"

"What did they do to them?"

"They took and gathered them up and sent them off, and they didn't have no right to!"

"Is that the reason you don't like them?"

"I don't see how I could after they have done that."

"When did they send these children away?"

"Last fall."

"Did Judge Wigginton and Mr. Carroll and Mr. Monroe have anything to do with that?"

Mr. Creal rose from his seat and said, "Objection, your honor. These men he named are not on trial here. What the witness thinks or doesn't think about them has no bearing on this trial."

Judge Richardson agreed and sustained the objection.

Returning to what had happened to Mandy's children, Mr. Bradbury asked, "Were they sent away by court proceedings?"

"Didn't seem like court to me, just ask a body what church they belonged to."

It was unclear what Lou was referring to, but Bradbury didn't inquire further. Instead he asked, "Were they brought there to Shepherdsville to be sent away?"

"Yes sir."

At this point Judge Richardson interjected a ruling that this line of questioning was immaterial on the question of feeling because the witness had already told that the feeling was bad and told why.

Changing tactics, Bradbury asked, "Lou, on Friday a week before your house burned down out there, where were you?"

"It's hard for me to say, I don't know."

"Were you and Mandy in my office in this town on that day?"

"I couldn't say whether it was that day or not."

"Didn't you and Mandy come in my office seeking to employ me to get those children back?"

"I don't think it was on Friday, but we did."

"I will ask you if on Friday before, you and Mandy were in my office, nobody being present but you, Mandy and myself, did you have a conversation with me in which conversation you said that John Bolton and Clarence Crenshaw had taken Mandy's children away from her, and that you were going to get even with them some way?"

"No sir, I didn't."

"And on the same day didn't you go to Attorney Funk's office and make the same statement to him, nobody being present but you, Mandy and Mr. Funk?"

"I didn't say I was going to get even with them."

"Did you come to the County Attorney's office that day?"

"I don't think I did."

"Didn't you and Mandy go to see Mr. Carroll that day?"

"No sir."

"Did you talk to Judge Wigginton on that day?"

"No sir, I didn't talk to Mr. Wigginton."

"In Funk's office didn't you say what I ask you and further say that you were going to get even with them if you had to take the law in your own hands?"

"No sir."

Despite her repeated denials, Bradbury's accusations were having an effect on the jurors.

"Lou, you say that on the night this house burned that Jim Harris came to your house; that isn't anything unusual is it?"

"He always had business every other time he come."

"What kind of business did he have at other times?"

Mr. Creal quickly objected to the question, and the judge sustained his objection, leaving the jurors to wonder just what this other business had been.

"You have known Jim Harris all his life, haven't you?"

Thinking literally, she answered, "No sir, not all his life."

When Bradbury asked, "You knew that Jim Harris wouldn't harm you at all?" the Commonwealth lawyers were quick to object, and the judge sustained their objection.

He next asked, "Lou, do you know Will Harris, Jim's brother?"

"Yes Sir."

"Did you go to Will Harris's after some seed potatoes?"

Judge Richardson, on his own motion, sustained an objection to the question on the grounds that the question was irrelevant.

Trying again, Bradbury asked, "Were you at Will Harris' a short while before this occurred?"

"I know I was there. I don't know when it was."

"Did you have a conversation with Will Harris on this occasion, the exact date I am not able to fix, in which you said that "Kate was getting so mean that you couldn't put up with her, and you were going to have to get rid of her," did you say that?"

"No sir, I never said that."

"And in that same conversation, did you say that Kate and Bennie were sleeping together and that Kate was ruining Bennie and that he wouldn't provide for you and that he wanted you to leave, and if he made you leave that house that it would go up in smoke?"

The comment about "sleeping together" produced audible gasps among the crowd, and the judge rapped for order.

Even Lou blushed a bit as she replied, "No sir. I would be a pretty thing to tell that on myself even if I did."

Despite her repeated denials, Bradbury needed to get these questions asked and answered on the record since he planned to call Will Harris as a witness later.

Bradbury next asked, "Where was the house that you lived in before you moved to this house that was burned?"

"Out in Mr. Willie Shaw's barn."

"What became of that house?"

"It was burned down," she answered reluctantly.

"Lou, how many houses have you lived in in that neighborhood that was either burned down while you were living in them or directly after you moved from them?"

"I don't know." was the even more reluctant response.

"I will ask you if as many as five haven't?"

Her face clouded over as she replied, "No sir, I don't think there have been that many."

Having made his point that places she lived had a habit of burning down, he next inquired, "The night that this trouble occurred, did you see Frank Hodge up at your house the afternoon before that night?"

Lou said "He was at our house about dinner time," referring to the noontime meal.

"Where did you see him?"

"Getting over the fence."

"Did he come in the house?"

"Yes sir."

"How long did he stay?"

"Not but a few minutes. I don't know exactly how many."

"Did you see him anymore that day?"

"No sir."

"That was the evening that you went with the officers to Elmer Crenshaw's still, isn't it?"

"Yes sir."

"Did you see him after you came back from the still?"

"Yes sir, we went up and raided the still that morning and he was there at dinner time, sure, and when he was there we were fixing to set out the dinner."

"Was Peachie there then?"

"Yes sir, and we was waiting for Bennie to come to dinner."

65

"Was Peachie at home the day before that?"

"Yes sir, he was working in the garden."

"That was Thursday?"

"Yes sir."

"Was he at home Wednesday?"

"Yes sir."

"Were you at home on Wednesday?"

"I was part of the day, it is hard for me to remember all that, but I know I helped make garden part of the day."

Next he asked the question he had been aiming for.

"What day did you go to Bardstown?"

"Best of my knowledge, it was Tuesday."

"Lou, you testified on the examining trial in regard to that didn't you?"

"I aim to tell the truth about it just like it is," she responded defensively.

"Didn't you say that you didn't remember what day you went to Bardstown?"

"As near as I remember, it was Tuesday."

"I will ask you if on the examining trial you didn't say that it was either Tuesday or Thursday?"

"I don't think so," she said reluctantly.

Bradbury asked, "Who had Peachie been working for lately up there?" He moved toward the defense table and picked up some papers as Lou replied.

"Different ones, just first one and then another."

Holding the papers in front of him, he asked "On page 13, question 152 of the examining trial this question was asked you, 'Lou, in reference to the day you went to Bardstown, what day in the week was that?' and didn't you make this answer that it was either Tuesday or Thursday and you didn't know which? Was that question asked you and didn't you make that answer?"

Lou appeared confused, but replied "No sir."

Keeping her off-balance, he then asked, "On Friday afternoon, when you went with the officers down the road, I believe you said that you saw John Bolton, didn't you?"

"Yes sir, I did."

"How far was he from the road?"

"A right smart distance."

"Did he say anything to you?"

"No sir."

"Did he say anything to the officers?"

"No sir."

"What was he doing when you went down?"

"He was up there in the field plowing."

"What was he doing when you came back?"

"He was down there in the field with the mules. I guess he was plowing."

"How far is that from the road."

"I don't know; it was a piece down in the field."

"Do you know whether he saw you or not?"

"No sir, he had his back to me."

Changing directions, he inquired, "You say you saw Frank Kinder that evening?"

"Yes sir."

"What time was that?"

"About four."

"Where was he then?"

"He was down there at home in the field."

"You saw him at home?"

"Yes sir."

"What was it you said that he said to you?"

"He ask me if I had joined the prohibition men and I says 'yes, don't you want to join them,' and he says 'you will be damn sorry for it.'"

Holding up the papers again, he said, "I will ask you if on the examining trial if you weren't asked this question, and if you didn't make this answer: question 170, page 14, you said that you were expecting this mob that you were going down the road and Frank Kinder asked you if you had joined the prohibition men and you said 'yes, don't you want want to join them,' and then he said that you will be damn sorry that you turned these men up, didn't you say that?"

"Yes sir."

"Did you add anything else to what I said?"

"No sir."

"Well, did he say anything else to you?"

"He said that I had better watch out."

"Why didn't you say that on the examining trial?"

"I think I did."

"Do you say that you said all then that you say now?"

"Yes sir, I am sure I did."

"What did you say?"

"It don't make no difference, go ahead."

Laying the papers down, he said, "On the night that this crime occurred Lou, what time did Ewing Browning come to your house?"

"He was there awhile before dark."

"Was Peachie there when he got there?"

"Yes sir."

"Had you already eaten supper when he came?"

"Yes sir."

"How long did he stay?"

"Not very long."

"When he left, who left with him, if anyone?"

"Peachie left with him."

"Do you know where they said they were going?"

"They said that they were going to Bud Pugh's."

"Did they leave before dark?"

"It was dusky dark when they left."

"Was it eight o'clock."

"I don't know for I ain't got no time piece."

"What time did they come back?"

"When Ewing come in he said it was eleven o'clock by his watch."

"How long was it after they left before Jim came?"

"Some little bit."

"Give us your best judgment."

"I don't know."

"Do you say that it was as much as a half an hour?"

"It might have been, I don't know."

"How long after Jim Harris came until Peachie and Ewing came back?"

"Not so long."

"How long?"

"I can't say for certain, not over twenty minutes I don't guess."

"And you say that it hadn't been over twenty minutes after Jim Harris was there until Peachie and Ewing came in?"

"That is what I said."

"When they came back, what did they do?"

"Ewing went home and Peachie went to bed."

"Did Ewing come in the house?"

"Yes sir."

"Where did he go then?"

"He said he went home."

"Is that the only place he and Peachie went? Didn't they go to the spring?"

"Yes sir, they went and got a can of water."

"How far is it from the house to the spring."

"It is in the edge of the yard."

"Just point to some object that will show about how far it is from the house?"

"About as far as from here to the jury."

"When was it you heard Ewing say that it was eleven o'clock, before he went to the spring or after he came back?"

"When he came in from Bud's."

"And he said that it was eleven o'clock?"

"Yes sir."

"After that they went to the spring?"

"Yes sir."

"Who brought in the water?"

"Peachie."

"Didn't Ewing come back to the house with Peachie?"

"If he did he didn't come in."

Bradbury next inquired as to where the various folks were when Peachie returned, and Lou said all of them were in the bed.

Confirming this, he asked "Rest of you were all at home in the bed but Peachie?"

"Yes sir."

"After the house caught fire, had you ever been asleep from the time Jim Harris was there?"

"No sir. I hadn't and Mandy said that she hadn't."

"After Ewing went home and Peachie had already come back from the spring, how long was it then until you discovered that the house was on fire?"

"Not very long. I can't say just how long it was."

"About how long had it been?"

"Jim Harris hadn't been gone from the door more than twenty minutes when I saw the fire."

"Lou, when you first saw the fire how much had it burned?"

"The whole top of the house was afire and it was all afire under the floor."

"When you first saw it?"

"Yes sir."

Bradbury asked who she called first after seeing the fire, and she said Peachie. He inquired if Peachie was asleep and she said he wasn't. The lawyer next wanted to know who she called next, and she said, "I never called anybody."

He then asked "What did Peachie do?"

"Went to the door and got the ax."

"Peachie got the ax first?"

"Bennie got it first and he give the ax over to Peachie."

"At the time they first shot through the door, who was chopping?"

"Bennie."

Bradbury wanted to know how many licks Bennie gave the door, and she said, "Three or four."

He asked what kind of ax Bennie was using, and she answered, "A double bit ax."

He asked if it was old or new and she said, "An old one."

His next question was "Did you have two axes in the house?"

She answered, "No sir, we just had the one."

Do you know how long you had had that ax?"

"No sir."

Continuing his interrogation, he said, "You say Bennie was chopping and then got shot and then who chopped next?"

"Peachie."

"How many licks did he hit with the ax."

"I don't know, he hit two or three licks and got shot and fell over between the beds and hollered 'oh Lordy, they have fixed me,' and then Angie took the ax and began to chop and she chopped the door open."

"Was Angie shot too?"

"Yes sir."

"Where was Peachie shot?"

"I don't know."

"Was he shot in the wrist?"

"I don't know where he was shot."

"Was there just one shot hit him?"

"Yes sir, I think so."

"Was it the shot or the piece off the door that knocked him down?"

"I don't know."

"Who finally got the door open?"

"Angie."

"How long was she chopping it open?"

"It looked like it was a long time."

"Did you see the wire on the chain that night?"

"Next morning I did."

"Lou, after the examining trial, the exact date I can't remember, I think two weeks ago today, weren't you up where the house burned down and didn't you see Ervin Funk and myself up there, and didn't we ask you about that chain, and you said that you didn't know what had become of it, didn't we ask you that?"

"Yes sir."

"Didn't you tell us you didn't know anything about the chain?"

"No sir, I saw the chain the next morning."

"When we asked you about it, didn't you say you didn't know anything about the chain, that you hadn't seen it?"

"No sir."

"Did you tell us anything about the chain having the wire on it?"

"No sir."

"Don't you know that you told us that you didn't know anything about the chain, that you never did see it?"

"No sir."

"After this door was open that night, who was the first one out of the house?"

"Bennie."

"Then who?"

"Me and Angie and Mandy and Kate all went out together."

"Who went first?"

"We all went out one right behind the other. I don't know."

"Which one of you took the lead?"

"That is hard for me to say, it is hard for a body to tell."

"When you got out, did you turn around to look and see who was there?"

"No sir, I didn't turn around."

"Where was Kate?"

"Standing up there at the house in the yard."

"Where did you next see Kate?"

"When they shot I heard her say 'I can't go any further, I am bound to fall.'"

"Do you know who shot her?"

"I don't know; that would be a hard matter to tell."

"Did Kate have her back to them?"

"Yes sir."

"Did she get shot in the breast?"

"Yes sir."

"The wound in the breast and head was inflicted while she was in the house?"

"Yes sir."

"Then she was shot that way in the house?"

"Yes sir, through the door."

"You say she was shot that way through the door?"

"I suppose she was. They shot her and I heard her say they have fixed me."

"Was that while she was in the house?"

"Yes sir."

"Then she wasn't shot any more until you got outside?"

"No sir."

"Where was Bennie?"

"He was done gone."

"How close were you all together?"

"Pretty close."

"How close were you and Kate together?"

"Tolerable close to her."

"As close as from me to you?"

"Yes sir."

"I believe you said that Kate said when she got up there apiece that she said that she was just bound to fall, that she couldn't go any further?"

"Yes sir."

"How far had she gone then after they shot her?"

"About fifty yards."

"Then you saw her drop out there in that little hollow?"

"I didn't see her drop, we found her out there the next morning."

"The next house from yours was Dena Browning's?"

"Yes sir."

"You followed that path up through by her house?"

"Yes sir."

"All of you together?"

"Yes sir."

"You and Angie and Mandy and Peachie were the four that were together there then?"

"Yes sir."

"You saw Dena as you passed her house didn't you?"

"Peachie was talking to her."

"When you went on up to Henry Browning's you saw him up there didn't you?"

"No sir."

"You didn't stop there?"

"No sir."

"You knew that Henry had a telephone, why didn't you stop there and telephone for the officers?"

"I was afraid that the mob would get us."

When Bradbury asked who lived at Henry Browning's place, she indicated just Henry, his wife, and son.

Inquiring about the son, the lawyer asked, "That is Ewing Browning, isn't it?"

"Yes sir."

"Is that the boy that was at your house?"

"Yes sir."

"Did you see him when you passed there?"

"No sir."

"Did you hear him?"

"No sir."

"Did you ask for Ewing?"

"No sir."

"Did you say anything to anybody either at Dena Browning's or at Henry Browning's?"

"No sir, I did not."

"You knew then that Kate had fallen?"

"Yes sir."

"That was a rainy night?"

"Yes sir."

"And it was cold?"

"Yes sir, well, it wasn't until after the shooting was done."

"You knew that Kate was back there?"

"Yes sir."

"Did you know that she was hurt?"

"I was bound to know that, there in the house."

"You didn't say anything to Dena or Henry's folks about going down there and rendering Kate assistance, did you?"

"No sir, I did not."

Bradbury paused to let the jury ponder that reply, and then asked, "Why didn't you?"

"What good would it have done?" was her pathetic response.

"You went on up the road about a quarter of a mile from there?"

"Yes sir."

"There you saw whom?"

"Selby Hodge and Frank Hodge."

"Where did you see them?"

"Up there on the road by Mr. Charlie Biven's barn."

He asked if her property was fenced, and she said, "Yes sir, wire fence."

"Was that fence torn down?"

"No sir."

To his questions about seeing any horses, automobiles, or buggies that night, her repeated reply was "No sir."

"Where did you spend the night that night?"

"At Charlie Biven's."

"You didn't see Frank Hodge before you got up to Charlie Biven's did you?"

"I seed him before I went back down to Charlie Biven's."

"Did you testify before that you didn't see either one?"

"He come out on the road and was talking to Peachie."

"You know where that road is that goes down to Elmer Crenshaw's place?"

"Yes sir."

"Which side of that road were you on when you saw Frank Hodge and Selby Hodge, between Charlie Biven's and home, or on the other side of Biven's?"

"On the other side, between his house and that road."

"Which side of the road was Frank on?"

"On the right hand side as you go up."

"Was that on his own ground?"

"Yes sir."

"If he had been down there at the house he couldn't have passed you, could he Lou?"

"Yes sir, he could."

"After you say you saw Frank Hodge up there you went back to Charlie Biven's?"

"Yes sir."

"You and Mandy and Angie?"

"Yes sir."

"You went to Charlie Biven's?"

"Yes sir."

"What was the first thing that you said when you got there?"

"I didn't say anything; Mandy done the talking."

"You didn't say anything to Dena Browning?"

"No sir."

"You didn't say anything to Henry Browning?"

"No sir."

"And you didn't say anything to Charlie Biven?"

"No sir."

"How long after you got there until you three got together there in the house and talked it over what you were going to tell about this shooting and fire?"

Mr. Creal had been silent for quite a bit of the cross-examination, but at this question he arose and addressed the court. "Your honor, I object to this question. It's leading, and assuming facts not in evidence."

When the court sustained Creal's objection, Mr. Bradbury then asked, "What time was it when you got up there?"

"It was twelve o'clock."

"How do you know?"

"I know it was twelve."

"Can you tell what time it is?"

"I sure can, do you think I am crazy?"

Bradbury paused and smiled at the witness; then turning toward the jury, he allowed his head to lift and dip slightly twice before turning back to the witness and asking, "Did Charlie and his wife get up?"

"Yes sir."

"Did they put their clothes on?"

"They did, yes sir."

"When they first saw you, what did they say to you, and you to them?"

"Miss Biven ask Mandy what was the matter, and she told her."

"What did you say?"

"I didn't say nothing; Mandy answered the question."

"How long had you been there before Mrs. Biven asked that question?"

"Not but a few minutes."

"Did you all go off and talk among yourselves about what to tell her?"

"No sir, we didn't."

"Did any of you tell Maggie and Charlie that Kate was down there hurt?"

"Sure, Mandy did."

"Did you ask them to go help her?"

"No sir."

"Did you see Peachie any more that night?"

"No sir."

"When you saw Peachie at the Coroner's inquest where had he been?"

"I don't know for sure, I just know what he told me."

"Did Peachie testify at the inquest?"

"No, I don't think he did."

"He didn't testify there?"

"No sir, I don't think he did. He can tell you more about that than I can."

"Lou, what time did you leave Charlie Biven's next morning?"

"Before sun up."

"Did you have breakfast there?"

"No sir."

"Did you tell them you were going?"

"Yes sir."

"How long had you been there before you went to sleep?"

"I never did go to sleep."

"Did you notice the clock when you left?"

"No sir."

"Was it daylight?"

"Yes sir."

"Where did you go?"

"To Charlie Browning's."

"In going down there you had to pass by where Kate was, didn't you?"

"No sir, we kept on down the road."

"You had to pass her."

"I couldn't see her."

"I ask you if you didn't have to pass her?"

"No sir, I went down the road."

Bradbury insisted, "You know that you passed her, didn't you?"

"I wasn't so close to her." she replied rather evasively.

"You went on the Charlie Browning's?"

"Yes sir."

"You hadn't been to see about Kate?"

"No sir."

"It was daylight?"

"Yes sir."

"You went over to Charlie Browning's, what did you go over there for?"

"I went over there and got him to go see about Kate."

"Was she still alive when they got over there?"

"Yes sir, they came back and told me that she was alive, but she was speechless."

"Then you went over there?"

"Yes sir."

"About what time was it when you saw Kate the next morning?"

"It was about seven o'clock."

"After you went over and found Kate, then where did you go?"

"Went up to Henry Browning's the first place."

"You found her about seven in the morning?"

"Yes sir, that is what they said it was."

"Why did you have to leave; why didn't you stay with Kate?"

"I had to call the coroner, or get somebody to."

"She wasn't dead, was she?"

"No, but she was dying when we got up there."

"Didn't you say at the examining trial that it was so cold that you couldn't stay up there, that you had to leave?"

"I ordered the coroner before I left."

"After you ordered the coroner, she still wasn't dead?"

"Yes sir, she died while I was down at Charlie Browning's."

"You didn't do anything to try to save Kate's life?"

"No sir."

"You went to call the coroner?"

"I went up there and she said that the line was cut, and she couldn't call."

"Did she try to call?"

"Said she did."

"Is the line cut now?"

"I don't know."

"When did she tell you that?"

"Next morning."

"You didn't find out that the line was cut that night?"

"No sir."

"Did you make any inquiry that night about what became of Ewing?"

"No I didn't."

"On Saturday, after the coroner's inquest, where did you go?"

"Went up to Jim Campbell's."

"Who is Jim Campbell?"

"My sister's child."

James Campbell was married to Cora Pugh, daughter of Bud and Nancy Jane (Browning) Pugh. Nancy was Lou's sister.

"Which ones of you came to this place?"

"Mandy, Angie and myself, and Peachie."

"Where was Bennie?"

"After we got there awhile, he come."

"That is the first time you had seen Bennie since the fire?"

"Yes sir."

"Bennie was the first one out, and you didn't see him any more until then?"

"No sir."

Bradbury then began hammering at a theme he would pursue with other witnesses later.

"Do you know Mrs. Roy Shaw?"

"Yes sir."

"A short while before this occurred, at Mrs. Shaw's residence with nobody present but you and Mrs. Shaw, didn't you have a conversation in which she asked you how Kate was and you replied that she was the meanest thing in the world, and that she was ruining Bennie, and that you would have to get rid of her, didn't you say that?"

"No sir, I didn't say that because the place wasn't mine, it belonged to my son; I couldn't have done that."

"Didn't you tell Mrs. Biven there on that occasion that Kate was getting so mean that you would have to get rid of her some way or other?"

"No sir, it didn't do no good to tell them."

"Do you know Mrs. Bud Pugh?"

"Yes sir."

"At her residence, nobody being present but you and her, didn't you have a conversation with her in which conversation you said that Kate and Bennie were sleeping together and that Kate was ruining Bennie, and that she was gettin so mean that you would have to get rid of her?"

"No sir, I never said that."

"Do you know Mrs. Ann Biven?"

"Yes sir."

"Didn't you have the same conversation with her?"

"No sir, how do you reckon I would get rid of her, the place wasn't mine."

"Do you know Mrs. Gabe McCormick?"

"Yes sir."

"Didn't you have a conversation with her in which you told her that Kate was ruining Bennie by sleeping with him, and that she was getting so mean that you were going to have to get rid of her?"

"No sir."

"Lou, I believe you said that you didn't see anybody there that night that you recognized?"

"No sir, but I heard some of them."

"You never did see anybody down there at the house that you recognized?"

"I knowed two of their voices."

"You didn't see them?"

"No sir."

In his final question for her, Bradbury asked, "Lou, John Bolton and his family have contributed to your support a good deal for some time, haven't they?"

"Yes sir." came the reluctant reply.

On cross-examination, Mr. Creal wanted to know, "Who is Mrs. Gabe McCormick?"

"She is Mr. Clarence Crenshaw's daughter."

"Did this same woman bring you some kind of word from Clarence Crenshaw about staying off his place?"

"Yes sir."

"Did she bring you any message from this defendant, any threats of any kind, if you didn't stay off his place?"

"Yes sir."

"I will ask you if you ever received any information from Clarence Crenshaw about staying off his place?"

The defense's quick objection to the question was sustained, and Creal tried a different tact.

"I will ask you if you received information from Clarence Crenshaw about you getting on his place, and what he would do if you were caught on it?"

"She said..."

"Don't tell me what this woman said, just tell whether or not you have information from Clarence Crenshaw about what he would do if he caught you on his place?"

The defense again objected and was sustained. Creal then said, "I have no further questions for this witness."

Mandy Jones Examined

Judge Richardson adjourned for the noon meal. Upon resuming the trial, he directed the Commonwealth to present its next witness, and they called Mandy Jones to the stand. After she was sworn in and took her seat, Mr. Creal went through the formalities of identifying her by asking her name and how she was related to Lou Browning, the previous witness.

He next asked, "Have you been married?"

"Yes sir," was the reply.

"Where were you making your home on the night of the fire at your mother's home?"

"There with them."

"How long had you been living there with them?"

"For a couple of years or more."

"Were you at home the night of the fire?"

"Yes sir."

"Who was living there?"

"My sister and mother, and my two brothers and my aunt." She counted them off on her fingers, a habit she had apparently picked up from her mother.

"Back before the fire that night, what time was it when you went to bed?"

"I don't have no idea, because I didn't have no time piece."

"Had you ever been asleep that night?"

"No sir."

"Who else was there and went to bed when you did that night?"

"My mother I believe."

"Where were the boys?"

"Bennie was there and Peachie was gone to his uncle's."

"Had you ever been asleep at the time of the fire?"

"No sir."

"Who did Peachie leave with that night?"

"Ewing Browning."

"What time did they leave?"

"It was about eight o'clock the best of my knowledge."

"Do you know when they came back?"

"Yes sir."

"According to your best judgment, what time was it?"

"Eleven o'clock is what Ewing said it was by his watch."

"Had you ever been asleep at that time?"

"No sir."

"When they got home, where were Kate, Angie, Lou, Bennie and you?"

"In the bed."

"Did anybody come to your house while Peachie was gone away?"

"Jim Harris was there."

"What did he do or say?"

Like her mother before her, Mandy described the scene in one breathless and continuous statement.

"He came to the door and hollered, and Bennie says 'who is that' and he says 'you know who it is,' and Bennie says 'is it you Jim' and he said yes, and then he said 'what would be the chance to get you to cut me some wood you and Peachie,' and Bennie says 'no chance at all for me Jim but I will see Peachie and maybe you can get him and Ewing to cut the wood,' and he said 'come in Jim,' and Jim says 'I will see about it and I will see you again Sunday morning,' and Bennie says 'all right Jim I will be here all day.'"

84

She had been leaning forward while reciting that statement; now she sat back in the chair to await the next question.

"Did Jim Harris come in?"

"No sir, he didn't come in."

"Did you have any lamp in the house?"

"There was a lamp there."

"All right, what did Jim do then?"

"He went away from the door and Mother says there is something wrong..."

"Don't tell me what your mother said to Bennie, but just tell what Bennie did when Jim went away?"

"He got up and went on the outside."

"What did he do that for?"

Mr. Bradbury spoke up, saying "Objection, your honor. that question calls for a conclusion by the witness." Judge Richardson agreed, and sustained the objection.

Continuing, Mr. Creal asked, "Did Bennie come back in the house after Jim left?"

"Yes sir."

"Did he go back to bed?"

"Yes sir."

"How long was it after Harris was there until Peachie and Ewing came back?"

"Just a few moments."

"When Peachie came, was that information given to him about Jim wanting the wood cut?"

"Yes sir."

"Where was Ewing after they came back?"

"He come back with him."

"Did he come in?"

"Yes sir, and then they went to the spring and got him and Peachie a drink."

"How long were they there together?"

"Just a few minutes."

"Then what became of Ewing?"

"He went home."

Working to get her to identify when the fire started, he next inquired, "According to your best judgment, how long was it after Peachie came in and went to bed until you discovered or had information that the house was on fire?"

"I don't have no idea. It wasn't over twenty minutes after Jim Harris left until the house was afire."

"Had you ever been asleep after Peachie and Ewing came in until you discovered that the house was on fire?"

"No sir."

"What was the first that you saw of the fire?"

"Mother hollered and said the house is on fire and I looked up and the roof was afire right up over the boys' bed."

"What did you do?"

"Jumped up and went to hollering."

"Was there any fire any other place?"

"Yes sir, under the floor." She was looking down at the courtroom floor, as if she were picturing the fire there.

"What part of the house was afire under the floor?"

"Over on the left hand side." She pointed.

"How big a place under the floor was it that was afire?"

"The best of my knowledge it was afire all over." She used both hands in an expansive expression.

"How high was that floor off the ground?"

"High enough for a chicken to go under."

"What kind of a house was that?"

"Just a one room log house."

"Were the logs seasoned or green?"

"They were green."

"How long had the house been built?"

"It was built along in the winter."

"What kind of roof was on this house?"

"Paper." she replied, indicating simple tar paper.

"What did you do toward trying to get out?"

"I hollered for the ax and Bennie took the ax and began to try to chop out."

"Did you try to get out at the door and found that it was fastened?"

Again Mr. Bradbury objected, saying "Your honor, he's leading the witness." His objection was sustained, and Mr. Creal moved to his next question.

"What did you try to do in order to get out?"

"Bennie took the ax and tried to chop the door open."

"How was this door fastened?"

"With a piece of wire."

"Was it fastened on the inside or out?"

"Both. We had a button on the inside and they had wired it up on the outside."

"How did you say that it was fastened on the inside?"

"With a button." The jurors all understood what she meant by a button; more like a simple latch that turned on a nail, or slide into a hole.

"Was it fastened in any other manner except with the button?"

"We just had it buttoned."

"Did the door come open when you went to pull it open?"

"No sir."

This time the defense's objection to the question was over-ruled, and Creal continued.

"Why didn't it?"

"Because it was wired up on the outside."

"How do you know?"

"I seed the chain laying there next morning with the wire twisted in it."

Again the judge over-ruled the defense objection to the question, and Mr. Creal pressed on.

"After you couldn't get the door open, then what did you do?"

"I says ..."

Creal interrupted and said, "Don't tell what you said, just tell what you did."

"Well, I ain't going to tell no lie about it, and I says 'get the ax and chop this door open so we can get out of here,' and Bennie took the ax and just as he struck the first lick they shot him right through the door in the face, and then Peachie took the ax and began to chop and they shot him, and then Angie took the ax and she got the door open."

Creal next asked a series of questions about who got shot and where, and learned from Mandy that Bennie was shot in the face, Peachie in the arm, and Angie in the face and head. Mandy indicted that she too was shot.

He then asked, "Did any of the rest of the family get shot there in the house before you got out?"

"Just what they told me is all I know about it." was her reply.

Creal wanted to know, "From the time you began using the ax, how many minutes or seconds were you in getting out?"

Mandy shook her head and said, "I don't have no judgment about that mister."

"How many shots were fired?"

"There was six through the door."

"What kind of door was that?"

"It was made out of cedar slabs and oak."

"How thick were they?"

"Oh, nothing like an inch."

"Was the door closed or open when they shot in at the door?"

"Closed."

"After you got it open, then what did you do?"

"We ran out."

"Do you know whether or not Kate got shot there that night?"

"I think she got shot there in the house the best of my judgment."

"What did she say there, if anything?"

"She put her hand up to her eye and says 'oh Lordy they have fixed me.'" indicating by her statement that Kate had been shot in the eye.

"Did you afterwards see her on the next day?"

"Yes sir, next morning."

"Tell the condition of her eye."

"Her eye was shot out."

Mr. Funk rose to object, stating, "She's stating a medical opinion, your honor."

Judge Richardson waved off the objection, and Creal continued.

"Was it her right or left eye?"

"Right."

"There in the house that night, when she threw her hand up over her eye and says 'oh Lordy they have fixed me,' which eye was that?"

"Right."

Turning to a new line of questioning, he asked, "After you got out, who was the first person you saw?"

"I saw John Bolton standing to the right hand side of the house, and I saw Clarence Crenshaw and Frank Kinder."

The jury members would recall that Lou Browning had heard, but not seen Bolton and Crenshaw.

"Where were they?"

"There in front of the door."

"Did John Bolton and Clarence Crenshaw have guns there that night?"

"Yes sir."

"What kind, shotguns or pistols?"

"Shotguns."

When he asked, "Did you see anybody else there?" she responded with the name of Selby Hodge.

"Where was Selby Hodge?"

"He was standing there in front of the door with that line of men."

"Did he have any gun?"

"Well sir, I just don't remember."

When he asked "Who else did you see there?" she repeated the four names mentioned before and added the name of Elmer Crenshaw to the list.

"Where were they?"

"Standing there in the line."

"Did Elmer Crenshaw have a gun?"

"I don't remember whether he had a gun or not."

Returning to her own shooting, he asked, "Did you get shot in the house?"

"No sir, I got shot on the outside."

"How many different places were you shot?"

"Three."

"Where?"

"On the arm, hip and ankle."

"Which arm were you shot on?"

"Right one." she said, hold up her arm.

"Which hip were you shot on?"

"Left one right along here where it joins my body." she pointed.

"Where else?"

"In the ankle."

"Which ankle?"

"My left one, right along here." She raised the foot and pointed to the ankle.

"How do you know that you were shot in those three different places?"

"I saw the shots and I felt them."

"How do you know that you were shot; did you see all three of these places at the same time?"

"I saw my foot bleeding and felt a smarting right on my ankle; my foot hurt me so bad I couldn't hardly walk."

"Were all these shots received at the same time or at different times?"

"I saw them all at the same time."

"Did you receive all the shots at the same time?" He repeated.

"I didn't seen my hip till next morning."

Changing direction, he asked, "How close were you to John Bolton?"

"Best of my judgment, it wasn't as far as from here to the window." indicating a distance about half way across the courtroom.

"Were there any other people there that you didn't know?"

"There were lots of them there that I didn't know at all."

"When did you find that Kate was dead?"

"The next morning we found her but she wasn't dead when we first found her."

"When you first got out of the house, which way did you turn, or did you go straight?"

"Turned to my right, up toward Mr. Henry Browning's."

"Did you go fast or slow?"

"We were walking off."

"You spoke of Jim Harris being there at the house that night before the fire, did you see him there any more?"

"No sir."

"Did you say anything to anybody else there that night?"

"To John Bolton. When I came out of the house I saw him standing there, and I says 'here stands that black ape John Bolton,' and he pointed a gun at me and pulled the trigger."

To the men of the jury who were familiar with shotguns, it may have surprised them to think that Mr. Bolton was such a poor shot that he only hit her with three pellets at that range.

Before they could dwell on that too long, Mr. Creal asked, "Did you hear any of the parties say anything there that night?"

"Yes sir, I heard John Bolton say, 'Clarence have you shot yet?' and Clarence said, 'No, but I am getting ready to.'"

"How much had the fire burned when you got out of the house; was it making a good light by that time?"

"It was making a pretty big light."

"At that time, was it moonshiny or dark?"

"It was a clear night."

"Next morning, was it still clear, or was it cloudy or how?"

"It had been raining, rained some Friday night."

"Have you told us all the people that you saw around the house there that night?"

"Yes sir."

"Anybody else that you heard that you didn't see?"

"Not to the house I didn't."

"Did you hear anybody else there that night?"

"I heard Frank Hodge and Selby up there on the road that night."

"Tell the jury just what you were doing and just where you were going."

This time her answer was more measured, with pauses as if she were recalled a conversation.

"Selby was over there in the field and I heard somebody keep whistling and Peachie stopped and I says, 'Go on Peachie maybe they don't know who we are,' and Frank Hodge come out there and says 'Who are you?' and Peachie says 'It is me Frank.' and he began shooting and Peachie says 'Let me go on Frank, I ain't going to hurt nobody. I am just hunting a place to stay all night.' and then Frank says 'Stop there or I will kill every damn one of you in a pile!' and then Peachie says 'Frank I am just hunting me a place to stay all night.' and Frank says 'If you go airy nother step up that road I will kill every damn one of you!'"

"What was Frank Hodge doing there besides talking?"

"Shooting."

"How close was he to you?"

"It was a mighty little piece, I tell you."

"How close did the shots come to you?"

"The balls rolled under our feet."

"What did you do?"

"He was standing there talking to Peachie and me and mother and Angie run."

"At the time you left, Peachie and Frank were standing there talking?"

"Yes sir."

"Where was Selby?"

"Over there inside the field."

"With reference to the house, was there any other way that they could have come that would have been nearer than the way that you did, and headed you off up there, and get up there without passing you?"

"Yes sir."

Mr. Funk said, "Objection. Calls for a conclusion."

To which the judge replied, "Over-ruled. The witness should be familiar enough with the area to be able to answer that question."

Creal continued, "Tell how they could have gone."

"They could have went by the old home place."

"Was that nearer or farther than the way you went?"

"A little farther than the way we went."

"How was the road across there, could they have traveled it all right?"

"Yes sir."

Inquiring about what happened next, Creal asked, "When you went back down to Charlie Biven's, who did you see down there?"

"Charlie and his wife and the baby."

"Did you spend the rest of the night there?"

"Yes sir."

"Then where did you go, back to the scene of the trouble?"

"Next morning we did, yes sir."

"What time was it when you got down there next morning?"

"I don't know; I couldn't say."

"Say you went down there before she died?"

"Yes sir."

"Where was she?"

"Laying down there in a little path."

"What time was it then?"

"It was real early, I don't have any idea what time it was."

"Was she alive or dead?"

"Alive."

"Did she know anybody?"

"No sir, she was speechless."

"Go ahead and tell whether or not you had any way of knowing whether she was conscious or not?"

"No sir, I did not; she was speechless."

"How long after you got there until she died?"

"Not but a few minutes."

"After she died, did you make any examination of her?"

"No sir."

"Who helped dress her?"

"Mr. Clarence and Mr. Ewing Crenshaw, and Mr. Masden and there was a bunch of other men around there, but I just can't say who they were because I wasn't right there."

"Mr. Masden, is that the coroner?"

"Yes sir, when they started to dress her I left."

Changing direction again, he asked, "Do you remember the day that your mother went to Bardstown?"

"Yes sir, for I was the one that sent her."

"You were the one that sent her?"

"Yes sir."

"Did you have information that there was a moonshine still in the neighborhood before you sent her up there?"

"Yes sir."

"How did you get that knowledge or information?"

"I saw the still myself, and I smelt the whiskey boiling."

"Do you remember what day it was that your mother went to Bardstown?"

"I believe it was on Tuesday."

"Do you remember what day it was when the Federal officers came out there?"

"Yes sir, it was on Friday."

"Did you ride with them any that day?"

"Yes sir."

"Who else was with you?"

"Me and my mother."

"Was that going to or coming away from the still?"

"Going to."

"Did you see them anymore that day?"

"Yes sir, when they had Elmer Crenshaw."

"Did you ride with them anymore after that?"

"Yes sir, they picked us up and took us home."

"Did you have any conversation with Elmer Crenshaw on the way from the still up to where you got out?"

"No sir, well he didn't say anything to me."

"Not a word?"

"No sir."

"What time of the day was it when they took Elmer away?"

"I don't remember."

"Did you see Frank Hodge anywhere that day?"

"Yes sir, he was at our house."

"What time was he there?"

"It was at dinner time." again indicating the noon meal.

"Do you know what he came there for?"

"Made out like he wanted some smoking tobacco."

"Was there anybody with him?"

"No sir, he was by himself."

"What did he do or say there that day?"

"He asked Bennie for some smoking tobacco and Bennie give him some old field tobacco and he says, 'No sir, I can't smoke that.' and then he got up and went and got him a drink and then he went and sat down and talked awhile, and he says 'I heard that they tore up a still today.' and then he says 'I believe I had better go home, Elmer Crenshaw might want to see me.'"

"That was about dinner time?"

"Yes sir."

"Did you see anything more of him until you saw or heard him up there on the road that night?"

"No sir."

"Did you see Frank Kinder any time after that still was raided that morning?"

"Yes sir, I saw Frank that evening."

"Have any conversation with him?"

"He ask my mother if she had joined the prohibition men and she told him yes and asked him if he wanted to join and he says 'You will be damn sorry of it.'"

"Who was there at the time?"

"My mother was there. He was talking to her and my Aunt was there. I don't know whether she was right there and heard it or not."

"Were any of his folks there?"

"His wife had just went in the house."

"Was there anything else said there at that time?"

"No sir."

"When Jim Harris was there that night, did you see him or hear him?"

"Just heard him."

"Did you know his voice?"

"Yes sir."

"After the fire that night, did you see him anywhere?"

"No sir."

Mr. Creal turned to the bench and said, "I have no further questions for this witness."

Mandy Jones Cross-Examined

Hobson L. James, the Hardin County attorney hired by the defense, rose from his chair and walked briskly toward the witness. He had been hired to help the defense relate to the Hardin County men on the jury.

In an attempt to show that Mandy and her mother had a specific reason for reporting Elmer Crenshaw's still, he began by asking, "Had you joined the prohibition enforcement crowd?"

"I don't understand what you mean," replied Mandy, taken aback by the question and his manner.

"Were you a member, or any prohibition enforcement officer?"

"I don't understand your question."

Sounding a bit exasperated, he tried again. "Had you had any arrangements with prohibition men to turn up stills?"

"No sir."

"Had you made any report of any before this time?"

"No sir."

"Had your mother?"

"Not that I know of."

"She went over to see Mr. Stanley and report Mr. Crenshaw's still?"

"Yes sir."

"And you sent her?"

"Yes sir."

Having shown that turning up stills was not something she ordinarily did, he now turned to the reason for doing it this time.

"You are the Amanda Jones whose children were sent to the Kentucky Children's Orphans Home, are you not?"

"Yes sir."

"Your feelings toward Mr. Crenshaw weren't very good, were they?"

"I worked for him some, but still my feelings were not the best in the world," she replied, still not admitting the hatred she felt toward Crenshaw.

"Your feelings were unkind toward Mr. Crenshaw and John Bolton?"

"I always liked them for a friend," She offered.

"Your feelings weren't very kind before you turned this still up were they?"

"Yes sir. I didn't have anything in particular against them."

Having heard her mother's testimony earlier in the day, the jurors would have a hard time believing this, James knew. He continued, "Was that the reason you reported that still?"

"I wanted it tore up. I want to get rid of this old moonshine out of the country."

There were audible murmurs throughout the courtroom at this statement. One matron who had managed a seat, rose slightly from it, saying aloud "Amen!"

The judge rapped for quiet as others either agreed with her, or laughed at what she had said. It was clear that there was wide disbelief at Mandy's declaration.

After the uproar had silenced, Mr. James asked, "When did you get the idea in your head that you wanted the stills out there torn up?"

"I have had that idea in my head all the time."

"You knew that there were others out there in that vicinity?"

"No sir, if I had I would have turned them up."

"You knew that there were other stills out there?"

"I had an idea, but I didn't know it, I didn't see it."

Hopeful that the jury had seen through her statements to the truth of why she turned up the still, he continued by saying, "Well you said awhile ago, I believe that you said that Frank Hodge was over at your house looking around the day that the still was turned up, the day he came down and asked for the tobacco?"

"Yes sir."

James continued with a series of rapid-fire questions.

"Did he seem to be looking for something?"

"Yes sir."

"Where was Peachie when he was there?"

"He was at dinner."

"Was Bennie there then?"

"No sir, but he came in while Frank was there, before he left."

"He wasn't there when Frank came?"

"No sir."

"What time of day was that?"

"The best of my knowledge it was twelve o'clock."

"Friday evening Peachie and Ewing got together over at your house and went out somewhere that night?"

"Yes sir."

"What time did Ewing come down there?"

"He come down after dark."

"And he and Peachie got together and left, and you don't know where they went?"

"No sir."

"They said that they went to Bud Pugh's?"

"Yes sir."

"And a short time before they came back Jim Harris was down there and wanted Bennie to cut some wood for him?"

"Yes sir."

James paused, then inquired, "Jim was making pretty frequent visits to your house wasn't he?"

"Yes sir, he come there a right smart."

"Bennie had worked for him some?"

"Yes sir."

"And I believe you say that, shortly after he was there, Peachie and Ewing came in and got the bucket and went to the spring and got a drink of water?"

"They come in and got the can and went and got a drink."

His next questions established that Ewing had left at eleven o'clock, and that all of them had gone to bed.

He then asked, "What was the next thing that occurred after Peachie came in and went to bed?"

"The house was afire. I never had gone to sleep, but I don't know about any of the rest but Bennie, but we had to shake him several times before we waked him up."

"And then when you did finally got him woke up, you said, 'get the axe and go to chopping,' and he was the first one to go to chopping?"

"Yes sir."

"Where was Bennie when you said get the axe?"

"He was there in the house."

"Had he gotten up?"

"Yes sir, he was standing there in the facing of the door."

"Was Peachie up?"

"Yes sir."

"Where were the others?"

"There in the house."

"When you told Bennie to get te axe, you hadn't heard anything on the outside?"

"No sir."

"You say then that a shot was fired through the door?"

"Yes sir."

"And then when he commenced to chop, a shot was fired and he hollered 'Oh Lordy, they have fixed me!'?"

"Yes sir."

"And then he stepped aside?"

"Yes sir."

"Peachie stepped up then?"

"Yes sir."

"And he said, 'Oh Lordy, they have fixed me!'?"

"Yes sir."

"Then he stepped aside?"

"No sir, he fell."

"The door hadn't been opened at that time?"

"No sir."

"Then Angie stepped up?"

"Yes sir."

"And she took the axe and began to chop?"

"Yes sir."

"How many shots were there before Angie went there and began to chop?"

"Two."

"How many were there fired altogether?"

"I couldn't tell you."

"There were two shots fired before she went up there and went to chopping?"

"The best of my knowledge there were."

"How many were fired after she got up there?"

"I don't know that."

"You didn't count those that were fired?"

"I didn't take time to count."

"You do remember those two that were fired?"

"Yes sir."

"Altogether, there were how many shots fired?"

"Six I think, while we were in the house."

"The door was finally opened?"

"Yes sir."

"Who went out first?"

"Bennie went first."

"Who was next?"

"I don't know that."

"Who went third?"

"I don't remember that either."

"Who came out last?"

"Peachie."

"Bennie was first and Peachie last, and the rest of you were in between?"

"Yes sir."

"Did Bennie say anything more after he said, 'Oh Lordy, they have got me.'?"

"No sir."

"Did Peachie?"

"No sir."

"Did Kate say anything more after she said, 'Oh Lordy, they have got me' until you all got out of the house?"

"No sir."

"You were not shot while you were in the house?"

"No sir."

"How long were you there trying to open the door?"

"Five or ten minutes."

"When you got out, it was light around there?"

"Yes sir."

"How many people do you say you saw there that night?"

"I saw about twenty-five, I guess; best of my judgment."

"Were they strange people that you had never seen before?"

"Yes sir."

"Never saw them before?"

"If I ever saw them before, I didn't know them."

"Nobody out there that night had on any mask?"

"No sir."

"How close were they to the house when you came out?"

"Right there close."

"Was it as close as from you to me?"

"It might have been as far as from here to the window over there."

"How were they standing?"

"Along in a line."

"Did they all have guns?"

"I don't know that they did."

"I believe you said that you saw John Bolton standing there and said, 'There stands that ape John Bolton.'?"

"That black ape, I says."

"What did he say?"

"Nothing, only he shot me."

"Take this stick and point it at me and show me just exactly how he shot at you."

"I don't know for I never shot a gun in my life."

"Did he hold the gun straight at you?"

"Yes sir."

"And you got shot in the ankle, hip, and arm?"

"Yes sir."

"At that time?"

"Yes sir, I did."

Once again the lawyer paused, hoping that the men of the jury would wonder how the blast of a shotgun that close by, from a shooter who knew how to shoot it, could result in so few pellets striking home.

"That is the only time that he shot?"

"That is the only time that I saw him shoot."

"Was he the only one up there that shot, that you saw?"

"He is the only one down there at the house that I saw, and there was Frank Hodge up there about a half a mile away."

"How many times did he fire up there on the road?"

"Well sir, I just don't know that."

"You didn't see anybody else shoot but those two?"

"No sir."

"Didn't see anybody else try to shoot?"

"No sir, nobody but John Bolton."

"There were five of you together, I believe you said?"

"Yes sir."

"Who were the ones along?"

"Peachie, Angie, and Mother and myself."

"Where were Bennie and Kate?"

"We left them. I don't know where they went."

"They didn't start off with you all?"

"No sir."

"You and your mother and Peachie and Angie started away to-gether?"

"Yes sir, me and Peachie and Angie and mother started away together."

"Which direction did you start?"

"To my right."

"Which way did Kate and Bennie start?"

"I don't know, they didn't start off with us."

"Neither of them were with you when you got out of the house?"

"No sir."

"You and your mother and Angie and Peachie walked out and walked along beside these twenty-five men, and none of them said anything to you?"

"No sir."

James turned his back on the witness, and facing the jury, shook his head in disbelief. Then he turned rapidly and faced the witness, asking as he turned, "After you said that you saw John Bolton, I be-lieve you said that Clarence Crenshaw was the next one that you saw?"

"Yes sir."

"Did Clarence have a gun?"

"Yes sir."

"Just show the jury how he had it."

"It was laying across his arm that way."

"That was a shotgun?"

"Yes sir."

"Who was the other man you saw with a gun?"

"John Bolton."

"Who else had a gun?"

"That is about all I remember seeing."

"Who else did you see that you knew?"

"I saw Frank Kinder and John Bolton there in front of the house."

"Were they in the line?"

"Yes sir."

"Where were they in the line?"

"About the middle of the line."

"Did Frank Kinder have a gun?"

"I don't know."

"Couldn't you see his hands?"

"Yes sir."

"Well, tell the jury whether or not he had a gun."

"I don't know whether he did or not."

James asked in disbelief, "You passed right by him and still you don't know whether he had a gun or not?"

"I never paid no attention," was her mumbled reply.

"Who else did you see there that night?"

"Elmer Crenshaw."

"He was the fellow that owned the still that you turned up?"

"Yes sir."

"Where was Elmer in the line?"

"Yes sir, he was there in the line."

"Lined up there in front of the door?"

"No sir, there were different places around there around the house."

"How many were in that line that Elmer was in?"

"I don't know," she hesitated, and then concluded, "about seven."

"You don't know exactly how many there were in that line?"

"No sir, I don't. I didn't count them."

"Tell us now just who it was that you saw there in that line?"

"John Bolton, Clarence Crenshaw and Frank Kinder."

"Didn't you say awhile ago that Frank Kinder was about the middle for this line of twenty-five men?"

"No sir," was her reply, contradicting what she had said before.

"Who else was there that you knew?"

"Clarence Crenshaw, Elmer Crenshaw and Frank Kinder."

"That was all you saw there?"

"That is about all I believe I saw there in the line."

"Clarence Crenshaw, Elmer Crenshaw and Frank Kinder?"

"Yes sir, there was three in that line in front of the door and John Bolton was to the corner of the house."

"Were there some more in that line in front of the door?"

"I told you about who I saw, that I knew."

"Did John Bolton get out of the corner and get in the line?"

"No sir."

"Did any of the other fellows say anything to you?"

"No sir." Mandy insisted.

"When you first saw this line where Clarence Crenshaw and Elmer Crenshaw and Frank Kinder were, how close were you to it?"

"I could have almost reached out and touched them."

"You walked right by them?"

"No sir."

"Which one of them was it now that you said had a gun?"

"John Bolton and Clarence Crenshaw."

"Now where was Clarence standing in that line?"

"Best of my judgment, he was standing about second or third."

"Now where was Elmer?"

"I believe he was first to the corner."

"Where was Frank Kinder?"

"He was along in the line in front of the door."

"Can you tell the jury whether Frank had a gun or not?"

Mr. Creal objected to the question on the grounds that it had already been asked and answered. His objection was sustained.

Mr. James then asked the witness, "Where was the other line?"

"Between Ewing Crenshaw's land and Henry Browning's."

"How far was that from the house?"

"Just a little piece."

"About how far?"

"About two yards, I suppose."

"They were right up there in your yard?"

"Yes sir, about two yards from the house."

"Who did you see in that line there that you knew?"

"I didn't know anybody in that line."

"Were there any other lines?"

"That is all I knew."

"Did anybody say anything to you?"

"No sir, not in that line."

"Did you see Bennie and your Aunt after you left there that night?"

"No sir, I didn't."

"Tell me where you were when you said that you started back to see about your aunt."

"Back up there to the corn crib."

"Where did Peachie and Angie and your mother go when you started back?"

"Kept on going."

"How far away from the house were you when you said you started back to see about your aunt, say you were close to Dena Browning's when you decided to go back and see about her."

"Yes sir."

"I believe she lives up there in Henry Browning's corn crib?"

"Yes sir."

"Then it was three or four hundred yards to the next house?"

"Yes sir."

"Was it in sight?"

"Yes sir."

"When you started back, you started towards your house?"

"Yes sir."

"Did you go all the way back to where the fire was?"

"I went in hollering distance to where it was."

"Didn't you say awhile ago that you got in about fifty or thirty yards of where the fire was?"

"No sir, I didn't."

"Didn't you say that you got within about as far as from here to the street to the house?"

"No sir, I didn't."

"Well, just how close did you get, you got up pretty close to that line didn't you?"

"No sir."

"Who was it that you said that you saw when you started down there?"

"I didn't see nobody; but I heard somebody."

"You got down to where you could hear them talking?"

"Yes sir."

"Then what did you do after you got down there?"

"I turned and started on back up to the road."

"Where did you go then?"

"On up above Charlie Biven's house."

"Did you go back to where your mother and brother and sister were?"

"Yes sir."

"Where did you catch up with them?"

"Up there close to Dena Browning's."

"Then you went there?"

"We had to go through her yard."

"Did you see her that night?"

"Yes sir, she was standing there in the door."

"You didn't tell her anything about any of this?"

"No sir."

"Did your mother say anything to her or tell her about Kate being down there?"

"No sir; Peachie was talking to her."

"Did she ask you what was the matter?"

"No sir."

"Your mother didn't say anything to her?"

"No sir."

"What did Peachie say to her?"

"He says they have been raising hell down there."

"Said that we have been having hell down there?"

"Yes sir."

"None of you stopped or asked for anything?"

"No sir."

"Next place you had to pass was Henry Browning's; didn't you stop there?"

"No sir."

"You didn't stop and tell them either place that Kate was shot up and needed assistance?"

"No sir."

"Did you see Henry Browning or his wife as you passed there?"

"No sir."

"Did you see Ewing Browning?"

"No sir."

"Did you call for him?"

"No sir."

"Why didn't you?"

"Because I was afraid to."

"You didn't think there was any danger up there did you?"

"I didn't know."

"You didn't holler?"

"No sir, not up there."

"Did you holler anywhere else?"

"Yes sir, I hollered 'Oh Lordy, the house is on fire; somebody come and help us!' when we were there in the house."

"Was that before you got the axe?"

"Yes sir."

"Just as soon as you saw the fire on the roof?"

"Yes sir."

"You didn't holler any more?"

"No sir."

"These men didn't offer to do anything to you?"

"No sir."

"You didn't call on them for help?"

"No sir, I just walked on by."

"Did you hear your Aunt Kate when she said that she couldn't go any farther?"

"No sir."

"You weren't along then?"

"No sir."

"Was your mother with you all the time?"

"Yes sir."

"After you went by Henry and Dena Browning's, you went up to Charlie Biven's didn't you?"

"Yes sir."

"You knocked and got them up and told them that you wanted to stay all night?"

"Yes sir."

"You went in the house?"

"Yes sir."

"They asked you what was the matter?"

"I don't know whether they did or not."

"You didn't say anything to them about this trouble?"

"I was talking to Mrs. Biven."

"Didn't you all have a talk among yourselves as to what you were going to tell about this before you told her anything?"

"No sir."

"You three didn't go off and have a talk?"

"Yes sir."

"You and Angie and your mother, after you had left Peachie up there in the road and went down there to Charlie Biven's, didn't you three get together and talk it over to see whether you were going to tell them or not?"

"No sir."

"You didn't talk to Angie and Lou about that?"

"No sir, I didn't tell them anything."

At this point Judge Richardson interjected, "Mr. James, you may cross examine the witness, but not about the conversation for that is not in chief," meaning that since the prosecution had not brought up the conversation in their examination, the defense was forbidden to do so in cross-examination.

James next asked, "Now when did you next see Bennie?"

"It was next day."

"What time next day was it when you next saw him?"

"Well, I don't know just what time it was."

"Morning?"

"Next evening."

"When did you see Peachie next?"

"Next morning."

"What time?"

"Along about eight o'clock."

"Now when you got up there on the road you saw Frank Hodge over there in his field and he made the bullets roll under your feet, I believe you said. Did you see them roll?"

"Yes sir."

"Tell me about that time that John Bolton shot, did you see the shots that time?"

"No sir."

Changing tactics, Mr. James asked, "Mandy, haven't you been in the asylum?"

"I have been at Lakeland, I reckon that is what you would call it. I think the ones that sent me there was crazier than I was; do you think I look like a crazy woman. I told them up there that I left the crazy ones back where I come from."

After the laughter had died down in the courtroom, Mr. James continued, "You have been there?"

"Yes sir."

Turning to the judge, Mr. James said, "I have no further questions for this witness."

Before Mandy could get up from the witness chair, Mr. Creal said, "One or two questions on re-direct, your honor."

Turning to Mandy, he asked, "How long did you stay up at Lakeland?"

"Two months."

"Is your husband still living?"

"Yes sir."

"Was that the time you had him indicted for child desertion and he had you tried and sent off?"

"Yes sir."

"How long did you say that you stayed up there?"

"Two months, and the city hospital one."

"How long has that been?"

"Two years."

Continuing with his questions, he wanted to know, "Before your home was burned, and before this still was raided, did you ever see any of these defendants hauling anything to that still?"

"I saw John Bolton go that way with a load of meal."

"A wagon load?"

"Yes sir, two-horse wagon."

Creal was finished with the witness, but the defense was not.

"How do you know that he was going there with it?" was Mr. James' first question.

"He was going that way."

"Doesn't he have to go that way to go home?"

"Yes sir, but he turned off of the road that goes toward his house and went down the road that leads to where the still was."

"Where was that?"

"About a half a mile from the still."

"What kind of meal was it?"

"I don't know. It was in the sacks."

"Did you see the meal?"

"No sir, I saw the sacks."

"What time of day was it that you saw him going over there with that meal?"

"About ten o'clock in the morning."

"Was there anybody with you?"

"Yes sir, my mother."

"Was there anybody with John Bolton?"

"No sir."

"Were you in the wagon?"

"No sir."

"How high was the bed?"

"High as any other wagon bed I suppose."

"How many sacks did you see?"

"The wagon was full."

"How do you know it was meal?"

"I saw it on the sack."

"Can you spell meal?"

"No sir, but I went by the other meal sacks I had saw."

"That is the same road that goes to John Bolton's house?"

"Yes sir, but he turned off and didn't go on toward home," she insisted.

Mr. Creal was not done with her either. After Mr. James sat down, Creal asked Mandy, "You say that the road that he was on went by his house?"

"Yes sir, but he turned off."

"Was that direction toward his house?"

"It was near his house, but he didn't pass it, he went away from it."

"Would there be any other houses that he would go by going back that way?"

"Yes sir. There was Mr. Jess Mann's and Mr. Walter Mann's and Mr. Sam Bealmear's."

Mr. Creal asked what kind of road it was, and she replied, "It is what we called the still road; it wasn't a pike."

"Say that it wasn't the pike road?"

"No sir."

"How long was this before the still was raided?"

"Three or four days."

Once again Mr. James rose and approached the witness.

"That was the reason that you reported that still, you saw John Bolton with those sacks and thought probably he might be mixed up in it, and you thought that you might get even with him that way?"

"Because I wanted to get rid of the old whiskey is the reason that I did it," she insisted.

"I believe you said that you knew Elmer Crenshaw was there that night the house was burned?"

"Yes sir, I knew him by his clothes."

"Was that the way you identified him there that night?"

"Yes sir, he had the still slop all over them."

"Was it the night of the fire that you saw him there with those clothes on that had the still slop on them?"

"Yes sir."

"Were those the same clothes he had on when he went to Bardstown?"

"Yes sir."

"Did you have your wound dressed?"

"No sir."

"Are there any marks on your arm?"

"Yes sir."

"Let me see it."

Satisfied that there was little to see, he said, "Please show that to the jury."

As she did so, Mr. James said, "We have no more questions for this witness."

When the prosecution concurred, the witness was excused.

Angie Browning Testifies

Angie Browning was the next witness called by the prosecution. After she took the stand, Mr. Creal asked her several questions of a general nature including her name and age (16), if she had been home the evening of the fire (Yes, she had), and then he asked, "Had you been asleep when they found the fire?"

She agreed that she had, and to his question of how long she had been in bed, she replied, "A right smart while."

When he next said, "I will ask you if you were at home when Jim Harris came down there?" she replied that she had been there, and that she had heard what he said.

Creal then asked, "Where was Peachie at that time?"

"He was up to Uncle Bud Pugh's."

"Who did Mr. Harris talk to?"

"He talked to Bennie."

Creal next inquired, "Now Angie, how long had Mr. Harris been gone until Peachie came home?"

She hesitated a moment, and then replied, "Not very long."

"Did you hear Peachie and Ewing talking when they came in?"

"Yes sir; they said that they were going to get a drink of water."

"Did you know about what time it was then?"

"Ewing said that it was eleven o'clock by his watch."

Happy to confirm the time with her testimony, Creal then asked, "Who was first to find the fire?"

"Mother."

"What did she say?"

"She told Peachie to get up, that the house was afire." Angie replied in a rush.

After establishing that they were all dressed except for their shoes, Creal asked, "What did you do when she gave the alarm of the fire?"

Angie leaned forward, took a deep breath, and then plunged into her reply.

"Mandy ask where the axe was and Bennie took it and began to chop on the door, and they shot him through the door, and then Peachie took the axe and began to chop and they shot him, and he fell back on the floor between the beds and says, 'Oh Lordy, they have fixed me' and then I took the axe and chopped the door open."

Finishing with a flourish she sat back and almost smiled at the prosecutor. He paused a moment, perhaps giving the jury time to digest what she said, and then inquired further, "How was the door fastened?"

"It was wired up."

"How do you know it was wired up?"

"Because we couldn't get it open without chopping it open," she replied, expecting him to see the obvious. However, he wanted her to explain it more clearly, and he continued questioning her about it.

"How do you know that you couldn't get it open without chopping it open?"

"Because it was buttoned on the inside and we turned the button and tried to pull it open and it wouldn't open and then we began to try to chop it open."

"Well, when you would unbutton the door and pull on it, would it come open any at all?"

"I don't know whether it would come open enough to get your hand through it or not."

After establishing again that they had to chop on the door to get it open, he asked, "When they commenced to chop on the door, what happened?"

"They began to shoot right through the door," she said, involuntarily touching the side of her face.

"Why were there so many of you people chopping on the door?"

"They would shoot them," was her almost whispered reply.

Returning her focus to the scene inside, Creal said, "Tell again what took place there in the house."

Condensing her earlier reply, she said, "Bennie took the axe and began to chop and they shot him, and then Peachie took it and began to chop and they shot him, and than I took the axe and chopped the door open."

"Did you get shot?"

"In the face and head and in the back," she answered, pointing at the spots as she did.

"Did you get any of your shots on the outside of the house?"

"I think I got them all on the outside."

"Where were you when you got shot the first time?"

"Out there at the road," was her response as she gazed at the floor, appearing to remember back to that night.

"Do you know who shot you?"

"Yes sir, I seed the man, but I don't know what his name was; I don't know him."

"Where were you shot the second time?"

"Up there in the road that goes by home."

"Indicate along your side and back where you were shot."

"All along down there," she again pointed.

Creal next wanted to know if she had seen anybody there that she knew that night, and she said, "Yes sir."

Turning to look toward the defendants, he asked, "Who did you see?"

"John Bolton and Elmer Crenshaw," was her reply, although she did not look toward the men.

"Where did you see John Bolton standing?"

"There at the corner of the house."

"Did he have a gun?"

"Yes sir."

"Was it a shotgun or a pistol?"

"It was a shotgun."

"Did Elmer Crenshaw have a gun?"

"Yes sir."

"What did he have, a shotgun or a pistol?"

"A shotgun."

"Did any of the other people there have guns that night?"

"I guess they did; I didn't notice them."

Seeking more identifications, he asked, "Did you see any more there that night?"

"No sir, I never seen any more." was her perhaps disappointing reply.

"Well, did you see anybody else that you knew there besides John Bolton and Elmer Crenshaw?"

"No sir, I didn't."

Deciding to move on, Creal wanted to know where Kate had been when she was shot, to which Angie replied, "She was in the house the first time."

"How do you know?"

"I heard her there when she hollered."

He then inquired, "When you went away from there, where did you go?"

"Went up by Mr. Henry Browning's, me and mother, and my brother and sister."

"What about Kate?"

"She was shot."

"Do you know when she dropped out, or when she stopped?"

"No sir, I don't."

"After you got up there on the road, did you see anybody up there?"

"No sir."

"Did you hear anymore shooting?"

"Yes sir, I think I heard about three shots."

"Where was that?"

"Up there above Mr. Charlie Biven's barn."

"Do you know who was doing that shooting?"

Almost as if she had been practicing this reply, she answered, "Frank Hodge and Selby was up there and Frank commenced shooting across the road and told us to stop or he would kill every damn one of us there in a pile, and he come over the fence and was standing there with Peachie talking to him, and me and mother and Mandy run back to Charlie Biven's and stayed there all night."

"Did you see Bennie any more?"

"No sir."

"When next did you see Aunt Kate?"

"I saw her the next morning; she was laying down there below the house."was her quiet response.

"Was she laying on the ground?"

"Yes sir."she whispered, causing the judge to encourage her to speak so the jury could hear her.

Creal gently asked, "Did you see her before she died?"

"Yes sir."

"Was she wounded in any manner?"

"Yes sir, I saw that her breast was all shot up."She shuddered as she spoke.

"Were there any other wounds on her?"

"No sir, I didn't notice anymore,"she replied, looking away as if to avoid the scene in her mind's eye.

"Was she alive when you got there?"

"She just barely was."

"What time of the day was it when you saw her?"

"It was about seven in the morning."

Changing direction, Creal asked, "When did you next see Peachie?"

"He come up there where the house was burned the next morning."Her voice was stronger now, more assured.

Returning her to the house on fire, he asked, "When you got up, where was this fire?"

"It was underneath the house and on top of it."

"What part of the roof was it that was afire?"

"Right about the middle."

"What part under the floor?"

"Right about the middle."

"Right about the middle of the house?"he confirmed.

"Yes sir."

Satisfied with his questioning of this witness, Mr. Creal said, "We have no more questions for this witness, your honor."

Then turning to the defense table, he said, "Your witness, counselors."

Erwin Funk had been waiting for this moment, and he asked, while rising from his seat, "What time do you say it was when Peachie and Ewing left your house that night?"

Instantly on the defensive, Angie replied, "I don't know what time it was the first time."

Funk wanted to know, "About how long had Peachie been at home that day before he left?"

"Been home all day that day."was her short reply.

"Was he at home all day the day before that?"

"Yes sir."

"He was at home for three days before this happened?"

"Yes sir."

"You testified in the examining trial of this case didn't you?"

"Yes sir, I guess so."

"In answer to a question that was asked you, didn't you say that he hadn't been home for two or three days and that he had just come home that evening?"

"No sir, I don't think I did."was her uncertain reply.

Picking up papers from his desk, Mr. Funk said, "On page 106 of the transcript of the examining trial, question 237, wasn't this question ask you and you made the answer, 'Where had Peachie been these two or three days that he had been gone?'and your answer was, 'I don't know where he had been.'?"

"I guess he was at home all that time. I might have made that statement." She seemed even less certain of her answer.

Pressing the point, Funk inquired, "I will ask you if on that occasion when that question was asked you, that you said the last few days that he hadn't been staying at home day or night?"

"He was at home all the time during the days and there most of the nights. He said he went over to Uncle Bud Pugh's that night."was her now more assured reply.

Mr. Funk next began a series of rapid-fire questions.

"That was the night that the fire occurred?"

"Yes sir."

"Angie, how long after Jim Harris was there until Peachie and Ewing came home that night?"

"Just a few minutes."

"It hadn't been a half an hour?"

"No sir."

"When they came back, did you say that they went down to the spring to get them a drink?"

"Yes sir."

"Did Ewing come back up there with Peachie?"

"Come back in the yard."

"When did Ewing say that it was eleven o'clock?"

"When he started home, he said that it was eleven o'clock, he was going home."

"Was that before or after he got the water?"

"After."

"Had any of you gone to sleep before this fire occurred?"

"Bennie was."

"Who discovered the fire?"

"Mother saw it first."

"What did she say?"

"Says 'Get up Peachie, the house is on fire!'" she shouted, bringing a brief frown to the judge's face.

"She told Peachie first?"

"Yes sir."

"Had you discovered the fire before that?"

"No sir."

"Did you hear any noise around there before you discovered the fire?"

"No sir, I didn't."

Pausing a moment, Mr. Funk next inquired, "None of you had been asleep except Bennie when you discovered that the house was on fire?"

"No sir, Peachie had to pull him out of bed."

"When Peachie pulled him out of bed, then what did he do?"

"Fell out on the floor, asleep again." There was scattered laughter throughout the courtroom at that response.

After the laughter had subsided, Funk asked, "What was the first thing that he did when he got up?"

"Tried to get the door open."

"Was Bennie the first one to try?"

"Yes sir."

"When Bennie finally got awake he ran and got the axe and began to try to get that door open because it was wired up?" Funk summarized.

"Yes sir, it was wired up."

"How was it wired?"

"There was a wire twisted in the chain."

"How was the chain fastened?"

"In a bolt or steeple or something of the kind."

"How was it fixed on the outside?"

"Fixed with a steeple to lock.

"How did you know that this wire was twisted in this chain?"

"I saw it in there."

"Did you examine it there that night?"

"No sir, I saw it laying there next morning."

"When you got outside who was the first one that you saw out there?"

"John Bolton."

"Who was the first one out of there that night?"

"Bennie was first and I was next and mother next."

"Who came out next?"

"Sister," she answered, referring to Mandy.

"Who was the last one out?"

"Peachie was the last one."

Mr. Funk continued his rapid-pace questioning, hardly giving her time to think before answering.

"Bennie got out first?"

"Yes sir."

"Where did he go when he came out?"

"He run."

"How far did he run?"

"I don't know." She shrugged her shoulders.

"Was it as far as from here to the end of the room?" he asked, pointing to the doors leading out of the courtroom.

"Yes sir, just about I guess," she answered reluctantly.

"Did you go on up to him then?"

"He was walking alone with me and then took out in a run."

"And that was about as far as from here to the end of the room?"

"Yes sir."

"Who of you were together then?"

"Me and Mandy and mother and my brother."

"Where was Aunt Kate?" he inquired, pointing out that she hadn't mentioned her aunt.

"She was coming."

"About how far were you from her?"

"About as far is from here over there," she replied, pointing in a general way toward the side of the room.

"When was it that Aunt Kate got shot?"

"There in the house."

"Was that the only time she was shot?"

"No sir, I think she was shot again after she got out of doors."

"Did you see her when she got shot?"

Shaking her head left and right, she answered, "Bennie said that he heard her when she got shot."

"Which way did you all go when you got out?"

"Up the road toward Dena Browning's, up past where she lived, and on up by Henry Browning's."

"What road did you go?"

"It wasn't any road it was just a plain little path up to the county road."

"Say this is the house," he said, pointing to the witness box, "which way from the house did Bennie go?"

"Up this way, toward the county road." She pointed.

"Did Bennie go up the same way that you all did?"

"No sir."

"Did you all go any part of the way together?"

"Not so awfully far."

"Then Bennie went one way and you all went another?"

"Yes sir."

"How did you get back to Mandy and the rest of them."

"I walked," she replied, to a few chuckles in the room.

"I believe you said that you started with Bennie?"

"Yes sir, but he was running and I couldn't keep up with him and then I got with mother and them and went on with them."

"How far was it after you got out of the house when you dropped off and couldn't keep up with Benny?"

"About as far is from here to the end of the court room."

"Was this as far as you went with him?"

"Yes sir."

"Was that from the door of the house?"

"Yes sir."

"Was that house about 14 or 15 feet long?"

"Yes sir."

"Was the door in the center of the house?"

"Yes sir, it was supposed to be."

"Did Aunt Kate get out of the house?"

"Yes sir."

"Now Angie, when you was out here with Bennie where was Aunt Kate?"

"She was out there in the yard with us before Bennie started to run."

"How far were you from the door when you were standing there talking?"

"About as far as from here to these men over there," she answered, pointing toward the jury.

"You weren't any farther from the door than that?"

"No sir."

"Angie, where were you when you got shot?"

"I think I got part of my shots in the house and part of them out of doors."

"Did you know when you got shot?"

"When they shot me in the face I did."

"Where were you?"

"I think I was out of doors."

"Whereabouts were you?"

"Up above the house a little piece."

"Was it while you were standing here with Bennie?"

"No sir."

"Who was the first one that you saw when you got out there in the yard?"

"John Bolton."

"Did he say anything to you?"

"No sir."

"What did he have in his hands?"

"A gun."

"What kind of a gun was it?"

"A shotgun."

"You saw Mandy when she came out of the house?"

"Yes sir."

"She came on out here to where you were?"

"Yes sir."

"John Bolton was standing right there beside Mandy?"

"Yes sir."

Funk next carefully asked, "Was he close enough that you could have touched him and that close to Mandy?"

"Yes sir."

"What did he do?"

"Never done anything that I seen," she answered, seemingly contradicting Mandy's earlier testimony.

"Did he say anything to you?"

"No sir."

"Who else did you see there?"

"Elmer Crenshaw."

"Where was Elmer?"

"At the other corner of the house."

"What did he have in his hands?"

"A gun."

"What kind of a gun?"

"A shotgun."

"How many shots were fired before you came out the door?"

"Six."

"How many were shot before you went to chopping?"

"About one."

"How many were fired while you were chopping on the door?"

"One, I think."

"Were there any fired after you chopped it open?"

"No sir, there were some shot before we went to chopping."

"Was there more than one shot before Peachie went to chopping?"

"Two before Peachie went to chopping."

"How many were fired before you went to chopping?"

"Three."

"How many were fired while you were chopping?"

"Two."

"Did those two shots hit you?"

"No sir, I guess not, I don't remember it if they did."

"Did you feel any shot hit you while you were chopping on the door?"

"No sir."

"Where was Aunt Kate while you all were doing this chopping?"

"Right over here in this corner, right over here (indicating the right-hand corner)."

"Now you say that Aunt Kate was right back here in this right-hand corner?"

"Right about middle ways of the house."

"Where was the floor burning?"

"Right about middle ways of the house."

"And the roof was afire right about middle ways of the house?"

"Yes sir."

"How long had Aunt Kate been back there where she was standing?"

"Just a few minutes, I don't reckon she had nowhere else to go."

"Were you chopping on the door at the time Aunt Kate was shot?"

"No sir, Bennie or some of them were."

"What did she say when they shot her?"

"Says, 'Oh Lordy they have fixed me.'"

"Was that the first shot that was fired?"

"About the second one I think."

"Was that before Bennie got shot?"

"Yes sir."

"Before Peachie got shot?"

"Yes sir."

"Was Aunt Kate the first one to get shot?"

"Yes sir."

"Then she went back there in that corner?"

"Yes sir."

"Did she fall down?"

"No sir, I don't think she did."

"Didn't Bennie fall when he was shot?"

"No sir."

"How come Bennie to give the axe to Peachie?"

"He was shot."

"When Peachie took the axe, did he get shot?"

"Yes sir, they shot him and he fell back between the beds."

Returning to the question of what she saw John Bolton do, he asked, "After you got outside did you see John Bolton fire any shots?"

"No sir, I didn't."

This time there were some glances among the jurors as they remembered Mandy's claim that he shot her.

"Did Aunt Kate ever leave there with you all."

"No sir."

"Did you ever at any time see her walking up the path?"

"Not after we started to run."

"You hadn't gotten to the path at the time you started to run had you?"

"Yes sir."

"You hadn't gotten out of the yard at that time had you?"

"No sir."

"That house was burning then wasn't it?"

"Yes sir."

"You could see all around there?"

"Yes sir."

"About how long after you came out of the house until Mandy came out?"

"We all come out just like this," she said, snapping her fingers.

"You stood out there in the yard for some few minutes?"

"Yes sir."

"Didn't get shot?"

"No sir, not then."

"Where did you get shot?"

"In the face."

"Whereabouts in the face?"

"Right here." she pointed.

"Are those shots still in there?"

"Yes sir, some of them are."

"Did you have a doctor take them out?"

"No sir."

Next, in response to his questions, she agreed that when she ran away from the house her back and left side where toward the people she saw there.

Then he asked, "And you got shot in the right-hand side of the face, some of them came out themselves, and you took some of them out?"

"Yes sir."

"Have any of them come out since the examining trial?"

"No sir," she said, and then agreed that she had taken three out on the day of the examining trial.

Funk next said, "I will ask you if, at the examining trial, you didn't state that you went home to dinner that day, and while you were there at dinner you took three shots out and you didn't save those shots?"

"No sir, I didn't save any shot."

"Didn't save any shots that came out of your side?"

"No sir."

"How much clothing did you have on that night?"

"Had on two dresses."

"Did any blood get on either one of those dresses?"

"I brought one of them here."

"Did it have any blood on it?"

"It did have but I washed it the other day."

"I believe you say that you went up to the road with Peachie, Mandy, and your mother that night?"

"Yes sir."

"Who was it that was up there on the road?"

"They say it was Mr. Frank Hodge, I never seen him."

"How far were you from your mother and them up there?"

"A right smart piece behind them."

"Did you stop?"

"Yes sir."

"Where was Peachie?"

"He was with mother and all of us."

"When did you get behind your mother and them?"

"They just walked faster than I did. I don't know when."

"You were all four together when you passed Dena Browning's house weren't you?"

"Yes sir."

"Did she say anything to any of you?"

"Peachie told her when we passed there, that they were raising sand down there."

"Didn't Peachie say to her, that we are having hell down there?"

"No sir."

"Then you went on by there?"

"Yes sir."

"You went on by Henry Browning's and on past Charlie Biven's?"

"Yes sir."

"Then someone began shooting up there and you then turned around and went back to Charlie Biven's?"

"Yes sir."

"Did you see any of the ones that were doing the shooting?"

"No sir, I didn't see them."

"Who did you first tell that you saw Elmer Crenshaw and John Bolton up there?"

"The coroner's jury."

"Is that the first ones that you told?"

"Yes sir."

"When you first got back up there to Charlie Biven's that night and got in at the door did you tell Maggie Biven and Charlie Biven anything that it happened down there?"

"Mandy did."

"When you all got down there and got in that house you all went off over in the corner and had a talk the first thing that you did, didn't you?"

"Yes sir," she answered reluctantly.

"And you talked it over and decided to tell that John Bolton and Elmer Crenshaw were down there?"

"Yes sir, and we never told any lie about it either," she insisted.

"You lay down there on the floor and went to sleep?"

"I did, I don't know about the rest."

"Where did you all go from there the next morning?"

"Charlie Browning's."

"What time did you get down there?"

"Just about daylight."

"This road that you had to travel to go down there passed right by the thicket where Kate was laying didn't it?"

"No sir."

"That thicket comes right up to the road doesn't it?"

"Yes sir, but she was at the other end of the thicket."

"She was in the same thicket but was at the other end of it?"

"Yes sir."

"Your mother told you about where Kate fell didn't she? "

"No sir."

"Didn't she tell you that Kate fell down there that night and tell you where she fell?"

"No sir, she didn't tell me nothing about it." Angie shook her head vigorously.

"You all didn't go back to see anything about Kate that night?"

"No sir, we were afraid to," she said, and then continued, "I thought she was dead."

"Who found Kate the next morning?"

"Charlie Browning. We sent him up there to see about her and he come back down there and said that she was still living but that she couldn't say anything and then we all went down there."

"You all hadn't been down there before that?"

"No sir."

"What did you think had become of Bennie? Did you think that he was dead too?"

"Yes sir I thought he was."

"Did you think that he had burned up in the house?"

"I didn't think that he was in the house."

"But you did think that he was dead?"

"Yes sir."

"You knew that Peachie wasn't dead didn't you?"

"I thought that he had got killed too."

"Peachie had gone with you up past Charlie Biven's house?"

"They were shooting up there, I didn't know whether he was killed or not."

"Up there that night was the last time that you saw Peachie until the next morning?"

"Yes sir."

"How many shots were fired up there on the road where you said they were shooting at Peachie?"

"About three," she answered doubtfully.

"Then you and your mother and sister ran back toward Mr. Biven's?"

"Yes sir."

"Now Angie you said that you didn't know but what one of these three shots killed Peachie didn't you?"

"I didn't know what become of him."

"How do you account for that statement, was it because those shots were fired?"

"Yes sir, and because he never did come back down to Mr. Biven's or nothing."

"How far were you from the Biven's house when those shots were fired?"

"Not so awful far."

"Were your mother and Mandy with you?"

"Yes sir."

Next Mr. Funk brought up the trouble the family was supposed to have been having.

"Now Angie, you and your mother and Mandy and Peachie hadn't been getting along with Aunt Kate had you?"

"Just a little family affair was all that had been the trouble."

"In that little one room log house, Benny and Aunt Kate had them a table to themselves and you and your mother and Peachie and Mandy all had a table to yourselves didn't you?"

"Yes sir," she agreed.

"Bennie brought in the grub, he was the only one in the family that was working, and he and Aunt Kate had a table to themselves and wouldn't let you all eat with them?"

"I didn't care much," she answered with an emphasis on the word "much."

"You all had quite a lot of arguments about it didn't you?"

"No sir" was her defensive reply.

"Didn't he tell you that you had to get out and get your own grub?"

"Yes sir," she admitted.

"Aunt Kate and your sister Mandy had quite a little trouble over that didn't they?"

"Yes sir, I reckon they had a little."

"You went with your mother down to have them arrested didn't you?"

"I went along with mother."

"The reason that you went down there was that Kate beat Mandy up, wasn't it?"

Refusing to agree out loud, Angie finally answered, "I didn't see nothing the matter with her."

"At that same time, didn't Bennie tell you all if you didn't stop the trouble that you would have to leave and your mother said that if she had to leave there that that house will go up in smoke?"

"I never did hear none of them say anything about that."

Funk's final question was "You were there most of the time weren't you?" to which she agreed.

As Funk headed for his chair, Mr. Creal rose and said, "A few questions on re-direct your honor."

Turning to Angie, he said, "You were asked about you all eating at different tables from Kate and Bennie; tell this jury if you had been doing this for two or three days before the fire took place?"

"We had been eating together for two or three days," she agreed.

Creal wanted to know how long the separate eating tables had been going on, and Angie replied, "A few weeks."

He asked, "How many meals did they eat over there by themselves?"

"I don't know, a lot of them."

"How long had you all been on good terms?"

"Two or three days."

Touching on the questions of firearms and jugs, Creal asked, "Did you all have any firearms about the place, a gun or pistol or anything of the sort?"

"No sir."

He then asked, "Did you all have any jugs there or borrow any?"

Angie shook her head, and replied, "No."

When both sides indicated they were through with the witness, she was dismissed.

Agent Frank Mather

Frank A. Mather, a prohibition agent, was the Commonwealth's next witness. After being sworn in, he took the witness seat, ready to answer questions.

Mr. Creal asked the usual questions to identify the witness by name and occupation before inquiring, "Did you make a raid in the county along about May 4, 1928?"

As the witness was replying, "Yes sir." the defense was already rising to object to the question and answer on the grounds that it was not relevant. The judge disagreed and over-ruled the objection.

Creal continued, "Whereabouts in the county was that?"

"Up in the Browningtown neighborhood."

In response to the next question, Mather indicated that he had arrested Elmer Crenshaw.

Creal next wanted to know, "Did anybody accompany you to this place to point out this still to you?"

"Mandy and Lou Browning." was Mather's reply.

Again the defense objected, and again their objection was over-ruled.

Creal continued, "Did they go with you part of the way to this still?"

"Yes sir, they went to the mouth of this hollow where the still was located up in about one hundred and fifty yards of the still."

"How far was this from their home?"

"About three or four miles I suppose."

Creal inquired if the Brownings had provided the information about the still's location, and Mather agreed.

Then Creal asked, "Who did you find there at the still with reference to these defendants?"

"Elmer Crenshaw."

"Was there anybody else there that you knew?"

"No sir."

"Was there anybody else there that you didn't know?"

"Yes sir, there was another man there."

"Did you catch him?"

"No sir."

"Have you learned his identity?"

Mr. Bradbury rose to object on the grounds it was immaterial to this case, and the judge agreed.

Creal next asked, "After you came back from the still, did you see the Browning women any more?"

Misunderstanding the question, Mather said, "They took us up the mouth of this hollow until we could track the rest of the way by the slop."

Clarifying, Creal inquired, "After you took Crenshaw into custody, did you see them any more?"

"Yes sir, I picked them up in the car and took them home."

"In the same car with Crenshaw?"

"Yes sir."

"Were there any other officers in the car?"

"Just Mr. Crenshaw and the two women and me."

"Were there any other officers out there with you?"

"Mr. Larkin was along."

"Do you know Frank Kinder?"

"I do now, I didn't at that time."

"If you do, did you see him on that day?"

"Yes sir."

"Where did you see him?"

"At home, Elmer sent him over after his father to tell him to come over to Bardstown to go on his bond."

"Did you pass any other house?"

"I didn't notice any other."

"I will ask you whether or not he stopped at any other house?"

"No sir."

"Was there any other house, any closer to Elmer Crenshaw's father's house than this one?"

"I couldn't state about this."

"Do you know where Frank Kinder lives and where Clarence Crenshaw lives?"

"Yes sir, but I don't know just how far it is."

"Did you see anybody else at any other house along there?"

"There are several other houses along there, but I don't remember whether I did or not."

"Do you know John Bolton?"

"Yes sir."

"Knowing John Bolton as you do now, did you see him on that day?"

"He was at a house a little more than a half a mile west of Kinder's place when we went down that morning."

"Were there any words passed between Elmer Crenshaw and John Bolton that day?"

"No sir, not that I know of."

"I will ask you whether or not you stopped at John Bolton's?"

"No sir."

At this point, Judge Richardson interrupted Mr. Creal, and spoke to the jury.

"Gentlemen of the jury the testimony of this witness relating to that still in the presence of Mr. Elmer Crenshaw there, and the conveying of him to Bardstown by the officers is not evidence in this case as to the guilt or innocence of this defendant on this charge. You may consider it as evidence as to the identity of Elmer Crenshaw and his motive if any and you will not consider it for any other purpose."

This concluded the Commonwealth's questions for this witness, and Mr. Bradbury rose, and asked the judge to exclude this witness's testimony from the jury, but was over-ruled.

Approaching the witness, he said, "You say that you found Elmer Crenshaw at the still I believe?"

"Yes sir."

"Did he ask your permission to change clothes there at the still?"

"I believe he said something about taking his overalls off."

"He turned them over to you gentlemen didn't he?"

"I wouldn't say about that, I don't remember."

"Do you remember whether or not you have his overalls now?"

"No sir, I don't."

"You do remember that he asked you about taking them off?"

"The best I remember he did."

"He had on a union suit didn't he over his other clothes?"

"I don't remember."

All this was to show that Crenshaw was not still wearing the slop-spattered clothes later that day.

Bradbury said, "I believe you say that you saw John Bolton that day?"

"Yes sir."

"Where did you see him?"

"At a house something like a half a mile after you turned off the pike."

"You say that you saw him standing here at this house as you came back?"

"Yes sir, he was standing right in front of his car there at the house something like 30 or 40 yards east of the house."

"Then when the Brownings say that he was up in the field plowing when you came back by they were mistaken?"

Creal objected to the question and was sustained; but Bradbury knew he had made his point with the jury.

Mather was dismissed, and the Commonwealth announced that it would next call Dena Browning to the stand.

Dena Browning Takes the Stand

Likely the last place Dena Browning wanted to be right now was here in this witness chair. But she'd made the mistake of being too curious about all the commotion the night of the fire. If she'd just stayed in bed instead of being at the door when Lou and her kids had come by ... but she hadn't, and now there was nothing to do but answer the lawyer's questions.

Mr. Creal began by establishing who she was, and that she was Dena Fox before she married.

He then wanted to know, "How close to this house that was burned do you live?"

"Right is sight. I can see the top of the house in daytime from my house," she replied.

"What is the nature of the ground between the place where you live and this house that was burned?"

"There are some trees, woods and bushes in there between my house and this one."

"Did you see any of the fire over there that night?"

"Yes sir."

"What was the first that you heard?"

"I heard the shooting."

"Was that before or after you saw the fire?"

"Before."

"Where were you at that time?"

"At home, standing in the door."

"When you first heard this shooting were you in the bed or where were you?"

"I was in the bed," she sighed. If only she had stayed there, she thought.

"Had you been asleep that night before that?"

"Yes sir, I had kind of dozed off to sleep."

"How many shots did you hear down there?"

"Seven or eight altogether something like that, three or four while I was in the bed and then there were seven or eight altogether, I guess."

Creal seemed pleased with the answer. He next inquired, "Then when you got up did you see any fire?"

"It wasn't burning much when I saw it."

"How long did you stay in there?"

"I don't know, it was burning pretty big before I left there."

"Did you hear any more shooting?"

"No sir."

"Did you see any of these folks that lived in this house that was afire?"

"Yes sir, they came up by my house."

"Who of them did you see?"

"Lou, Angie, Mandy and Peachie."

"How were they traveling?"

"Walking pretty fast."

"Who was in front?"

"Peachie."

"Did they stop there at your house?"

"Peachie stopped and says that they are raising sand down there."

"Were the women folks with him?"

"Yes sir."

"Was Aunt Kate along?"

"No sir."

"Did you see either of these three women there at that time to tell whether or not they were shot?"

"No sir."

"Did you see them anymore that night?"

"No sir."

"See them next morning?"

"No sir," she replied, and then volunteered, "I saw all of them down there where Kate was."

"Did any of them have any indications of any wounds anywhere?"

"Looked like Angie was shot. I could see the blood on her face."

"Which side of her face?"

Dena thought for a moment, and then said, "Both sides I think."

"Did any of the others have any such indications?"

"I never did see any place."

Creal then inquired, "Did you see Ewing Browning there that night?"

"Yes sir."

"What time was he there?"

"About nine o'clock."

"Which way was he going?"

"He was going toward his home."

"Did you have any conversation with him?"

"Yes sir."

"Was that the first time that you had seen him that night?"

"Yes sir."

"Was he going toward or away from the house that was burned?"

"Going toward his home."

"From the house that was burned?" Creal sounded a little puzzled.

"Yes sir."

Creal noted that Bradbury was making a note on the paper in front of him, and realized that he too had recognized the discrepancy between the eleven o'clock mentioned by Lou and her kids, and the nine o'clock testified by Dena.

He turned back to the witness, and asked, "How long had it been since you had been down to the Browning home where Aunt Lou and the rest of them live?"

"I hardly ever did go down there."

"When they passed your house that night did any of the Brownings have any firearms, guns or anything of that kind?"

"No sir, I didn't see any."

"How close were you to Peachie?"

"About as far as it is from me to you," she indicated, a distance of only a few steps.

"Was it clear or cloudy that night?"

"The moon was shining."

"I will ask you after they passed on if you heard any shooting anywhere else?"

"That was out at Charlie Biven's that I heard a dog barking at them."

"Did you hear any shooting?"

"Yes sir."

"What did they sound like a gun or pistol?"

"I can't hardly tell."

"How many shots were fired up there?"

"Three or four, four or five, I couldn't tell they were shooting so fast and I never paid much attention."

"What direction was that from where you were, the direction that these folks went or the other direction?"

"Right on up the road the way they went."

"Do you know whether or not they had their shoes on?"

"No sir, I do not."

Deciding he was not getting any more useful information from the witness, Mr. Creal turned and walked away, saying "Your witness, counselor."

Attacking the last question first, Mr. Bradbury asked, "They go barefooted most of the time don't they?"

"The women do."

"So you live close to that house?"

"Yes sir."

"When you first discovered the fire there that night was when you heard the shooting, wasn't it?"

"Yes sir."

"How long was it before you went to the door after you got out of bed?"

"I got right up and went to the door."

"How long until you saw them coming?"

"The house was burning pretty big when they came by."

"When you first got up was the house burning pretty big? "

"Not very big, when I first got up."

"After you got up you heard two or three more shots?"

"Yes sir."

"How long after you heard these last shots until these people came up there by your house?"

"I don't hardly know."

"Was it half an hour?"

"No sir, I don't guess it was over ten minutes."

"After you went there to that door, did you stay in there all the time?"

"Yes sir."

Bradbury then asked her a question that puzzled her.

"Did you hear any automobiles pass your house that night?"

She thought about it a bit, and then replied, "No sir."

"Did you see any?"

"No sir."

Then he wanted to know, "Did you hear anybody hollering?"

"I heard somebody," she said vaguely.

"Where they talking to somebody?"

"Sound like they were talking to somebody or hollering at them."

"When you heard that, where were you?"

"Up there in the road."

"How long was that after they passed?"

"Ten or fifteen minutes."

"Did you see anybody else come up by your house before they came?"

"No sir."

"When they came along what did Peachie say to you?"

"He says that they are raising sand down there."

"He didn't ask you for any assistance?" asked the lawyer, in a tone that suggested he was shocked that they hadn't.

"No sir."

"Henry Browning has a telephone doesn't he?"

"Yes sir."

"Did they stop up there?"

"No sir."

"Did you hear them talking before they got to your house?"

"Yes sir."

"Could you understand anything they were saying?"

"No sir."

"Were they all in a bunch together or were they scattered out?"

"They were all one right behind the other."

"Peachie was first and who was the next one?"

"I don't know, I never paid no attention."

"How long had it been since you heard the last shots?"

"Ten or fifteen minutes, something like that I guess."

"When they went on out the road toward Henry Browning's, did they walk pretty rapidly or pretty slow?"

"Pretty fast."

Returning to the subject of Ewing Browning, Bradbury wanted to know, "Do you know where Ewing was that night?"

"He was at home."

"How do you know?"

"I was up there."

"Did you see him?"

"Yes sir. He was in bed., but with the lamp burning I could see him."

"I believe you say that you saw him pass your house that night going home about nine o'clock?" Bradbury asked, with an emphasis on the word "nine."

"He was going that way."

"When you went over there and saw Ewing there in the bed that night did he get up or not?"

"No sir."

"Did you see Henry?"

"Yes sir."

"Did he say anything about what was going on down there?"

"Yes sir."

"Ewing never got up at all?"

"Not while I was there."

Bradbury paused thoughtfully, and then quietly asked, "Dena, Ewing is your brother-in-law isn't he?"

"Yes sir."

"You have been married twice I believe?"

"Yes sir."

"He was a brother to your first husband and also a brother to your present husband?"

At this point Mr. Creal arose and objected to the question on the grounds that the witness's personal life was not relevant to the matter at hand. Judge Richardson agreed and sustained the objection.

Satisfied that he had made his point, Mr. Bradbury thanked the witness for her testimony, and returned to his seat.

The Coroner Testifies

C. A. Masden, the county coroner, was next called as a witness for the Commonwealth and sworn in.

After preliminary questions about his identity, Mr. Creal asked the witness, "Did you hold an inquest at the Browning home sometime about May 4 over one Kate Browning?" to which the witness said he had.

When asked whether Kate was alive or dead when he arrived, he replied, "She was dead."

Creal next asked, "Where was she?"

"Just about 50 yards from the house."

"Did you make any examination of the body?"

"I did."

"What kind of examination did you make?"

"We examined and found that she was shot up pretty badly in the breast and then we turned her over and found that she had been shot in the back too."

"Which was the greater wound in the back or front?"

"In front."

Creal wanted to know "How deep did the shots go that struck her in the back?"

"Not very deeply, just barely did get through the flesh." was Masden's answer.

When asked how deep the shots went that struck her in the breast, his reply of "pretty deep" caused Mr. Funk to rise in objection.

However his objection that the witness was not qualified to judge the nature of the wound was over-ruled.

Pursuing the issue, Creal asked, "How big was the wound across her breast?"

"Covered a right smart space."

"Were there few or many shot holes?"

"Many."

"Did it indicate that the holes were made with bullets or with shot?"

"Shot."

His next questions elicited the information that there were no powder burns that Masden could see; that there may have been one or two shots close enough to the surface to pick out; and that the wound was on the left side of her breast.

He then asked, "Where were they with reference to the heart?"

"My judgment would be that they were right over the heart."

Mr. Funk again arose to object. "Your honor, the witness is not a medical expert." However, the judge was not impressed, and over-ruled the objection.

When Creal then asked "From your examination of her what in your judgment produced her death?" Mr. Bradbury objected that the witness was not a doctor, and had no way of knowing what had caused Kate's death.

This time the court agreed, and sustained the objection.

Creal then inquired, "Were there any other wounds of any kind other than what you have described?"

"Not that I know of, I didn't see anymore."

"Did you look for any others?"

"Yes sir."

"As to the amount of blood, could you tell whether or not she had bled much or little; was there much blood around there?"

"A right smart of blood around there."

"Where was it?"

"On her clothes."

"Was there any anywhere else?"

"I never noticed whether there was any there on the ground or not."

"Are you a physician?"

"No sir."

"Could you tell from the wounds on the left side of the breast that you saw there whether or not they had gone in very deep, or how deep they had gone by looking at them?"

"No sir."

"How big a hole did they make?"

"Look like a right good size hole."

"Something like the size of a dollar?"

"Probably something like the size of a dollar." the witness agreed.

"How deep was the main place?"

"I couldn't tell you."

"From your examination of that wound would you say that hole was made all at one shot, or whether it was shot from more than one gun?"

Again Mr. Bradbury objected, stating, "Your honor, how could the witness possibly know that?"

"I agree," replied the judge, and looking at Mr. Creal he said, "Rephrase your question, or move on."

Trying another tactic, Creal said, "Other than the large deep wound on this left-hand side of the breast, what other character of wound was there on the other side of the breast?"

"Just a few scattered shot."

"Did they penetrate as deeply as the main one?"

"I don't know exactly, I wouldn't say."

"Was she cold or warm when you got there?"

"Cold."

"Was that wound, in its location and the depth of it, sufficient to cause death?"

"Objection, your honor," protested Mr. Bradbury, "The witness has indicated that he is not a physician; therefore he is not qualified to make that judgment."

Judge Richardson agreed, and told Mr. Creal so.

Asking another question, Mr. Creal inquired, "Did the wound enter the body, that is go through the flesh on into the body?"

"Yes sir."

Bradbury again objected on the same grounds, but his objection was over-ruled.

Creal continued, "The wound on her back, how big a space did that cover?"

"There weren't many shots struck her back."

"About how many would you say?"

"I wouldn't want to say, I don't know."

"What part of the back was it on, side, center or what?"

"Seemed to be right along here." he indicated, pointing to the place.

"Could you tell whether or not she had received two wounds or that the same wound had come and gone?" asked Creal, seeking to determine if the wounds front and back were from the same shot.

"It looked to me like there were two wounds."

"Tell what you saw in the back. Did you see any shots in the back?"

"Yes sir, I did."

"Did the shot in the back go deep or shallow?"

"Shallow."

Changing direction, Creal asked, "Did you see Angie Browning there that day?"

"I did."

"What time of the day was it that you saw her?"

"Something like ten o'clock."

"Did you notice whether or not she was wounded in any manner?"

"She was wounded in the face."

"Anywhere else?"

"No sir."

"Did you examine any other members of the family?"

"No sir, I didn't examine any of them."

"Did you see Peachie Browning that morning?"

"Yes sir, but not until after the inquest was held."

Mr. Creal thanked the witness, and turned him over to the defense.

Following up on Creal's latter questions, Mr. Bradbury asked, "Say you never examined any of them?"

"No sir."

"You don't know whether Angie was shot or not?"

"Blood was running down her face."

"You don't know what caused that?"

"My judgment was that she was shot."

"What time did you say that you got there?"

"About ten o'clock, something like that."

"Was it raining when you got there?"

"Yes sir."

"Was it a cold, disagreeable morning?"

"It was a little cool."

"That's all. Thank you Mr. Masden." With that Mr. Bradbury returned to his seat, and Mr. Creal announced that the prosecution's next witness would be Bennie Browning.

Bennie Browning Testifies

The prosecution would rather have avoided putting Bennie and Peachie Browning on the stand, but judged that to not do so might make the jury wonder why they were avoiding to testify. Still, Mr. Creal began his examination of the witness with a certain hesitancy.

He began with the preliminaries, identifying the witness as Ben Browning, son of Lou Browning, and determining that the witness had been at home the night of the fire.

He then asked, "What was the first thing that you saw or heard of the fire there that night?

"I saw the fire on the roof first."

"Who gave the alarm that there was a fire there that night?"

"My mother."

"Just go ahead and tell the jury what you saw there that night."

"I saw the fire on the roof and under the floor."

"What did you do when you saw that?"

"I got up and got the axe and went chopping on the door."

"What did you do that for?"

"So that I could get out." was the response, spoken as if he thought the lawyer couldn't see the obvious.

Mentally cautioning himself that the witness needed careful handling with relatively simple questions, Creal next inquired, "Why did you have to chop the door to get out?"

"It was fastened on the outside."

"How was it fastened?"

"Wired."

"Did you try to get out before you went to chopping?"

"Yes sir, I did."

"How was the door fastened on the inside, or was it fastened at all?"

"It was fastened with a button."

"Who was the first of your family to that door?"

"I was."

"Just go ahead and tell just what you did." Creal asked, hoping to get a coherent reply.

"As soon as I went to chopping they went to shooting." was Bennie's straight-forward response.

"Which did you try to do first, pull the door open or begin chopping on it?"

"Tried to pull it open."

"Tell everything that took place there while you were trying to chop the door open."

"My sister got the axe and give it to me, and I began to chop and they got so hot for me I had to give it up, and I give the axe to my brother and he got shot, and then my sister took the axe and finally got the door open."

"What do you mean when you say that they got so hot for you?"

"They were shooting at me."

"From where?"

"Outside there some place."

"Did that shot bother you any?"

"Yes sir."

"What kind of door was that?"

"Oak."

"Where was this shooting, close to the house?"

"Pretty close."

"What was Angie doing?"

"Standing back there in the floor."

"Did any of you do anything else toward trying to get out?"

"My sister did."

"When you got the door open, then what did you do?"

"Went out of the house."

"Where did you go then?"

"I stopped out in the yard to look at the fire, and then they started shooting at me again."

"How many shots were fired altogether?"

"There were six through the door."

"How many were fired at you after you got out?"

"There were two or three fired at me after I got out."

"Could you see any of the shots that were fired at you there who fired them?"

"Golden Hodge."

Once again, Bennie brought out the name of Golden Hodge, although none of the others mentioned seeing him at the scene.

"Did any of the shots hit you that time?"

"No sir!" was his proud reply.

"Who else was out there that you knew when you got outside?" Creal asked, hoping that Bennie would get the answer right.

"Jim Harris, Elmer Crenshaw, Frank Kinder, and Arthur Hodge," was the reply.

Hoping for more, Creal inquired, "Who else?"

"Frank Hodge."

"Who else?"

"Selby Hodge."

"Who else?"

Eager to please, Bennie volunteered, "I heard John Bolton talking."

"What did you hear him say?"

"Some of them ask him if he was ready and he says yes."

"Who was it that asked him if he was ready?"

"I couldn't tell who it was." Bennie seemed disappointed that he didn't have another name to give.

"What did he say?"

"Said yes."

"Was there anybody else that you saw there?"

"No sir."

"Did the rest of the members of your family go in the same direction that you did?"

"None of them went the same direction that I did, I don't think."

Cautiously Creal inquired, "Where was Golden Hodge?"

"Standing up there at the corner of the house."

"How do you know that he shot at you?"

"Because I know that he did." Bennie blustered.

"He didn't hit you, did he?"

"He come pretty near it." he insisted.

"Where did the shot hit?"

"On the ground there right by me."

"Where were the rest of your folks at that time?"

"There at the house."

Thus far, the witnesses had been rather vague about just how Kate had received her fatal wound, and Creal thought that Bennie might be the one to provide an answer.

"Where did you last see your Aunt Kate?"

"Right there where I left her in the yard when we were standing there talking."

"Do you know when she was shot?"

"They shot me and her both at the same time."

It was not clear in the minds of the spectators when this occurred. Was it while everyone was in the house and Bennie was chopping on the door, or was it after they got out of the house?

Creal asked, "How do you know they shot her at that time?"

"I heard her holler."

"About how far were you away from the door?"

"About ten steps."

"Did you see who shot her?"

"No sir."

"When she was shot, was she shot from in front or behind?"

"In front."

"Where were the people that shot her?"

"In front of the house."

"What did she do?"

"Hollered."

"What did she say?"

"Oh Lordy."

"Then what did she say?"

"I left her then, I don't know what she said."

"Where were the rest of your folks then?"

"They were in the house then, standing in the door, my mother and them the last account that I had of them."

"Did you come out in front of them or behind them?"

"In front."

"Then where did you go that night?"

"I slept in Mr. McClure's barn that night."

"How long did you stay there?"

"Until daylight."

"Did you go back to the place of the fire then?"

"No sir."

"Did you go back to the place of the fire the next day?"

"No sir."

"After you say that your aunt was shot, and after you left over there that night, did you hear any more shooting that night?"

"Over there where the fire was."

"How many shots did you hear?"

"Four."

"Was that a shotgun or a pistol that you heard?"

"A shotgun I think."

"Was there anybody stayed there in the barn with you?"

"No sir."

"When did you next get with the rest of your family?"

"Next evening."

"Did you see Angie that evening?"

"I saw all of them except my aunt and she was dead."

"What about Angie, did she have any wounds?"

"Had some in her back and face."

"Did you see the ones in the back yourself?"

"No sir."

"Did you see the ones in the face?"

"Yes sir."

"Which side of the face was it on?"

"If I am not mistaken, it was on the left side."

"What about Peachie, where was he shot?"

"One hit him on the wrist, he said."

Judge Richardson had been patient with the lawyer asking somewhat leading questions due to the mental state of the witness, but now he interrupted, and said, "Gentlemen of the jury, as to what Peachie said would not be competent, and you will ignore it."

"The place that you saw on Peachie's wrist, what kind of a place was that?"

"Just a little bit of a place."

"Did you see any other places anywhere about him?"

"No sir."

"These men that you saw there that night that you have named that you recognized, how long have you known these men?"

"A pretty good while."

"How long?"

"For years."

"Which one is that that you have known for years?"

"Clarence Crenshaw."

"Did I understand you to say that you saw Clarence Crenshaw there, or didn't see him?"

"No sir, I didn't see him there that night."

"Those that you saw there, how long have you known them?"

"I have knowed Frank Hodge and Selby Hodge and Frank Kinder about four years?"

"How long have you known John Bolton?" asked Creal.

"Ever since I have been in the world."

"Did you ever work for John Bolton?"

"Never did that I know of."

"Did he live in that same neighborhood?"

"Yes sir, but not very close to us."

"How long have you known Frank Hodge?"

"About four or five years."

"How long have you known Arthur Hodge?"

"About four or five years."

"How long have you known Jim Harris?"

"Ever since I was born."

"Known him all your life?"

"Yes sir."

"Was there anybody else there that you saw or heard that you recognized that you have not testified about?"

"No sir, I don't think there is."

"Did you at that time, or any of the other members of your family have any guns, pistols or firearms of any kind there in your home?"

"No sir, I had a gun and sold it sometime last summer."

"Did you have any jugs in there at all?"

"No sir."

"When did you next see the house after it was burned?"

"About two weeks ago."

"I mean did you see it next day or how soon did you see it?"

"I didn't see it the next day nor the next one."

Not believing he could gain by asking this witness any more questions, he turned him over to the defense.

Bennie Browning Cross-Examined

As Mr. Funk approached the witness, Bennie sank back into the chair, his brash manner of before becoming suddenly defensive.

"What time did you get home that night?" was Mr. Funk's first question.

"I got home before dark."

"Who was there?"

"My mother and aunt and two sisters and Ewing Browning."

"How long did Ewing stay after you got there?"

"Just a short while."

"Did anybody go away from there with him?"

"Him and Peachie went somewheres." He shrugged as he answered.

"Where did you go when you came home from work?"

"Henry Browning's."

"Is that Ewing's father?"

"Yes sir."

"Was Ewing at home when you were up there?"

"No sir."

"When you went from there, where did you go?"

"Home."

"What time did you get off from work?"

"About six."

"Did you come by Henry Browning's?"

"No sir I went home first."

"You went home and then back to Henry Browning's?"

"Yes sir, I come home and had my supper and then went up to Henry Browning's."

"Ewing was gone from home when you were up there?"

"Yes sir."

"Then you went down to your house and found him down there?"

"Yes sir."

"Then right away after you got there he and Peachie left?"

"Yes sir." Bennie sounded a little resentful, as if he would like to have been invited to go with them.

"When did you see them next before this fire happened?"

"I seen Peachie just before it happened."

"Were you awake?"

"No sir."

"Did you hear them when you came in?"

"No sir."

"You don't know how long you had been asleep when they got there?"

"No sir."

"How long had you been asleep when you found out the house was afire?"

"Not very long."

"Did they come home after Jim Harris left?"

"Yes sir."

"Who woke you up to let you know that the house was afire?"

"My mother."

"How did she wake you?"

"Came over there and shook me and hollered at me."

"How long before you got up, did you get right up as soon as you were awakened?"

"No sir, it was a right smart while, I just felt so sleepy I just couldn't hardly get up." he replied sheepishly.

"Did you get up and go get the ax?"

"I got up and went right straight and got the ax."

"And the next thing that you did you went and went to chopping on the door?"

"Yes sir."

"You were the last one in the house to wake up?"

"Yes sir."

"You went right straight and got the axe and went to chopping and the rest of them were there trying to wake you up?" Funk's question was deliberately confusing.

"I was done up before I got the axe." Bennie insisted.

"They hadn't gotten any axe before you got up?"

"No sir."

"Where did that shot hit you?"

"In the face."

Mr. Funk picked up some papers before asking, "You testified in the examining trial didn't you Ben?"

"Yes sir."

"I will ask you if on the examining trial you were asked this question and made this answer, page 43 of the transcript, you said that you were shot in the face and Mr. Creal ask you this question, "Anywhere else?" And your answer was "in the arm," was that the question asked you and you made that answer?"

Trying to remember back, Bennie finally mumbled "Yes sir."

"Did you get shot with the door fastened, I believe I understand you to say that you got shot when the door was shut?"

"Yes sir that is right." he agreed.

"Were you shot in the arm?"

"Yes sir."

"Which arm?"

"The right one."

"When you woke up did you have any clothes on?"

"I had on my pants and shirt."

"Did you go to bed this way?"

"Yes sir, I was expecting this mob."

"Did you have information that there was a mob coming there that night?"

"Yes sir."

"Who gave you that information?"

"Ewing Browning."

Ewing's name kept coming up, and both prosecution and defense would like to have spoken to him, but neither side had yet found him to summons him to court.

"Were you expecting this mob before Peachie and Ewing left your house that night?"

"Yes sir."

"What time did they come home?"

"I was asleep when they come home, I don't know."

"You didn't have information later on that the mob wasn't coming did you?"

Confused by the question, Bennie finally answered, "I didn't wake up when they come in."

"You were awake when Jim Harris was there at your house?"

"I was laying there in the bed awake."

"After he left what did you do?"

"I went out of the house and looked for him but I couldn't see anything of him, I thought maybe there was something wrong."

"How long had he been gone before the fire?"

"About twenty minutes."

"You had gone back in the house and gone to bed and gone to sleep when Peachie and Ewing came in?"

"Yes sir."

"Who did you say that you saw there that night?"

Bennie started ticking them off on his fingers. "Jim Harris, Elmer Crenshaw, Arthur Hodge, Selby Hodge, Les Hodge and Golden Hodge and I heard John Bolton talking and I saw Frank Kinder there."

"Did you see Golden Hodge?"

"Yes sir."

"Arthur Hodge?"

"Yes sir."

"I will ask you if on the examining trial this question wasn't asked you and this answer made? What men were out there that night that you knew and your answer was Frank Kinder, Elmer Crenshaw, Walter Crenshaw, Arthur Hodge, Selby Hodge, Jim Harris and Golden Hodge, didn't you make that statement?"

"Yes sir."

"So you heard John Bolton talking down there?"

"Yes sir."

"Someone asked him if he was ready and he said yes?"

"Yes sir."

"That is the only words that you heard John Bolton say?"

"Yes sir."

"What made you leave Walter Crenshaw out when you named them this time?"

"Just forgot him."

"You just forgot him?"

"Yes sir."

"Have you forgotten anybody else?"

"No sir."

"Didn't see anybody else there at all?"

"There was a lot more there but I didn't know who they were."

"Where did you see Elmer Crenshaw?"

"Up there above the house."

"Was he out in front of the door?"

"Yes sir."

"Where did you see John Bolton?"

"I didn't see John."

"Where did you see Frank Kinder?"

"Up in front of the house."

"Where did you see Jim Harris?"

"Up in front of the line."

"Were these men lined up?"

"Yes sir."

"Lined up just like this row of men?"

"Yes sir."

"Did you see Frank Kinder with a gun that night?"

"No sir."

"Did Jim Harris have any?"

"No sir."

"Did Shelby Hodge have any?"

"No sir."

"Did Walter Crenshaw have any?"

"No sir."

"Did you see anybody have any gun except Golden Hodge?"

"No sir."

"What was Golden doing with his gun?"

"Pointing at me and shot at me."

"How far away from you was he?"

"About 100 yards." There were some chuckles and a few shaking heads at the distance mentioned. Some thought he was confusing yards with feet, and others just thought he didn't have the sense to properly judge the distance.

"Isn't that place covered with thicket, brushes and briars?"

"Just a few scattered trees, not no thicket."

"Was that house burning pretty bright when he shot at you?"

"Yes sir."

"There were some trees around there?"

"Yes sir, a few scattering trees."

"Was there anybody else there that you saw that had a gun?"

"No sir."

"Who was with you when Golden Hodge shot at you?"

"I was by myself."

"Who came out of the house next to you there that night?"

"My aunt was next to me."

"Where did you go when you came out of the house?"

"Stopped there are in the yard."

"Which side of the house was it on?"

"Right-hand side."

"How far did you go before you were shot at?"

"About ten steps from the yard there."

"About how far away from this door were you?"

"About ten steps." he insisted.

"Then you were still in the yard?"

"Yes sir."

"About how many steps from the right-hand corner of the yard?"

"I don't know, I didn't step it."

"How long was that house?"

"About 16 or 18 feet."

"The door was in the middle of the house?"

"Aimed to be."

"You walked about ten steps after you got out of the house before you stopped?"

"Around the right-hand corner of the house." he pointed.

"That is when Golden Hodge pointed his gun at you and shot?"

"When I left Golden shot at me."

"When you left?"

"When I was leaving out of the yard."

"How long did you stay there before you left?"

"About ten minutes." Again there were shaking heads among the spectators, and a few of the jurors. Ten minutes was a long time to wait before fleeing someone trying to shoot you.

Emphasizing the word "ten" Funk asked, "During the ten minutes that you were standing up there looking at these man, was Golden Hodge the only one that you saw with a gun?"

"Yes sir, he was the only one that I saw."

"When Aunt Kate came out of there, where did she go?"

"Right behind me."

"Did she come to the right-hand side of the house?"

"Yes sir."

"Aunt Kate came to the right-hand side of the house?"

"Yes sir."

"You stood there at the corner of the house for ten minutes?"

"Yes sir."

"You were looking at these men?"

"Yes sir."

"When did she get shot?"

"Back down the hill toward the spring."

"Where were you when she got shot?"

"I was there with her."

"When Aunt Kate got shot, did you get any of those shots?"

"I couldn't tell."

"Which direction did the shots come from?"

"Up above the house."

"Which way were you facing?"

"Down the hill this way from the house." he pointed again.

"And I believe you say that you were shot in the right arm?"

"Yes sir."

"Did you have on your clothes when that shot was fired?"

"I had on my shirt and a pair of pants."

"You introduced the shirt in the examining trial I believe?"

"Yes sir."

"Were there any shot holes in it?"

"I didn't see any."

"Did you go to a doctor?"

"I went to Mr. Holbrook."

"Did he take any shot out of you?"

"No sir."

"Did you, yourself take any out?"

"Yes sir."

"When was the last that you took out?"

"About two weeks after this was done, since the examining trial."

"You were asked particularly about that in the examining trial?"

"Yes sir."

"About how long do you say it has been since you got any shot out?"

"About two weeks."

"Do you have any mark or scar on your arm now?"

"I have got some places on there."

"Let's see them."

"All right, feel right there."

"How many shots did you say went in your arm?"

"Six."

"How many did you say you picked out?"

"About one."

"What became of the rest of them?"

"I don't know, I picked out one of them."

"You turn that shirt over to Mrs. Wallace the stenographer at the examining trial didn't you?"

"Yes sir."

"If Mrs. Wallace brings that shirt here before this trial is over would you be willing to introduce it as evidence in this trial?"

"Yes sir, if it is the same shirt I will."

"After you came out in the yard where did Lou, Mandy, Angie and Peachie go?"

"My mother and two sisters were in the house."

"The door was already chopped down when you came out and they were in the house ten minutes after you got out?"

"Yes sir." Bennie had settled on the answer and continued to stick by it.

"When they came out, were you still in the yard?"

"Yes sir."

"Did Angie run up the path part of the way with you?"

"No sir."

"Which direction did you go?"

"I went up toward Dena Browning's house and turned right to my right when I got up there to the forks of them roads."

"Are there two roads up there at that fork?"

"Two little roads."

"Roads or paths?"

"Paths."

"How far from where the house burned?"

"I don't know exactly."

"Was there anybody right behind you?"

"Not as I seen."

"Anybody say anything to you?"

"No sir."

"Did anybody speak or say anything at all to you?"

"No sir."

"The house was burning and all the yard was lit up?"

"Yes sir."

"You could see all these men and yet none of them said anything to you?" Funk asked in a manner that suggested he found it hard to believe.

"No sir." was the insistent answer.

"Did any of the members of your family say anything to you?"

"Not after I got out of the house."

"What was it Aunt Kate said when the shot was fired?"

"Hollered 'oh Lordy!'"

"Was that on the outside?"

"Yes sir."

"Did she say the same thing on the inside and out both?"

"Yes sir."

"Did you ever see Aunt Kate anymore?"

"No sir."

"Didn't even see her the next day?"

"No sir."

"You have never seen her until this day?"

"No sir."

"Where did you go when you left the house?"

"Went on to the barn."

"Who's barn?"

"Jim McClure's."

"How far was that from this place?"

"About a mile."

"You stayed there the rest of the night?"

"Yes sir."

"What time did you get up the next morning?"

"I don't know what time it was."

"Was the sun up?"

"Yes sir."

"How far is that from Jim McClure's barn to Jim Campbell's house?"

"It is a long ways."

"How many miles?"

"I don't know, I don't have no idea."

"Which road does he live on?"

"The Shepherdsville Road."

"Is that before you get to Cedar Grove Church?"

"Yes sir."

"Going which way?"

"Coming this way it is." he answered, meaning toward town.

"What time did you get over there next day?"

"About two o'clock I guess."

Keeping Bennie off-balance, Funk then asked, "When did you first come to the conclusion that Golden Hodge was there that night?"

The prosecution objected to the question, and was sustained. The judge instructed Mr. Funk to rephrase his question or move on.

Funk then asked, "Who did you first tell that Golden Hodge was there that night?"

"I don't remember who it was."

"Bennie, how long have you been working for Ewing Crenshaw?"

"Off and on for about four years."

"Since you had moved into this new house had you been working for him all the time?"

"No sir."

"Since you had been working with him had you and Aunt Kate had any trouble with the rest of your family?"

"No sir."

"Hadn't you and Aunt Kate been eating at different tables and wouldn't let the rest of them eat at the same table with you all?"

"They could have if they wanted to." he mumbled defensively.

"Didn't you all have some trouble about that?"

"No sir." he insisted.

"Didn't your mother and Mandy and Aunt Kate have some trouble in your presence about that?"

"I don't know what they done."

"You don't know?"

"No sir."

"Didn't you tell them if they didn't quit having all that trouble around there that they would have to leave?"

"Yes sir." he agreed reluctantly.

"Didn't your mother tell you that if she had to leave there that that house was going up in smoke?"

"I heard somebody was going to burn it." was the only reply he would make.

"When did you move into this new house?"

"The fifteenth of January."

"This happened on May 4th?"

"Yes sir."

Mr. Funk indicated that he was finished with the witness, and Mr. Creal rose for a few questions on re-direct.

"Bennie, you were asked about what word Mr. Bolton said, and you said that he only said yes, what did the other man say to him?"

"Some of them asked John was he ready and John said yes."

"Tell the exact words as near as you can as to what this man said."

"Ask John was he ready was all that I heard."

"What words did the man speak?"

"Ask John was he ready."

"How do you know that it was John Bolton?"

"I heard him call him John Bolton."

"Which did he call him, John or John Bolton?"

"John Bolton."

Mr. Bradbury objected to the question on several grounds, but was over-ruled.

"Did he say John Bolton are you ready, or what did he say?"

"He says, 'John Bolton are you ready', and John said 'Yes.'"

Bradbury was hopeful that the jury had caught that Bennie's answer contradicted that of his mother on who asked who the question of being ready to shoot.

Through with this witness, Mr. Creal recalled Lou Browning to the stand for a few questions.

"Lou, did Kate eat supper there with the rest of you folks that night?"

"Yes sir."

"Did she eat dinner that day?"

"Yes sir."

"Was she well otherwise when she got shot?"

"Yes sir, she had been at work places."

Taking this opportunity, Mr. Bradbury then questioned Lou about the jug that was said to have been seen near the burned-out house.

"Lou, I believe you say that you saw a jug on the outside of the house that night?"

"Yes sir, I did."

"The day you testified that you were up there and saw Mr. Funk and myself up there, did you see a jug in the building that day that had been burned and broken to pieces?"

"Yes sir."

"Was there a jug laying there?"

"Yes sir, there was a stone jug laying there."

He then turned to the trouble the family had been having amongst themselves.

"Lou, you folks have had a lot of trouble up there haven't you?"

"Not then, we were on the best of terms."

"You went up to Mr. William Lanham's to get him to call the sheriff to get him to come down there and keep peace in the family not long ago, didn't you?"

"Yes sir." she answered reluctantly.

"And you folks hadn't been eating there together for some little time had you?"

"I don't see no sense in asking that kind of questions; we didn't eat there together sometimes for some little bit."

"At the time you went over to Mr. Lanham's to call the sheriff, Kate and Bennie were in trouble with Mandy weren't they?"

"Kate and Mandy had a little trouble, it was all family affairs, nothing to that."

Satisfied the jury had understood his point, Mr. Bradbury ended his cross-examination.

Mr. Creal stood and addressed the court. "The Commonwealth now called Dr. R. N. Holbrook to the stand."

Dr. Raymond Holbrook Testifies

Dr. Raymond N. Holbrook had been in Shepherdsville for almost two years, after graduating from the University of Louisville medical school in 1926. A native of Graves County, he and his wife Mary, a registered nurse, were newcomers to Bullitt County, but had been warmly welcomed.

Following the routine identifying questions, Mr. Creal asked him, "Have you made an examination of Bennie Browning?"

"Yes sir, I think that is his name, I am not sure about that. I made two examinations of one of the Browning boys."

"When did you make the first one?"

"The second day of the examining trial here."

"Have you made one more recently?"

"Yes sir, this afternoon about five o'clock."

"What kind of examination did you make?"

"Just kind of an inspection and an attempt to remove some shot owing to the fact that I couldn't use my x-ray, but this afternoon I made an x-ray examination using the fluoroscope."

"I will ask you to state whether or not you found any shots?"

"Four."

"Where were they located?"

"In the right arm, about here." He pointed to his upper arm.

"Did you make that examination to see whether or not the shot were there the first time?"

"Yes sir."

"How did you make that examination?"

"By feeling, some of the shot I could feel, I could feel the one here and the one in the top of his arm and there was a shot under the eye and the eye was black but those places have cleared up now."

Creal turned and faced the defense table, but directed his question to the witness.

"Doctor, assuming that a woman 60 years old that was able to work and had eaten the usual dinner and supper and had retired at the regular time and later between that and 12 o'clock at night was shot with a shotgun in the breast over or near the heart, the shot sprinkled over a considerable portion of the breast, the main part of the wound being as large perhaps as a dollar or a little less, and the shot penetrating to such a depth that they could not be seen penetrating the flesh, and then upon examination after that were found on the back other places which merely entered through the skin, and that on later examination no other wounds were found on the body, and the woman having received that wound in the breast somewhere after 12 o'clock and then the next morning near about seven she died, on last May 4, or in the morning of May 5, and that she lay on the ground from the time she received the wound until her death about seven the next morning, Doctor what in your opinion was the cause of her death?"

"I think that it is perfectly obvious if she was shot that it was the result of a gunshot wound."

Smiling, Mr. Creal said, "I have no other questions for this witness, your honor."

Mr. James rose from the defense table, and said, "Just a few questions, your honor."

Turning to the witness, he said, "A woman, age 60, is likely to have any organic disease isn't she doctor?"

"Yes sir." Dr. Holbrook answered carefully.

"Might have heart trouble?"

"Yes sir."

"Apoplexy?"

"Yes sir."

"Without knowing her previous condition of health and the depth of the gunshot wound you couldn't tell whether her death resulted from the gunshot wound or something else could you?"

"No sir. I would have to know the condition of her health previous to that time and the depth of the wound of course."

"You would have to know these things before you could answer that question wouldn't you?"

"Yes sir, but he in his question gave me an idea of her previous condition of health and everything and something about a gunshot wound the size of the dollar, it is almost obvious to me from the question that the gunshot wound was what caused her death, but of course I couldn't say without knowing all these things. He gave me the circumstances and I drew the conclusion."

"Doctor, did you assume that the shot entered a vital organ?"

"Yes sir."

"If you don't go on the idea that the shot entered a vital organ you can't come to that conclusion can you?"

"No sir." was his quiet response.

Mr. James also smiled, and said, "That's all, your honor."

Almost before the word left his mouth, Mr. Creal was on his feet with a question.

"How far from the outer portion of the body is the heart?"

"About three-fourths of an inch to an inch." Dr. Holbrook said, holding his thumb and index finger about that far apart.

"Is the heart of such a nature that if a gunshot should enter it as far as the center that it would produce death?" Mr. Creal was thinking this was true, but the doctor's reply was negative.

"There are instances where even a bullet from a pistol has entered the heart and the patient is still living."

"Then it is possible for a shot to pass into the heart without producing death?" Creal asked, almost disbelievingly.

"Yes sir."

"No more questions, your honor. The Commonwealth wishes to ask Mr. Mather a few more questions, your honor, if he could be recalled to the stand."

Mr. Mather retook the stand, and Mr. Creal asked him, "Were you at the Browning home on the next day after the fire?"

"Yes sir."

"How many of them did you see there that day?"

"All of them, I took them to Bardstown."

"How many of them, if any, did you see that had wounds?"

"They all had been shot, or at least they had marks that appeared to be shot marks."

"Since that time have you talked with them sufficient to know Bennie and Peachie apart?"

"Yes sir."

"Could you tell where they were shot?"

"Bennie was shot in the face and he said that he had some shot in his arm, I didn't see them, and Peachie was shot in the face."

"What about Angie, was she shot?"

"Yes sir, she was shot in the face."

"What about Mandy?"

"Mandy and Lou were shot in the feet."

"How could you tell?"

"They didn't have on any shoes and I could see the places where the shot went in, and then I could see them limping."

"Was any of the house left when you got there next day?"

"No sir."

"I think that's all for this witness, your honor."

When the defense indicated it had no questions, Mr. Creal said, "Your honor, we call Peachie Browning to the stand."

Peachie Browning Testifies

Mr. Creal approached the witness stand, and inquired, "What is your name?"

"Peachie Browning." was the slow reply. He almost said "Jerry Browning" because that was really his name; but everybody, including his mother insisted on calling him Peachie, a nickname that he'd received as a boy for a reason nobody had ever bothered to explain to him.

In the next few questions, he agreed that he was a brother of Bennie Browning, and that he was at home the night of the fire.

Creal then asked, "How long had you been home that night before you discovered that there was a fire?"

He thought for a moment, and replied "About ten minutes."

"Had you gone to bed?"

"I had just got in the bed and I had never been asleep."

"Who saw the fire first?"

"Mother, I guess. She was the one that hollered at me."

"Go ahead and tell us just what you did."

"I got the axe after I got up and Bennie says, 'give me that axe,' and I handed it to him."

"Then what did you do?"

"They commenced to shooting through the door and they shot Bennie and then I took the axe and began to chop on the door and they shot me."

"How many licks did Bennie chop on the door?"

"I remember three or four." was the hesitant reply.

"Say, if you know, why he quit chopping?"

"He got shot."

"Then what did he do with the axe?"

"Give it to me."

"Then what did you do?"

"I took the axe and begin to chop and they shot me and I fell back between the beds."

"Then what did you do?"

"I was standing there waiting for them to get the door open so I could get out." He slipped forward in the chair like he was ready to run away then.

"How did you get shot?"

"A gun shot me in the wrist and something hit me right here in the breast," he pointed, and then continued "I don't know what that was."

"Then what happened after that hit you there?"

"I fell back behind the bed."

"Then what did you do?"

"Lay there until the rest of them got out then I got up and run out and Frank Hodge was the first man that I saw out there when I got out."

"Who else did you see?"

"Selby Hodge, Les Hodge, Arthur Hodge and Elmer Crenshaw and I heard Walter Crenshaw talking and Frank Kinder," he identified each one as he ticked them off on one hand before raising the index finger of his other hand when he came to Frank Kinder.

Creal had never been satisfied that Walter Crenshaw wasn't there, despite his alibi, and decided to pursue this line of questioning.

"What did Walter say?"

Peachie slumped back in the chair and shook his head, saying "I heard him talking I don't know what he said."

"How long have you known Walter Crenshaw?"

"Three or four years."

"How was he talking, loud or low?"

"Pretty loud."

"Talking fast or slow?"

"About like anybody else would talk."

This didn't seem to be going anywhere, so Creal changed directions, and asked, "Did they have guns?"

"Yes sir, they were standing there with guns."

"Was there anybody else there besides these men?"

"Not that I know."

"How many people were there in your best judgment that you didn't know?"

"About 50 the best I could know."

"How much had the roof caught by that time; was the flame up high enough that you could see everything pretty plain?"

"Yes sir, you could've picked up a pin there in the yard."

"Did they shoot at you anymore after you got out?"

"Yes sir, but they didn't hit me anymore." he smiled.

"Did you hear anybody say anything?"

"I heard someone say shoot him again Selby and he said I can't, I have done emptied my gun. I couldn't tell who it was that said that."

"Where were you at that time?"

"Going across the yard."

Creal asked, "Were the rest of them in sight of you then?" meaning the rest of his family.

"I didn't see them no place."

When asked where he met back up with them, he indicated "Way up there above the house."

Creal asked who was there, and he replied "Mother and them, Angie and Mandy. That's all I seen." He also indicated that he never saw Bennie anymore that night.

"Did you see Aunt Kate when she got shot?"

"Yes sir, out there in the yard."

"How far was that from the house?"

"About fifty yards something like that."

"What did she do when she got shot?"

"I heard her holler 'Oh Lordy.'"

"Did you know which one of them that it was that shot her?"

"I didn't know who he was; he was standing back in them trees."

"Did you see anybody that was there with him?"

"No sir."

"How close was the fellow that shot your Aunt Kate; how close was he to her?"

"Sixty or seventy yards, something like that."

"Did you receive any more shots after you got on the outside?"

"No sir."

"Where did you next see Frank Hodge that night after you left down there at the house, did you see him again?"

"Yes sir, up there in the road above Mr. Charlie Biven's."

"Where were you going when you saw him up there?"

"Some place to hunt me a place to stay the rest of the night."

"Where were the women folks at that time?"

"About four feet or something like that behind me."

"You were in front?"

"Yes sir."

"Were are you going fast or slow?"

"Walking pretty fast."

"How do you know that was Frank Hodge?"

"I was talking to him, he had a gun up there shooting across the road in front of us and somebody whistled and then he says 'Who is that?' and I says 'It's me Frank.' and he says 'Where are you going?' and I says 'I am hunting me a place to stay all night Frank.' I says 'I ain't going to hurt nobody.' and he says 'Stop there or I will kill every damn one of you right there in a pile.'"

"What was he shooting with?"

"A pistol."

"How many shots did he fire?"

Peachie held up one hand with the fingers spread and said, "Five."

"What became of the women folks?"

"They said they went to Charlie Biven's."

"What became of you?"

"I went to Aunt Vina Biven's." he replied, indicating his mother's sister who was married to John Biven.

When Creal inquired as to where Frank Hodge was when he was shooting at Peachie, the witness indicated that Frank was coming through the wire fence around his own property, and out onto the road the last Peachie had seen of him.

Creal wanted to know, "Where were you, in the field or in the road?"

"In the road."

"What did you do?"

"I run." Peachie said with a rush.

"What kind of fence was that?"

"Barb wire."

"Were there any more shots fired?"

"Yes sir."

"How many?"

"One more that I can remember of."

"Where did you run to?"

"I run on down through the woods."

"Then where?"

"John Biven's."

"Was he up or in the bed when you got over there?"

"In the bed."

"Were there any of the folks up over there?"

"No sir."

"Did you see any of the women folks that night, Angie, Mandy or your mother?"

"No sir, I didn't see them anymore until about dinner time the next day."

"Where did you next see Bennie?"

"Down at Jim Campbell's."

"Did any of you folks have any guns pistols or firearms of any sort that night there at the house?"

"No sir."

"Had you been at home all day that day?"

"I was working in the garden that day."

"What kind of clothes did you have on when you ran out of the house that night?"

"Overalls and shirts, no shoes."

"When you say you saw Bennie next day what time of day was it when you saw him?"

"I don't know exactly what time it was."

"In the morning or evening?"

"Evening I think."

"Did you see what kind of clothes Bennie had on then?"

"Yes sir, he had a pair of overalls and a shirt."

"Have on any shoes?"

"Yes sir, he had on a piece of a pair."

"Did you see Angie next morning?"

"Yes sir."

"Where?"

"Up there where the house burned."

"I will ask you whether or not Angie received any hurt or wounds of any kind?"

"Yes sir, I guess she did."

"Did you see any place where she had been shot?"

"Yes sir."

"Where was that?"

"In the face."

Feeling he had done all he could with this witness, Mr. Creal turned him over to the defense for questioning.

Cross-Examination of Peachie Browning

C. P. Bradbury rose from his chair and asked, "How old are you Peachie?"

"Twenty-one."

"Where have you lived practically all your life Peachie?"

Peachie shrugged, and muttered, "Different places."

"Where mostly?"

"I lived up on Mr. Will Trover's place a while, and up in Browningtown most of my life, and I lived up on Mr. Cochran's place."

"Did you ever live anywhere else besides Bullitt County?"

"I don't know of no other place." he insisted.

"Don't you know that you have lived out of Bullitt County?"

Peachie's face darkened in a scowl as he almost shouted, "I stayed there, I never did live there!"

Bradbury inquired mildly, "Where?"

"At Frankfort." was the reluctant reply.

"Where did you stay in Frankfort?"

Peachie hesitated, and then replied, "At the feeble minded institute."

"How long since you came back?"

"I don't know." He shook his head.

"Don't you have any idea?"

"About four or five years I guess."

"Since you have been back what have you been doing?"

"I can't remember that far back."

"Who have you worked for up in that country?"

"Nearly everybody up in there."

"You all lived in this little one room house together, all six of you?"

"Yes sir." Peachie didn't care for this man or his questions.

"Six of you living there in one little room?"

"Yes sir." The scowl deepened.

"Two boys and four women?"

"Yes sir." was the muttered reply.

"Say you were at home on Friday before this happened on Friday night?"

"Yes sir."

"Worked in the garden?"

"Yes sir."

"You saw Ewing Browning there that day?"

"Yes sir."

"Did he come over to your house sometime that day?"

"Yes sir."

"What time?"

"He came over there sometime about dinner time." Peachie replied, indicating the noon meal.

"What did he come for?"

"I don't know." he shrugged.

"How long did he stay?"

"Not but a few minutes."

"When did you next see him?"

"I seen him the night the fire took place."

"Was he over at your house that time?"

"Yes sir."

"How long did he stay?"

"Until about eleven."

"Tell the jury, if you please, where the two of you went."

"We went down to the spring and around by the sawmill and come back home."

"About what time was it when you left home, was it dark?"

"Yes sir."

"Then the first place that you went was to the spring?"

"Yes sir."

"From there where did you go?"

"We went from there to Bud Pugh's."

"How long did you stay there?"

"A right smart while."

"Did you stay there an hour?"

"No sir, I don't guess we did."

"Stay there about a half an hour or something like that?"

"Something like that."

"Then where did you go?"

"Up past Mr. Ewing Crenshaw's silo barn."

"You were in up there with Ewing Browning?"

"Yes sir."

"Did you go in Bud's house?"

"No sir."

"Did you see him?"

"No sir, I heard him talking in the house."

"Did you go in Bud Pugh's house that night at all?"

"No sir."

Bradbury proceeded to ask a number of brief questions that determined that Peachie had not seen Mrs. Pugh, that he and Ewing Browning were in the Pugh yard, but didn't knock on their door, but just stood talking in the yard.

When Bradbury asked what the conversation was about, Peachie replied, "I don't know what we were talking about."

"What were you and Ewing Browning standing there in Bud Pugh's yard talking for a half an hour there that night for?"

"Just talking like anybody else would." he replied, shrugging his shoulders.

"What did you go there for?"

"No certain thing, just went to be going."

"When you left Bud Pugh's, what direction did you go?"

"Back east to the silo barn."

"Did you stop there?"

"No sir."

"You went from the silo barn to the sawmill?"

"Yes sir."

"Did you find anything there?"

"I saw a lot of lumber there." He grinned at the scattered laughter in the courtroom.

Bradbury was not amused. He continued, "You hadn't been working there had you?"

"No sir, not that day. I had worked there."

"Not lately had you?"

"Not for a right smart while."

"How long did you and Ewing stay there at the sawmill?"

"Not but two or three minutes."

"Did you go through the gate up there?"

"Yes sir."

"Did you go up past John Greenwell's?"

"No sir."

"Then where did you go?"

"Down through the field by Lee Biven's."

"What direction from there did you go?"

"Straight on to my right."

"And you say you got back home about what time?"

"About eleven."

"When you got back home did Ewing go in the house with you?"

"No sir."

"What did you all do when you got down to your house?"

"We went down to the spring and got a drink and when we come back he looked at his watch and said it was eleven o'clock and he was going home and going to bed."

"Did he go in the house at all?"

"Not when we came back he didn't."

"How long did he stand there in the yard with you?"

"Not very long."

"Did you all go to the spring and get a can of water."

"No sir."

"Ewing went into the house, didn't he?"

"No sir."

"Where was he?"

"Standing out there in the yard."

"How close was he to the door?"

"About ten feet."

The next few questions revealed that after Ewing left, Peachie went to bed, that his mother was awake, but Bennie was asleep, and that his mother had told him about Jim Harris being there and wanting some wood cut.

Bradbury inquired, "Did you see Jim Harris?"

"No sir, I didn't."

"When you went into the house did you go to bed?"

"Yes sir."

"How long after you went in the house until you discovered that it was afire?"

"About ten minutes."

"Did you see Ewing when he left there that night to know which way he went?"

"Up the path that leads from the house toward his house."

"Did you see Ewing anymore that night?"

"Not after he left."

"You went to bed and went to sleep and never knew any more until your mother called you?"

"She never called me."

"How did you come to discover the fire?"

"I heard it roaring on the roof."

"Nobody called you at all?"

"If they did I didn't hear them."

"Who called Bennie?"

"Me, and then he got the ax first, I picked it up and he said give it to him and I did."

"And you were the first one to get the ax?"

"Yes sir."

"How come you to give the axe to Bennie?"

"He says give me that axe."

"How thick was that door?"

"I don't know exactly, I don't guess it was an inch."

"What is it made of oak slabs?"

"Yes sir."

"It was pretty hard to chop down wasn't it?"

"Yes sir."

"What kind of axe was that?"

"A double bitted axe."

"Was it a new one or an old one?"

"I don't think that it was a brand new one."

"What happened to Bennie?"

"He got shot and then Angie got the axe and chopped a while and then I took the axe and chopped a while and I got shot and I throwed the axe down and then she took it again and chopped the door open."

"How many times did you cut at the door?"

"Three times the first time and twice the last time."

"Three licks the first time and then two the last time?"

"Yes sir."

"Who had chopped at the door?"

"Angie had after I got done."

"Didn't you hand Bennie the axe?"

"Yes sir, I did the first time."

It was clear that Peachie's rendition of the sequence of chopping on the door wasn't the same as that given by the others, and Bradbury encouraged him to continue, saying, "Now tell the jury so that we can understand it?"

"After I chopped, Bennie chopped."

"Then Angie chopped?" Bradbury offered.

"Yes sir."

"Then Bernie chopped again?"

"Yes sir." Peachie agreed.

"After Angie got the door cut down, who was the first one out?"

"I don't know." He shook his head.

"Do you know whether they were all out when you got out or not?"

"No sir."

"Who went out right ahead of you?"

"They was all done out before I got out."

"When you came out where was Aunt Kate?"

"Walking up the road."

"Did you get ahead of her?"

"Yes sir."

"You didn't see this fellow that shot her did you?"

"Yes sir, I did."

"You didn't see him when he shot at her did you?"

"Yes sir."

"Did he shoot her with a shotgun or a rifle?"

"Shotgun."

"Now Peachie was it men that you saw out there or was it fence posts standing out there?"

"Elmer Crenshaw was the only one in that bunch there in front of the house that I know."

"Did you see the line of the other side of the house?"

"They wasn't in any line."

"Who was in that bunch that was scattered around there?"

"Arthur Hodge, Selby Hodge, Frank Hodge and Les Hodge."

"How many of them had guns?"

"Everyone."

"When you got outside, did you stop?"

"Yes sir, I'll stop there on the doorstep a minute."

"Did you say anything to anybody when you stopped there on the door sill?"

"No sir."

"When you got to the door did you see anything of your mother and Mandy and Angie?"

"Yes sir."

"Where were they?"

"Up there in the yard walking off."

"Where was Bennie?"

"I never did see him anymore."

"Did you see Bennie anymore at all after you got out of the house?"

"I didn't see Bennie anymore at all."

"Was Kate shot while she was in the house?"

"I heard her holler 'oh Lordy.'" he replied without actually answering the question.

"Was she shot in front or in the back?"

"I never did take time to look."

"Did she fall right there?"

"Just dropped right there." he said, another contradiction to earlier testimony.

"What did you do when you saw Kate fall?"

"I run."

"Where did you pass your mother and Angie and Mandy?"

"Caught up with them and went up to Charlie Biven's with them."

"When you passed Dena Browning's who was in front?"

"I was."

"Did you tell her anything about the trouble?"

"I told her that they was raising hell down there."

"Did you tell her anything about having seen Kate fall?"

"No sir, that is all I said."

"Did you see anybody at Henry Browning's?"

"No sir."

"You didn't stop there?"

"No sir."

"And Ewing had just left your house, just about ten minutes before the fire?"

"Yes sir."

"You didn't stop and call for him?"

"No sir."

"You and he had been out together that night?"

"Yes sir."

"When you passed Henry's what happened then?"

"I run on up there past Charlie Biven's and they commenced hollering for me to stop."

"And I believe you said that you saw Frank Hodge down there?"

"Yes sir."

"You said that he was down there at the house didn't you?"

"Yes sir."

"Well then, did he pass you on the road?"

"No sir."

"How did he get up there then?"

"He could have gone another way through by Mr. Ewing Crenshaw's and on up through Mr. Charlie Biven's yard."

"Where did you go after you say you saw Frank Hodge up there?"

"I went to Jim Campbell's."

"How long did you stay there?"

"Until next morning."

"Where did you go then?"

"Started to Mount Washington, I got up as far as the pike."

"What were you going to Mount Washington for?"

"To tell something about this."

"Then where did you go when you got back?"

"Up by the graveyard."

"When you come to the graveyard did you know who all was there?"

"I didn't know who all was there."

"Did you see Charlie Biven there?"

"Yes sir."

"Did you see Hugo Maraman there?"

"Yes sir."

"Did you see Charlie Browning there."

"I don't know as I did."

"I will ask you if out there at the graveyard you didn't tell these men, Charlie Biven, Charlie Browning and Hugo Maraman that you shot a man over there in the thicket that night and that when you shot he hollered 'oh Lordy' and you threw your gun in the ditch and ran, I am asking you if you didn't say that?"

"I didn't say I did."

"Do you say you didn't?"

"I say I didn't kill none."

"Did you tell them you did?"

"If I did, I don't remember it."

Bradbury shook his head in disbelief. Turning to the judge, he said "I'm finished with this witness, your honor."

Judge Richardson inquired of the prosecution if they wished to adjourn for the evening, but Mr. Creal replied that they were close to finishing their case, and would likely need no more than another hour or so to do so.

Prosecution's Case Continues

Sam Greenwell was the next prosecution witness. Sam was a son of John and Elizabeth Greenwell. Elizabeth, known in the family as Aunt Bets, was Lou Browning's aunt.

Mr. Creal's first question was "Mr. Greenwell, where were you on the night of the fire at the Browning home?"

"I was at home."

"Did you see or hear any shots that night?"

"No sir."

"Did you see any of the Brownings early the next morning?"

"Yes sir."

"What time was it?"

"About seven or eight o'clock."

When asked who he had seen that morning, Mr. Greenwell named Lou, Angie, Mandy, Henry and Vina Browning, and Kate's body.

When Creal asked if he had seen any wounds on Angie, he replied "I think she was shot, she had scars on her face that looked like shot wounds."

"Did you notice any shots anywhere else?" Creal asked.

"I just noticed them, I didn't see any more."

"Did you see Aunt Kate's wounds?"

"I saw the shots on her."

"Where do you say she was shot?"

"In the breast and in the chest."

"Did any of the others have any wounds?"

"I never noticed any scars on Mandy, and I never saw the boys, and I think the others had a few shots."

"You heard no shots there that night?"

"No sir."

"How far do you live from there?"

"About a mile and a half."

"Thank you sir." Mr. Creal finished, indicating that he was finished with the witness.

Mr. James rose from his seat at the defense table and asked, "Did they see you around there that night?"

Greenwell looked at him sternly and said "I was at home that night."

"Did you see blood on these people the next day?"

"Yes sir."

"That is all you saw?"

"Yes sir."

"No further questions, your honor."

Mr. Creal called for Henry Browning to take the stand. After he was sworn in, and identified as Henry Browning, father of Ewing Browning, Mr. Creal asked, "Were you at home on the night of the fire down at Lou and Kate Browning's that night?"

"Yes sir." was the careful answer.

"What did you see or hear about it?"

"I heard guns going on in three different places, but I didn't hear none down there where the house was burned," he said, and then added "but I saw the fire."

"What time of the night was it when you got up?"

"Twelve o'clock."

"How do you know that it was twelve?"

"I looked at my clock when I got up."

"Where was Ewing Browning?"

"He was in the bed and his mother went and woke him up."

"Is your house a one story house?"

Anticipating a question about where Ewing slept, he replied "We all slept below."

"About how far is your house off the road?"

"About forty yards off the road."

"Did you see any of the women folks that night?"

"No sir."

Mr. Creal indicted he was finished, and Mr. James asked the witness, "You didn't go to the fire that night?"

"No sir."

"Ewing didn't either?"

"No sir."

"Are you kin folks of Kate and Lou?"

"Yes sir."

"Do you know what kin?"

"Cousins."

Mr. James thanked the witness and took his seat.

Charlie Biven was the prosecution's next witness, and Mr. Creal asked him, "Do you remember the night of the fire at the Browning home?"

"Yes sir."

"Did you see any of the Brownings that night?"

"Yes sir."

"Which ones?"

"Lou, Angie, and Mandy."

"Did they come to your house?"

"Yes sir."

"Did you hear any shots?"

"Yes sir, out at my barn about forty or fifty yards from the house."

"How long after that until these women came to your home?"

"I got up and went to the door and looked out and saw them coming through the yard and then I went back to bed, and they hollered at Maggie to let them in and I told her to get up and let them in."

"After they came in your house, did you have a light?"

"Yes sir."

"I will ask you whether or not any of them had any wounds?"

"Angie had some blood down on the side of her face."

"You didn't see any wounds that the others had?"

"No sir, only the wounds on Angie's face."

"I will ask you whether or not they told you then that they were shot?"

"Hear-say testimony, your honor," objected Mr. Bradbury, and the judge agreed.

Creal tried again, asking "Did you make any inquiry of them there as to who it was shooting at them up there on the road?"

Mr. Bradbury objected again, and was sustained.

Creal then asked, "You are a brother-in-law of Frank Hodge I believe?"

"Yes sir." he agreed. His sister Mary Stella was Frank's wife.

"Were these folks all together when they came in your house?"

"Yes sir, they all came in about the same time."

With that, Mr. Creal turned the witness over to Mr. James who asked, "Did you see Peachie down there at the grave yard the next day?"

"Yes sir."

"Make any statement to you down there that day in which he said that he shot one man up there last night and he threw up his hands and hollered 'Oh Lordy'?"

"Yes sir."

"Did he say that he threw his gun in the ditch and ran?"

"Yes sir."

"Thank you, sir." Mr. James said as he retired to his chair.

Mr. Creal was quickly out of his chair. "A question or two on re-direct, your honor."

Turning to the witness, he inquired "When you had a conversation with them in reference to somebody shooting at them down there, where were they with reference to being close together?"

Mr. Bradbury's objection was quickly sustained, and Mr. Creal moved on.

"Did they have a conversation among themselves that you didn't hear?"

"They were kind of whispering among themselves."

"You didn't hear what they said?"

"No sir."

"That's all, your honor. We now call Maggie Biven to the stand."

After identifying her as Maggie Biven, wife of Charlie Biven, Mr. Creal asked her, "Did you see any of the Brownings the night their home was burned?"

"Mandy, Angie and Lou were at my house."

"Were you in bed or up when they came?"

"Up."

"Say you were up?"

"Yes sir, I heard somebody shoot twice up toward my barn and I got up and went to the door; that is how come me up."

"Did you hear any other noise?"

"No sir, but I sure heard two shots."

"How long after you heard these two shots until these three women came to your door?"

"Just a second."

"Did you see anybody else out there besides these three women?"

"No sir."

"Did they come in?"

"Yes sir."

"When they came in, did you see any blood or any wounds on any of them?"

"No sir."

"None of the three?"

"No sir, well Angie's face looked like she had been shot in the face."

"Where?"

"Right kinda in her mouth."

"Did you see any wounds on either one of the other two?"

"Mandy showed me a place on her knee."

"What did it look like?"

"Looked like a little round hole there in her knee."

"Any other places that you saw?"

"Aunt Lou showed me a little blue place."

"Was there any blood?"

"Not that I seen."

"Could you tell whether or not there was any shot in those places?"

"No sir, I couldn't."

"You are not any kin to Frank Hodge are you?"

"No sir."

"Is your husband any relation?"

"Frank married his sister."

When the defense indicated it had no questions for her, Mr. Creal called his next witness, Sheriff Monroe.

Sheriff Monroe Testifies

"Sheriff Monroe, did you receive any information on Saturday morning, May 5th, about some shooting that took place down at Browningtown?"

"Yes sir."

"About what time of day was it?"

"The first time, I suppose it was about eight o'clock."

"What did you do?"

"I didn't pay any attention to it because they are always having trouble up there." There were several knowing nods at that statement.

He continued, "And directly another fellow come to me and told me about it, and I still didn't pay much attention to it then; but I went up there, it must have been about nine o'clock or something like that when I left here."

Mr. Creal then inquired about John Bolton, and determined that Monroe had seen Bolton at home on the way to the scene, had stopped and asked Bolton if he wanted to go with him, and had been told that he didn't have time, and didn't think that there would be any use of him going?

Creal then asked, "When you got out there did you see any of the Brownings?"

"I saw Aunt Kate, she was dead."

"Did you see any of the rest of them?"

"I saw Lou, Angie and Mandy."

"Did you see either of the boys?"

"Before I left, Peachie came in."

"Had Aunt Kate been moved?"

"I don't think so."

"What kind of wounds did she have, if any?"

"She was shot all through the breast."

"See any shot about the eyes?"

"I don't remember whether I saw any shot about the eyes or not."

"What did you do then, did you do any washing?"

"We washed her breast off and then turned her over and found out that she was shot in the back."

"About what size shot were those in the back; did you pick any of them out?"

"Yes sir."

"About what size shot were they?"

"About No. 7."

"What about the wound in the back, how deep did it go?"

"Just barely went through the skin; but the one in the breast went in pretty deep."

"Which side of the breast were they on?"

"She was shot all over her breast, but mostly on the left hand side."

"Where were they in reference to the heart?"

"Right over the heart."

"Where was the main part of the load centered with reference to the heart?"

"The main load, I think, was right about over the heart."

"Was the shot any thicker there?"

"Yes sir, some thicker."

"Did you get any shot out of her breast?"

"Yes sir, one or two."

"Did you look at the size of those?"

"They were about the same size."

"Did you see any powder burns?"

"No sir."

Creal next inquired about Angie. The Sheriff indicated that she had had shot wounds in the side of her head, and on the side of her face.

Creal wanted to know, "Did either of the others have any wounds that you could see?"

"Aunt Lou and Mandy had blood on them."

"Where were they shot?"

"There was some blood on Aunt Lou's arm and some on Mandy's arm."

"What about Peachie?"

"I wouldn't swear for sure, but I think Peachie had blood on his right arm."

"Did you see Bennie that day?"

"No sir."

"Did you look around there to see if you could find any shells or anything?"

"I found five shells."

"How were they located?"

"Scattered about over the yard."

"What was the condition of the house when you got there; was it burned up or was there any of it left?"

"It was already burned up, but there was still a lot of fire."

"Were there any jugs around there anywhere?" Creal kept coming back to the jug, believing that it had contained what set the house on fire.

"I believe I saw one there in the fire, melted and broken."

"What color and kind was it?"

"White stone."

"How far was Aunt Kate from the house, do you know?"

"Yes sir, I stepped it and it was fifty-two steps by my steps."

"Do you know where Dena Browning lives?"

"Yes sir."

"When you are standing in the yard of the Browning place, can you see anything laying in the yard on the ground?"

"No sir."

"Why can't you?"

"For the trees and bushes."

"You can't see down there?"

"I can stand up at Dena Browning's and see the top of this house before it was burned."

"Could you see anybody from up there if they were standing on the ground?"

"No sir, I don't think so."

"From Dena Browning's over to the Lou Browning home about how far is that on an air line?"

"About a hundred and fifteen or twenty yards."

"That's all, your honor" Creal indicated, and Mr. James arose to question the sheriff.

"Say you found five shells there?"

"Yes sir."

"Number twelve gauge?"

"Yes sir."

"Winchester repeaters?"

"Two or three of them were."

"Do you have the shells Mr. Monroe?"

"The court has them here somewhere."

Mr. James walked to the evidence table, picked up the shells and showed them to the sheriff.

"Are these the shells that you picked up out there?"

"Yes sir."

"Three of them are Winchester repeaters?"

"Yes sir."

"Do you understand that there was just a bunch of holes like shot holes scattered about, no big holes like a bunch of shot had gone in?"

"No sir." Sheriff Monroe disagreed.

"Did they look like they had been shot from a distance?"

"Yes sir."

"Of course you couldn't tell how far?"

"No sir."

"Thank you Sheriff Monroe."

As Mr. James returned to his seat, Mr. Creal rose and inquired of the witness, "Could you tell whether or not they were fresh shells or old shells when you picked them up?"

"Looked like they had just been fired."

Satisfied, he returned to his seat, and Mr. James asked the witness, "You didn't find any more shells around there?"

"No sir, I didn't look very good, but I picked up all I saw."

Mr. Creal stood up once again, and said, "Re-direct, your honor."

"Sheriff Monroe, were there any other folks there that day?"

"Yes sir."

"How many were there?"

"About fifteen or twenty."

"Any of the nine defendants there?"

"I saw Mr. Crenshaw and Selby Hodge and Frank Kinder there, three of them."

"I will ask you whether or not you saw the chain with which the door was fastened, or the wire?"

"No sir."

As Creal seated himself, Mr. James arose again, and asked, "Did Clarence Crenshaw assist in dressing the dead body?"

"Yes sir."

"And these other men were assisting in doing things around there?"

"Yes sir."

Once again Mr. Creal stood up, and inquired, "What assistance did Frank Kinder render?"

"I saw Frank there, but now I can't say that I saw him doing anything."

"What assistance did Hodge do, did any of them do anything except Clarance Crenshaw?"

"No sir, that is the only one."

One last time, Mr. James stood and asked the sheriff, "Those men assisted to bury this woman, didn't they?"

"Mr. Crenshaw did, I don't know about the rest."

"Didn't Kinder and Hodge assist in putting the boards and things in the grave?"

"I don't know; I didn't go over to the grave."

And that seemed to end the questions.

Mr. Creal announced that the prosecution rested, and Mr. Bradbury arose to move that the court to instruct the jury to find each of the defendants not guilty. This was a procedural move, and no one was surprised when Judge Richardson denied the motion.

Judge Richardson then announced that the trail was adjourned until the next morning when the defense would begin presenting its case.

A Late Night

At two in the morning, C. P. Bradbury sat alone in his office, making some last minute notes. James and Funk had headed for their beds thirty minutes ago, after the trio spent several hours rehashing the first day's testimony.

While there were some hopeful points made, with the Brownings having contradicted one another here and there, Bradbury had to be honest and admit that things did not look good for his clients.

For one thing, there was this Hardin County jury. Strangers to the community, they were less susceptible to feelings of sympathy for the defendants and, more important, contempt for the Brownings that anyone who knew them would hold. He would certainly have to make sure the jurors understood the low esteem their neighbors had for Lou and her family.

And then there was the consistency of the family's testimony to combat. He had to admit that, for a bunch of illiterate, ignorant people, they had stood up well under cross-examination. Well, if they spoke well, maybe they lied well too. It was common knowledge among those that knew them that lying came easy to their lips. He would have to make sure the jury knew that.

He stared at his notepad at the words "liquor haters" and the jury names beneath it. Mr. James had been brought in to provide some contact with and information about the men on the jury, but even he was unsure just how many of the jurors felt about prohibition.

That liquor law had caused a divide in the nation that was not easily crossed. Would the Crenshaw arrest for moonshining cloud the judgment of jurors. He hoped not.

The three lawyers had decided the order in which they would present their clients for examination. Jim Harris would go first. The potential evidence against him seemed the weakest. Then they would follow with John Bolton, a popular man, generally well liked in the county, and hopefully a man who could handle himself on the stand. After that it would be Clarence Crenshaw's turn, followed by the others in turn.

Bradbury knew the alibis that each man would present, but while they were well thought-out, they depended a little too much on family and close friends for his liking. He knew the prosecution would attack that point vigorously.

He laid his pen down, deciding there was little more he could do to prepare, and headed off to his bed. Morning would come too soon for all of them, he thought, as he dimmed the light.

The Defense Case Begins

Before eight o'clock that morning, Tuesday, June 5th, the courtroom was occupied by bleary-eyed lawyers, defendants, and spectators. The room's seats quickly filled, with additional folks forced to remain in the halls, hoping to hear the proceedings.

It began raining as the session began promptly at eight o'clock when Judge Richardson called the court to order and invited Mr. Bradbury to call his first witness.

"I call James Harris as a witness in his own behalf," answered Mr. Bradbury.

Harris was sworn in and took the stand. Bradbury began by asking, "What is your name?"

"J. P. Harris."

"Where do you live?"

"Up in Leaches, Bullitt County."

"Do you know the prosecution witnesses, the Brownings?"

"Yes sir."

"Do you know where they lived on the night of May 4th?"

"Yes sir."

"How far is it from where they live to where you live?"

"Two and a half or three miles."

"The night that Kate Browning is said to have been killed, on the night of May 4th, where were you that night?"

"I was out there." he admitted.

Bradbury quickly asked, "About what time were you out there?"

"About half past seven."

"What were you out there for?"

"To get the boys to cut me some wood."

"Did you see them?"

"I saw Bennie."

"Did you see Peachie?"

"No sir."

"How long were you there?"

"About five minutes I guess."

"Where did you go then?"

"Back home."

"Did you stop anywhere on the road?"

"At Claude Coleman's a minute."

"Then where did you go?"

"On home."

"What time did you get there?"

"About eight or half past."

"What did you do when you got home?"

"Fed and washed, and ate my supper, and then went to bed."

"Did you shoot Kate Browning?"

"No sir, I did not." Harris said emphatically.

"Did you aid, abet or assist anybody else to do so?"

"No sir." again emphatically.

"Were you over there any other time that night?"

"No sir." was his final, again emphatic reply.

Having established his client's alibi and his denial of having anything to do with Kate's death, Mr. Bradbury turned the witness over to the prosecution.

Mr. Creal stood at his seat and inquired, "Who did you work for that day?"

"Clarence Crenshaw."

"Who do you live with?"

"Me and old Aunt Susan Crenshaw."

"Is she related to Clarence?"

"Well, I guess she is distant related to him."

Seeking to question just when Harris had stopped at Coleman's place, Mr. Creal asked, "At the time you stopped at Claude Coleman's, you hadn't been to Brownings' at that time had you?"

"Yes sir."

"Were you there twice that night?"

"No sir."

Creal stared at the witness for a long moment, and then declared, "No other questions, your honor."

Mr. Bradbury rose and announced that his next witness would be John Bolton.

After establishing his name, and that he lived six miles east of Shepherdsville, and about three miles from the Browning place, Bradbury asked, "Mr. Bolton, you heard about the killing and trouble that occurred down in Browningtown on Friday night of May 4th?"

"Yes sir."

Plunging immediately to the crucial question, he asked, "Did you shoot Kate Browning?"

"No sir."

"Did you counsel, aid, advise or assist anybody else to do so?"

"No sir."

"Did you shoot Mandy Jones?" This in response to her earlier charge.

"No sir."

"Where were you that night?"

"At home."

"What time did you go to bed?"

"Somewhere between eight and nine o'clock."

"Did you go away from home any more at all that night?"

"No sir."

Turning to Creal, he said, "Your witness."

Creal first asked "Are you related to Clarence Crenshaw?" to which he received a positive reply.

When he asked, "Were you interested in this still of Elmer's?" Bolton said he wasn't.

He then asked, "When did you first learn of the fire and killing over at Brownings'?"

Bolton appeared to think for a moment, and then replied, "Saturday morning between seven and eight o'clock."

"Who told you about it?"

"I think Calvin Crenshaw told me about it down at the shop."

"Did you go over there?"

"No sir."

"You hold the office of magistrate of this county I believe?"

"Yes sir."

"Did you hold it at that time?"

"Yes sir."

"What information was brought to you?"

"I just heard that they had a killing in town."

"Who told you about this?"

"Calvin Crenshaw runs a shop down there and I was down there at the shop next morning, and I believe he was the first one that told me about it."

"Later on in the day, did the sheriff and county attorney come along by there and ask you to go over there with them?"

"Yes sir."

"Did you tell them what had happened up there?"

"I asked them where they were going and they said that they had heard of a killing up at Browningtown and asked me if I wanted to go up there with them."

"They asked you to go with them?"

"I asked them if they would need me and they said no, they reckoned not, and I was busy and didn't go."

"Later on you were arrested on a federal charge, charging you with intimidating government witnesses?"

Bradbury quickly objected to the question on the grounds that it was prejudicial. His objection was sustained.

Creal continued, "After you were charged with this offense, did you afterwards visit the scene of the crime?"

"No sir, I didn't have time; I was arrested on Sunday."

Bradbury again objected, but Judge Richardson allowed the question.

"Weren't you out a few days on bond after you were arrested?"

"Objection, your honor! Counsel is revisiting what you already ruled was inadmissible."

Judge Richardson agreed, and told Mr. Creal to move on.

"You had an opportunity to go from your home over to that place didn't you?"

"No sir."

"When you came here to Shepherdsville, didn't you come from your home here to Shepherdsville?"

"Yes sir."

"How long had you been at home?"

"I stayed there that night."

"Hadn't you been there the day before that?"

"I had been to Louisville on Monday."

"You came here what day?"

"Wednesday morning."

"You have never seen the place where this happened since that night?"

"I have never seen it at all."

"Since the night it was committed, you haven't seen it since?"

"No sir."

"Why didn't you go over there with these folks? You were the nearest magistrate?"

"I took the attorney's word for it; he said that he didn't think there would be any use of me going."

"Did you testify on the examining trial of this case?"

"Yes sir."

"Didn't you testify that you were getting ready to sow millet that morning?"

"Yes sir."

"Wasn't it too wet?"

His answer of "It wasn't too wet to have been fixing plows." received a few smiles and chuckles.

"Who came to your house that morning except that first man that told you about it?" Creal asked, attempting to trap the witness.

"I was down at the shop when he told me about it." was the measured reply.

"Who was there after the officers came by?"

"I don't know, there was always a crowd gathering around after they went by."

"I will ask you if, on the examining trial, you didn't state that there was just a bunch of children coming down to the mail box that morning?"

"Yes sir."

"I will ask you if this question wasn't asked you on the examining trial and you made this answer, question 67 page 212, "Have you asked any of the neighbors or friends about this trouble or have you made any investigation of any kind about this matter?" and your answer was "No sir." Did you make that answer?"

"Yes sir. I didn't think that it was any of my business, all of them were already taken up before I knew anything about it."

"Who was at your house that day?"

"Mr. Lutes came by there, and Mr. Harris came by."

"Which Harris?"

"Will Harris. I have a shop up there within about a half mile of the house and people are always passing and stopping."

"You were at home all day that day?"

"Yes sir."

"You were not over at the coroner's inquest?"

"No sir."

"On the night of the trouble, I believe you say you were at home that night?"

"Yes sir."

"Did you hear any shooting across there?"

"No sir."

"The next day after this house burned down over there, did you see any of these eight defendants?"

"I saw Frank Kinder go up the road there; he stopped and passed a few words and then drove off."

"Did he say anything about the killing?"

"He didn't have time, he wasn't there long enough."

"He didn't talk to you about it?"

"No sir."

"Did you see any of the other defendants?"

"Not that day."

"Did you see the officers that evening that they took Elmer Crenshaw away?"

"No sir."

"Did you hear about Elmer getting caught that evening?"

"Yes sir, I heard it."

"Who told you about it?"

"Frank Kinder."

"Any of the other defendants talk to you about it?"

"No sir."

"Did you know who was going on his bond?"

"No sir."

"Were you asked to?"

"No sir."

"On the day following the trouble, did you have any conversation with any of the defendants?"

"No sir."

"Hadn't you heard about the inquest and heard that they were accusing you?"

"No sir."

"None of your friends told you about it?"

"No sir."

"You never got any information at all as to whom they suspect-
ed?" Each question was being asked with an increasing tone of disbelief.

"No sir."

"You didn't make any inquiry?"

"No sir."

"Why didn't you?"

"Because I didn't think that it was worthwhile."

"Did you see the officers come back from over there?"

"No sir."

"Did you see Sheriff Frank Monroe or the County Attorney as
they came back?"

"No sir."

"You didn't try to see them to see what they had found out?"

"No sir."

"When did you first learn that you were being charged with the
crime?"

"Sunday evening about two o'clock."

"Who told you?"

"The United States Marshall."

"None of the defendants told you?"

"No sir."

"The first information that you had was when the warrant was
read to you?"

"Yes sir."

"What business are you engaged in?"

"Saw mill, threshing, and farming."

"What other business do you have besides those?"

"Work on the road."

When Creal asked "Are you engaged in the moonshine business?" Mr. Bradbury objected strongly and his objection was sustained.

However, Bolton had already replied, "No sir."

Creal continued through the objection, "When did you quit?"

Bradbury shouted, "Your honor!"

Before he could continue, Judge Richardson prevented Bolton from replying, and reprimanded the prosecutor, sustaining the objection.

Mr. Creal apologized to the judge, and then inquired of the witness if he knew an Arvin Burba of LaRue County. Bolton admitted knowing the man who had worked for him for four or five months. Whatever connection Mr. Creal wished to make between Bolton and Burba was not pursued further.

After getting Bolton to say that Clarence Crenshaw was his first cousin, Creal abruptly asked, "Do you know where this still was located?"

"No sir."

"Did you see anything of Clarence or Elmer either on Saturday or Sunday following the Friday that he was caught?"

"Yes sir."

"Did Elmer tell you where they caught him?"

"No sir."

"What did he say about being caught; did he say whether or not he was at work?"

"I didn't get to say anything to him; the prohibition fellows had him in one car and me in another one."

"You have been intimately associated with him here in jail every since?"

"Yes sir."

"Did you learn from him where he was working when they caught him?"

"No sir."

"What did he tell you about it?"

"He didn't tell me anything."

"Did you know about it without asking him?"

"No sir, I didn't know exactly."

"Did you ever see the still or have any interest in it?"

"No sir."

"You never even thought enough about it to ask whose land it was on?"

"No sir."

"Was it on your land or his?"

"I don't know."

"How many tracts of land do you own?"

"Two tracts, about one hundred and forty-four acres."

"How many acres on the home tract?"

"About four acres."

"About how far is the other tract away from that?"

"I guess it is about three acres long."

"About three acres between them?"

"Yes sir."

"The remaining hundred and forty acres, what shape does that lay in?"

"Mostly knob land."

"Is there some running water on it?"

"Yes sir."

"How often do you go over that land back there?"

"I was over it in February."

"Haven't been over it since?"

"No sir."

"So that still could have been on your land and you wouldn't have known it?"

"Yes sir, it could have been." Bolton admitted.

"And you hadn't even looked over it since February?" Creal asked in a tone of disbelief.

"No sir."

As Creal retired to his seat, Mr. Bradbury rose and said, "One question, your honor."

Turning to the witness, he asked, "Did you haul any meal to this still?"

"No sir." replied the witness who was then excused.

The Defense Case Continues

Clarence Crenshaw and Frank Hodge were next to take the stand on their own behalf. Crenshaw's questioning didn't take very long, but Frank Hodge would be subjected to a lengthly cross-examination.

Bradbury began his questioning by determining that Crenshaw was fifty-four, and lived in the Leaches District about seven miles from town. He then asked, "How far is it from your house to where Lou Browning lived?"

Crenshaw responded, "The way you have to go around the road, it is about five miles."

"How far do you live from Squire Bolton?"

"It is about a mile from my house to the church and about a half mile from the church to his house; that would make it about a mile and a half."

"On the night of May 4th, the night that Kate Browning is said to have been shot, where were you?"

"I was at home."

"Did you shoot Kate Browning?"

"I did not." He too was empathic in his response.

"Did you counsel, aid, advise, or assist anybody else to kill Kate Browning?"

"No sir, I did not."

"Were you up at Brownings' that night?"

"No sir."

"What time did you go to bed that night?"

"Between eight and nine o'clock."

With that, Mr. Bradbury turned the witness over to the prosecutor who inquired, "You are the father of Elmer Crenshaw?"

"Yes sir."

"What interest did you have in Elmer's still?"

"None."

Turning to the judge, Creal announced, "I have no further questions of this witness at the moment, but reserve the right to question him further in the future."

Bradbury then asked Crenshaw, "The next morning, after this trouble is said to have occurred down in Browningtown, where were you?"

"Stayed at home until about nine o'clock."

"Then where did you go?"

"Over to Ewing Crenshaw's."

"Where does he live?"

"About three and a half miles east of my place."

"How close to the Browning house?"

"A short mile."

"Did you go over to the place where the house burned?"

"I did."

"When you first got over there, what did you do?"

"Helped to wash old Aunt Kate and helped take her and bury her."

"What caused you to go over there?"

"I went over to Ewing Crenshaw's and asked for him, and they said that he was over there, and I went on over there then."

"Did you get your information there that Aunt Kate had been killed?"

"Yes sir."

"Thank you. That's all your honor."

Mr. Creal stood and approached the bench, saying "Just a moment, I do have additional questions for this witness."

Turning to the witness, he inquired, "Did you go to Bardstown with your son Elmer to make bond for him?"

"I didn't go with him."

"Did you go afterwards?"

"I did."

"What time did you get home that evening?"

"About five o'clock."

"The same day?"

"Yes sir."

"Did you see Frank Kinder that evening?"

"Yes sir."

"Did you have a conversation with him?"

"I stopped and asked him about a male hog that he had there."

"Was that all the conversation that you had with him?"

"Yes sir."

Directing his attention to the judge, Creal indicated that he was finished with the witness. Then the defense called Frank Hodge to the stand, and Mr. James arose to question him.

In his initial answers to James' questions, Hodge testified that he lived about three and a half miles from Cedar Grove Church, and about three quarters of a mile from where Lou Browning lived. He further testified that he had a wife and four children, and lived on a farm.

Mr. James then asked, "I will get you to state to the jury whether or not on the night that Kate Browning is said to have been killed you were there at her house?"

"No sir."

"Tell the jury whether or not you shot her?"

"No sir, I did not." Another emphatic answer.

"Did you aid, abet, assist, counsel or advise anybody else to do so?"

"No sir."

"Where were you that night?"

"At home."

"Tell the jury whether or not you were in your field out near the road?"

Mr. Creal rose to object to the question, stating that the lawyer was leading the witness. His objection was sustained.

James then asked, "Did you do any shooting that night at all?"

"No sir."

"Were you out in your field near the road when Peachie Browning, Lou Browning, Angie Browning, and Mandy Jones came along?"

"No sir, I never seen none of them."

Indicating he was finished with the witness, Mr. James gave him over to the prosecution for questioning.

Mr. Creal immediately wanted to know, "What were you doing over to the Browning home about an hour or so after this still was raided?"

"Mr. Charlie Samuels' store was broken into a night or two before that, and he sent me over there to look for some meat that had been stolen."

"What time did you have information that Elmer Crenshaw was arrested?"

"Mandy told me about it when I was over there."

"You knew when you went over there that Elmer had been arrested." Creal challenged.

"No sir, I never." was the immediate reply.

"Did you ask them if they had joined the prohibition men?"

"No sir, I did not; I didn't ask them anything."

"What did they tell you about it?"

"Aunt Lou said if she had known that they were prohibition officers she wouldn't have turned this still up for ten dollars." At this there was considerable laughter in the courtroom among the spectators. It quickly quieted when the judge rapped for order.

"She said if she had known it she wouldn't have turned them up for ten dollars?" Creal repeated in a disbelieving tone.

"Yes sir, that is what she said."

"Did she say that she didn't know that they were prohibition officers when she went down there with them?"

"Yes sir."

"She denied knowing that they were prohibition officers?"

"She said that she knowed after they got back."

"When she said that she wouldn't have gone down there with them for ten dollars, what did you say?"

"I didn't say nothing."

"How long did you talk to them on that subject?"

"I didn't talk to them or ask them any questions about it."

Changing direction, Creal inquired, "Where did you look for any meat?"

"Over there in a thicket I judge to be something like a hundred yards from the house, and I found some meat over there."

"Were you still looking for meat there in the house?"

"I went in to get a drink and there was a great big bunch of stuff covered up there in the bed."

"Don't you know that that was a sack of meal that Frank Mather gave them?" Creal insisted.

"No sir."

"The next night after this happened you had some people coming down there to guard your house, afraid that you were going to be mobbed, didn't you?"

"I heard that Peachie Browning had gone to Mount Washington to get a mob and mob me."

"How far is Mount Washington from where you live?"

"About twelve or thirteen miles."

"You weren't afraid of anybody in your neighborhood were you?"

"I knowed he couldn't get nobody in my neighborhood; I thought maybe he might slip up there and burn my house."

"Did you think he might have gotten a mob?"

"He might have." Hodge said quietly.

"Peachie has been in the feeble minded institution hadn't he?"

"Yes sir."

"And his reputation for truth and veracity is very bad?"

"Yes sir."

"Did you believe what he said about going to Mount Washington and raising a mob?"

"I didn't know what he could do."

"You believed what he said about it then?"

"Just what he said is what I told you."

"You hadn't done anything to be mobbed for?"

"No sir."

"You hadn't done anything to Peachie?"

"No sir."

"Weren't at his home that night?"

"No sir."

"Had you ever had any other trouble with him?"

"No sir."

"Had you had any trouble with him since?"

"No sir."

"How come you to think that he might burn your house?"

Hodge shrugged his shoulders and held up both hands. "I didn't know what he might do."

"He never did burn any houses for you, did he?"

"No sir, he didn't burn any for me."

"Did he ever burn a house for anybody?"

"No sir, not that I know of."

"The house that he lived in was burned?"

"Yes sir."

"You never did know of any house that Peachie burned down?"

"I know of several that they have lived in burning down; I don't know how come them to." Hodge replied, attempting to leave the impression that he really did suspect the Brownings of burning places down.

To counter that, Creal said, "That was done whenever the people in the community wanted to get rid of the Brownings, wasn't it?"

"I don't know anything about that." was the defensive reply.

"You don't know that any of the Brownings ever did it themselves?"

"I know that there were four or five houses burned down that they lived in; I don't know who did it." He insisted.

"What time did you hear of the trouble and fire down there?"

"About six o'clock on Saturday morning."

"Who told you about it?"

"R. H. Crenshaw was the first one to tell me about it next morning."

"What did he tell you about it?"

"He came by and asked me if I had heard about the trouble down in town and I asked him what kind of trouble, and he says, 'Kate got killed down there last night,' and I says 'Well that's too bad.'"

"Did you really think that it was too bad?" Creal asked with mild sarcasm.

"I hated to hear of poor old Kate getting killed." Hodge said, shaking his head.

"You hated to hear it?" Again Creal's voice was mildly sarcastic.

"Yes sir." Hodge's reply sounded sincere.

After Hodge indicated that he had heard of Kate's death about six the next morning, Mr. Creal asked if he had immediately gone over there, to which Hodge replied, "No sir, I didn't."

When Creal wanted to know the reason he hadn't, his reply was "I had to go up to the store and get some groceries."

Creal stated, "I thought you were just up there the day before."

"I was up there on Thursday."

"And you had to go right back over there on Saturday morning again?"

"Yes sir. I was up there every two or three days. I had a machine up there."

"What did you do on Friday afternoon?"

"Mr. Charlie Samuels come to my house on Friday evening and we went down there to look for that meat."

"And you went lickety split right back down there to that store the first thing you did as soon as you heard of this fire?" The sarcasm was full-blown now.

When Hodge answered "Well, I didn't have no business only to get a few groceries." Creal peppered him with questions designed to trip the witness. He wanted to know what kind of groceries Hodge got, who waited on him, how much sugar he bought, what kind of tobacco, and so on.

Despite the rapid-fire questioning, Mr. Hodge had a reasonable answer to each inquiry.

Creal then asked, "How long were you up there?"

"I left home about eight o'clock and stayed until about the time the ten thirty train run." This was the train that ran from Bardstown Junction to Bardstown and Springfield.

Continuing his questions, Creal elicited from Hodge that he had gone home, arriving about noon, and eaten his noontime meal.

Creal then said, "Then you fixed up and went over there where Aunt Kate was?"

"No sir."

"It was too bad about Aunt Kate getting killed and you were in high sympathy with the family, yet you never went over there?" Creal asked with more sarcasm in his voice.

"No sir."

"When did you go over there?"

"I didn't go over there at all."

"You didn't go over at all?"

"No sir."

"Did you go over there the next day?"

"No sir."

"How far do you live from there?"

"About three-quarters of a mile."

"The next morning did you go over there to see the fire?"

"I haven't been over there until yet."

"You've seen people passing your place from Shepherdsville going down there, haven't you?"

"I have seen people passing along down there in machines; they travel that road all the time."

"You haven't seen the Browning home at all since the night of the fire?"

"No sir, I have not."

"Did you see a fire down there that night?"

"I could see a light down there."

"What time of night was that?"

"Along about twelve o'clock."

"What were you doing up?"

"My wife was sick."

"Didn't you go up and get your mother-in-law to come down and stay with your wife that night?"

"Yes sir."

"Why did you do that?"

"I thought maybe I would have to go get a doctor or something and I didn't want to leave her there by herself."

"When did you ever go after your mother-in-law before this to come down there and stay with your wife?"

"Maybe probably two weeks."

"Do you know when that was?"

"No sir. I can't read mister, and I can't put things like that down in a book." Hodge's voice sounded angry.

"Well you know whether you ever went down there after her at all or not?"

"Yes sir, I have gone several times."

"Why did you always go up there and get your mother-in-law to come down there and help with your wife?"

"She had cramping spells and she always wanted her mother."

"How long would they last?"

"Sometimes they would last probably eight or ten days."

"Would your mother-in-law stay with you all that time?"

"Not while we lived in Bardstown she didn't."

"On that night what time did you go after your mother-in-law?"

"Maybe, probably it was eight and might have been eight thirty."

"Where was your wife then?"

"At home."

"At twelve you were up?"

"Yes sir, I was up all night with the exception of laying down on the floor a little while, I think it was about three in the morning when I finally laid down."

"When you saw the fire up there that night could you tell where it was?"

"No sir, I couldn't; me and my mother-in-law was talking about it and we thought that it was a little too far to the right for Browningtown."

"You didn't go over there to see?"

"No sir."

"Did you hear any shots that night?"

"I heard some shots, sounded like they was in a house."

"Did you hear those shots up there close to your house?"

"No sir, I didn't hear no shots up there."

"Those pistol shots that were fired up there close to your house, did you hear those?"

"I heard some shots that night but I don't know where they was."

"Did you go out to see whether it was pistols or shotguns?"

"No sir."

"That shooting down there, did you hear any hollering going on?"

"No sir."

"You didn't hear any hollering at all?"

"No sir."

"You didn't step out on the porch to see who it was doing that shooting?"

"We was out in the yard."

"Who was out there?"

"My mother-in-law first discovered the fire and called me out there."

"Then you went out and you saw the fire down there?"

"I couldn't see the fire after she mentioned it, I could just see the light."

"When did you go back in the house?"

"Off and on back in the house; I would go out and look at the light and then I would go back in the house."

"Did you go out and look to tell where those shots were?"

"I couldn't tell where they was; there is a hill between me and that house down there."

"How many shots do you think you heard up there close to your house?"

"I have done told you." was the stubborn reply.

"Do you mean that all the shots that you heard were at the same time?"

"No sir."

"Which did you learn about first; did you see the light over there or hear the shots?"

"The first I seen the light and then I heard shooting."

"Were you standing looking at the light?"

"I was, after my mother-in-law drawed my attention to it."

"How many shots did you hear down there?"

"From the racket I heard, I judge that there was seven or eight shots, possibly six or seven."

"Did you hear any more shots any more after that?"

"Might have been some more shots went off and I didn't hear them; I might have been in the house and couldn't hear them."

"How far is it from your house up there to Charlie Biven's?"

"Best of my judgment it is about seven or eight hundred yards."

"Charlie Biven is your brother-in-law?"

"Yes sir."

As the questioning continued, the jury learned that Hodge had been up all night, except the time when he laid down on the floor; that he was awake at both eleven and one o'clock; that he owned a forty-five colt pistol, and a sixteen gauge shotgun. When questioned about the pistol, he declared that it was in the house somewhere, and that he had not seen it for six or seven weeks.

Creal then wanted to know, "Did you see it any time during the night of the fire?"

"No sir, I did not."

"Isn't it a fact that you were at the Browning home that night?"

"No sir."

"You weren't there?"

"No sir, I was not and haven't been."

"You were at the Browning home around twelve that night?"

"No sir, I was not." Hodge nearly shouted.

"You were over there the day that this still was raided, weren't you?"

"On Friday, yes sir, I was over there that day."

"Weren't you down there solely for the purpose of finding out whether or not these women had turned up this still?"

"I didn't know a thing in the world about the still until I went down there!" he did shout this time, and was cautioned by the judge.

Creal then inquired, "Did you have any conversation at all except about these revenue officers raiding this still?"

Mr. Hodge collected himself, and launched into a description of the events of that day.

"I was coming along there about as close as to the back of the court house and Lou Browning looked off down there and seen me coming and took back in the house, and I walked up to the door and I believe Mandy asked me in, and I went in and sat right down by the door, and I sat there and I wanted to smoke and I asked Peachie, I says, 'Peachie have you got some tobacco?' and he says, 'I have got some long green,' and I says, 'I can't stand that, I never could smoke it.'"

He paused a moment to take a breathe before continuing "And I got up to get me a drink and I happened to glance my eye over on the bed and I seen something covered up made a big hump in bed, and then she up and mentioned about the prohibition officers coming by and picking them up and taking them over to Elmer Crenshaw's still with them, and then she said that if she had known that they were prohibition men she wouldn't have went with them at all."

"As soon as you got that information you left?"

"Yes sir."

"What were you doing over there?"

"Looking for some meat that had been stolen."

"You didn't ask anything about any meat then?"

"No sir."

"Did you ask anybody's permission or have a search warrant to look for that meat?"

"I didn't ask permission. I just went over there in that thicket and looked."

"What did you go in the house for?"

"They asked me in."

"Why did you go up to the door?"

"I was passing by there and Mandy was standing in the door and I stopped to talk and they asked me in."

"Then you got up and went to get you a drink and you saw this something covered up over here on the bed?"

"Yes sir."

"You don't know what that was?"

"No sir."

"Don't you know that it was a sack of meal that Frank Mather, the prohibition agent, gave them?"

"No sir, I don't know."

Abruptly returning to Hodge's trip to the grocery, Creal asked, "Did you see Charlie Samuels at Deatsville that morning when you went up there?"

When Hodge said he had, Creal wanted to know where Samuels was, and Hodge said, "Well, he was standing on his porch when I first got there."

Creal then asked, "What were you doing running up to Charlie Samuels' so much; are you partners in any kind of business together?"

"No business, only I go up there to buy my groceries and stuff like that."

"Have you any other business together except that you go up there to buy your groceries?"

"No sir."

Mr. Creal continued to pepper him with short questions about the trip, wanted to know who waited on him where Mr. Samuels was at the time, where the store was located, and when he left there. Patiently, Mr. Hodge answered all of the questions, frustrating Creal a bit.

Creal then asked, "Who was the first fellow that came to your house the next morning?"

"Mr. Frank Kinder was the first fellow."

"What did he say about this killing and burning down there?"

"He didn't say a word because I don't think that he knowed it."

"Didn't he tell you then that there was a fire over there?"

"No sir."

"What time was he there?"

"I judge it to have been about six o'clock, just a few minutes before Mr. Crenshaw was there and told me about it."

Trying to confuse and trip the witness up, Creal asked a series of questions beginning with "He didn't say a word about it?" When Hodge said no, Creal then asked "Did you tell him about it?" and received another negative response.

Creal then asked, "Did you tell him about seeing the fire?" and received another no answer.

"Did you tell him about hearing any shooting over there?" produced a like response.

Then Creal asked, "Who did you say the first man was that told you about this the next morning?"

"R. H. Crenshaw."

"Who else informed you about the fire after Crenshaw had told you about it?"

"I don't think anybody else said anything to me about it until Sunday we got picked up."

"During the day Saturday, did you hear that you were being charged with being in this mob?"

"Well I won't say for sure, I won't say that I didn't."

"If you heard it you didn't give it any thought?"

"I told you, right now at the present time, I don't remember it."

"Don't you know that you were accused of being in it Saturday?"

"No sir, I don't know it."

"Nobody told you?"

"No sir, I don't remember it if they did."

"Didn't tell you a thing about it?"

"Probably they did and it just passed over my mind."

"Heard that you were accused of murder and still you never gave it enough thought to remember whether you heard about it or not?"

Hodge shrugged his shoulders again and answered, "I knowed that I was at home and never done it, and I never did give it a thought because I was at home tending to my own business; if I had been down there it would have been different."

"You never paid any attention to a thing like that?"

"No sir."

"Never paid any attention to seeing that fire down there and hearing all that shooting?"

"There is so much of that shooting and camp fires down there that I never pay any attention to it."

Creal then surprised the witness by asking, "Do you know who the other man was that was working with Elmer over there at that still?"

Although surprised at the question, his answer was sure. "No sir, I don't know a thing about that still."

"Do you know who that man was that ran away?"

"No sir, I do not."

"Did Elmer ever tell you who he was?"

"No sir, he didn't."

"Did you know who it was without him telling you?"

"No sir."

"When did you say you saw that pistol last?"

"About five or six weeks ago."

"The night that you had those men there guarding your house, didn't you have that pistol out?"

"No sir."

"What kind of gun did you have?"

"I had my shotgun."

"Who did you have there helping you to guard the house?"

"H. D. Perkins and John Cripps."

"Did they stay all night?"

"Until about maybe five the next morning."

"Nobody ever did come?"

"No sir."

Mr. Creal thought for a moment, and then declared that he was finished with this witness.

Elmer Crenshaw Testifies

Mr. Bradbury knew that Elmer Crenshaw was facing a stiff cross-examination when he called him to the stand.

With gentle questions, he elicited from him that Elmer was twenty-eight, a son of Clarence Crenshaw, and that he lived on Cedar Grove Road, just a little below Cedar Grove Church.

Continuing to question the young man, Bradbury let his answers inform the jury that he was home the night that Kate Browning was killed, that he had not shot her or anyone else that night, that he had not been a party to the shooting in any way, that he had been home in bed when it happened.

He then asked, "Do you know anything about what occurred up there at the Browning home that night of your own personal knowledge?"

"No sir."

"How far do you live from the Browning house?"

"About four miles I judge."

"Do you live on the main road from Shepherdsville to Bardstown by way of Deatsville?"

"Yes sir."

"Which side of Cedar Grove Church do you live on?"

"West side." was the reply, indicating the side closest to Shepherdsville.

With that he concluded his examination, and Mr. Creal stepped forward to begin questioning the young man.

"That day as the officers took you away from the still, did you see anything of the Browning women?"

"Yes sir, after we got up there in the road."

"Did they ride part of the way with you in the machine?"

"Lou and Mandy did."

"Did you say anything to them?"

"No sir."

"Did they say anything to you?"

"No sir."

"How far did you ride in the same machine with them?"

"Three or four miles."

"And you didn't say a word to one another?"

"No sir."

"What time in the day were you caught at that still?"

"About ten o'clock."

"How many of you were there working when you were caught?"

"Two."

Creal then wanted to know on whose land the still was located, but Crenshaw said he didn't know. Feinting surprise, Creal asked him if he wasn't born and reared in that country which Crenshaw admitted. He next asked, "Now you knew that neighborhood well enough to know whose land that was didn't you?"

"No sir."

"Don't you know that it is Cousin John Bolton's land?"

"No sir."

"How close was this to his land?"

"I don't know just how close, my farm and his join."

Creal asked, "Anybody own any land between you all?" and the reply was no. Creal sounded puzzled as he pondered how the still could not be on either Crenshaw or Bolton land.

Then he asked, "Mr. Crenshaw, who owns land out there where you were running that still except John Bolton?"

"Well, Jess Mann owns some land in there and Sam Bealmear lives out there."

"Do you know where Jess Mann's land is?"

"I know where part of it is."

"Were you running this shine on either one of them?"

"I don't know."

"How long had you been running that shine?"

"Four or five days."

Creal quickly asked, "Who was that other man that got away?"

"Well I don't know him personally."

"How long had he been working for you?"

"Two days."

"Where did you happen to meet up with him?"

"He come to my house."

"What did you call him?"

"Called him George."

"Have you ever seen him since this raid?"

"No sir."

"Did you ever see him before he came there?"

"No sir."

"What kind of a looking man was he?"

"A white man, about my size."

"Where did he stay while he was there?"

"Stayed with me."

"And you never found out his name?"

"No sir."

"Where did you get your meal?" Creal asked, changing the subject.

"Got it in Louisville."

"Who brought it out to you?"

"Ice milk truck."

"Where did you get your still?"

"Got it in Louisville."

"Have you ever made any real whiskey on it before you were caught?"

"Yes sir."

"What time did that fella come to your house?"

"He came there late one evening and went to work next morning."

"What evening did he come there?"

"Wednesday evening."

"When did he go to work?"

"Thursday morning."

"Did you send for him or did he come and apply for the job."

"He came out there for a job, a fellow that I had sold whiskey to, a fellow by the name of Johnson brought him out there so he could help make the whiskey and make it to suit his customers." Crenshaw replied with the longest answer he had yet given.

Mr. Creal asked a few more idle questions about the mystery man before inquiring, "What kind of hat did that fella have on?"

"He didn't have on a hat, he had on a cap."

"Did you see that hat laying there at the still that these officers picked up?"

"No sir."

"Didn't you see them pick up a hat there?"

"No sir."

"Was there one there?"

"I do not know."

"When they took that still away, did they take away any meal?"

"No sir."

"Don't you know that they took a bag of meal away from there with them and gave it to these Browning women?"

"Not when I went."

"Was there any meal there when they got the still?"

"Yes sir."

"You saw them pick up the meal and put it in the machine didn't you?" Creal challenged.

"No sir." was Crenshaw's stubborn reply.

"When they put the Browning women out of the car, did they have any packages?"

"No sir, they didn't have any."

"What time did you get back from Bardstown?"

"About a quarter after five."

"Who went your bond?"

"My father."

"Who did you stop and send your father word to come over there to go on your bond over there that morning, who did you send?"

"Frank Kinder."

Continuing to jump about in his kind of questions, Creal asked, "The man that you sold the whiskey to, what else was his name besides Johnson?"

"I don't know."

"Where was he from?"

"Louisville."

"Did you take it in there to him or did he come out here after it?"

"He came after it."

"Do you know his address?"

"No sir." It was clear to everyone in the courtroom that Elmer was not going to give any information about either George or Johnson.

"After you came back from Bardstown and went home, where did you go after you got home."

"Nowhere. Stayed at home."

"When did you first hear of this trouble?"

"Saturday night."

"Saturday did you hear that they held an inquest over Kate?"

"Yes sir."

"About what time?"

"How about seven o'clock Saturday night."

"Did you employ Mr. Bradbury as your attorney?"

"Yes sir."

"Where were you when you employed him?"

"At home."

"Who was with him?"

"He was by himself."

"Before you were informed of this trouble out there that you were being accused, had you already made arrangements for an attorney?"

"No sir."

"Who spent the night at your house besides your own folks the night that this trouble occurred?"

"My uncle and aunt were there for a while."

"They came and stayed a little while?"

"Yes sir."

"Was there anybody else there that night?"

"My brother came by there."

"That was Walter?"

"Yes sir."

Deciding he had gotten all he was going to get from this witness, he returned to his seat, and Mr. Bradbury stood up to ask a question on re-direct.

"The time that the officers arrested you at the still, did you or not change your clothes at the still?" he wanted to know.

"Yes sir."

"Another question your honor," announced Mr. Creal.

"When you got back home you didn't keep on your best clothes did you?"

"I didn't have on anything except a suit of overalls."

"You had on overalls and a shirt?"

"Yes sir."

Then Mr. Bradbury wanted to know what had become of the overalls he had on at the still, and he replied "I just left them laying there."

Mr. Creal had the last question, inquiring "You had other overalls at home didn't you?"

Elmer Crenshaw agreed that he did. And that concluded his testimony.

Frank Kinder & Selby Hodge Testify

Frank Kinder took the stand to be examined by Mr. Funk. They quickly established that he was thirty-two years old, and that he had lived close to the Cedar Grove Church for about seven years. He indicated that his residence was about three-quarters of a mile from where Lou Browning lived.

Mr. Funk asked him the, by now, standard questions about whether or not he shot Kate Browning, or had any part in her shooting, or was even there at the time of the shooting; to all of which he responded, "No sir."

He declared that he was at home all night after arriving there about eight o'clock.

Then Mr. Creal began his cross-examination with the question, "Did you see Lou and Mandy Browning the afternoon the officers had raided that shine down there, and didn't you ask them if they had turned prohibition agents?"

"Yes sir." Kinder didn't deny it.

"What else did you tell them there, did you tell them that they would be damn sorry?"

"I told them, I says, 'Lou, as poor as you are, you will be sorry you turned this still up,' for I knew that Mr. Crenshaw's folks had always helped them."

"Did you know anything about them turning up this still?"

"My wife and Della Browning told me, I think they had told them about it."

"Did you hear it from any other source?"

"No sir."

"Were you over at Clarence Crenshaw's that day?"

"Yes sir."

"What did you go over there for?"

"Elmer had me to go over there and tell his father to send bond over to Bardstown for him."

"What time in the evening did you have this conversation with Lou?"

"It was about four o'clock."

"Did you have any other reasons for thinking that she would be sorry?"

"No sir. She had worked for Mr. Crenshaw and every time she would go out there to work she would come back with a load of stuff that they had given her."

"Did Mr. Crenshaw tell you anything about putting Lou out of business?"

"No sir, I didn't see Mr. Crenshaw. I left word with Mrs. Crenshaw."

"Did you see him that evening as he came back, or after he came back?"

"Yes sir, he stopped at my house and wanted to buy a male hog that I had there."

"Was that before or after you saw these Browning women?"

"After."

"How long after?"

"About an hour."

"Where was he going?"

"He had been and got Elmer and they were going home."

"Who gave you the first information that you had about this affair?"

"Della Browning gave me the first that I had."

"Where were you going when you heard about it?"

"I was coming to Shepherdsville and I went by her house to get the money to get her some groceries that she wanted me to get for her."

"You hadn't heard this until then?"

"Yes sir."

"What information did you have before?"

"I heard that Kate was stabbed."

"Did you go down there?"

"Yes sir."

"Who was the next person that told you about it?"

"R. H. Crenshaw told me about the house being burned up and Kate being killed."

"What about Sam Greenwell, did he tell you anything about it?"

"He said that he got word over the telephone that they found Peachie up there dead."

"Did he tell you about Kate being killed and the house being burned?"

"No sir."

"Did you tell him?"

"I told him about what Della told me about Kate being stabbed."

"Then did you come to Shepherdsville?"

"No sir, Sam Greenwell, Henry Greenwell and myself went up there."

"Frank, do you know or did you know then whose land the still was located on?"

"No sir, I don't know whose land it was on."

"Weren't you at Frank Hodge's the next morning after the fire?"

"Yes sir, before I went up to Della Browning's."

"What time were you up at Frank's?"

"About 5:30. I had been plowing for him and I tore my plow up and I told him that I couldn't finish plowing that day."

"You didn't have to go up there to tell him about tearing your plow up, did you?"

"I went so I could give him a chance to get somebody else."

"Why did you go so early?"

"I had to come to Shepherdsville."

"Did you come to Shepherdsville?"

"I did after the inquest."

"You went down there and were on the corners jury?"

"Yes sir, the coroner Mr. Masden summoned me."

"He summoned you?"

"Yes sir."

"You sat on the coroner's jury and heard the testimony?"

"Yes sir."

"The night of this fire did you see Selby Hodge?"

"Yes sir."

"Where did you see him?"

"Over on Mr. Hardy's farm to milk."

"Who all was over there?"

"Vina Browning, Dena Browning, H. D. Perkins and my oldest son and myself."

"Was that on Friday evening before this happened?"

"Yes sir, before that happened on Friday night."

"Was there any discussion there that evening about these women turning that still up?"

"Some of them asked me if it was so about them turning the still up."

"What did you tell them about it?"

"I told them I didn't know but that I had heard it."

"What did Selby say about it?"

"He wasn't there at the time we were talking about it."

"What was H. D. Perkins doing there?"

"Standing there talking."

Mr. Creal concluded his cross-examination, and Mr. Funk then called Selby Hodge to the stand.

On examination, Selby testified that he was twenty-two years old, and that he lived between a mile and a half and two miles of the Browning place and about the same distance from the Cedar Grove Church.

Funk then asked him a series of questions, each designed to let him deny that he was there when Kate Browning was killed, and that he didn't know anyone who was there. He further denied that he was with his brother Frank or anywhere near Charlie Bevin's place that night.

For a change, Tot Carroll rose to question the witness. After hearing that Selby lived on the old George Hurt farm that was about a mile and a half or two miles from Browningtown, Mr. Carroll inquired, "You knew Friday night of the raiding of Elmer Crenshaws still?"

Selby denied it, and Carroll then asked "Hadn't Frank Kinder been over to your house that night?" which was also denied.

"Well, did you see him?" queried the lawyer.

"Yes sir, I seen him over there at Mr. Hardy's barn when I went over there to milk."

"How long did Frank Kinder stay over there?"

"About three-quarters of an hour."

"How long did you stay over there?"

"No longer than I was milking my cow."

"During all that time Frank Kinder never mentioned a thing to you about that still being raided over there?"

"Not that I know of, no sir."

"Who all was there?"

"H. D. Perkins, Vina Browning and Henry Greenwell's oldest boy."

Carroll next inquired, "Next morning you went over to Brownings'?"

"Yes sir, sometimes between 10:30 and 11 o'clock."

"Weren't you there when the sheriff came?"

"I think I was, yes sir."

"Where did you learn first about this fire over there that night?"

"Henry Grindle's oldest boy told me."

"Where were you going when he told you about it?"

"I was starting to my brother Frank's."

"When did you last see Frank before this?"

"On Tuesday."

"Where did you see him?"

"I helped cut some sawlogs up there."

"When you went up to Brownings, did you see Frank Kinder anywhere that morning?"

"Yes sir."

"Where did you see him?"

"Up there where Kate was shot."

Mr. Carroll kind of surprised the witness with the question, "What did you do with this axe that you got out of this fire?"

Selby denied getting an axe, but indicated that H. D. Perkins had found it. He also agreed that it looked burned, but he didn't know if the axe handle had been burned out of it or not. He at first denied knowing what Perkins had done with the axe, and then agreed that Perkins had taken it to Vina Browning and left it there.

Carroll wanted to know why Selby hadn't told the authorities about the axe, and he answered, "It wasn't my place to speak up."

He insisted that it was Perkins who removed the axe, and when Carroll wanted to know "What made him take that axe away?" the defense objected to the question on the grounds that the witness couldn't be expected to know why another person did something. The objection was sustained.

Carroll then asked, "Do you know why he took it?"

"He just took it up to Mr. Browning's and left it there." Selby shrugged as he said this.

"What kind of an axe was it?"

"A double bitted axe."

"After Crenshaw's still was raided and before the night of the fire, had you received information that this still had been raided?"

"I heard my wife and Mrs. Browning talking about it; me and H. D. was in the yard."

"Didn't you hear anything they said about it?"

"I just heard them talking about Lou and them turning up a still but I didn't know whether it was Elmer Crenshaw's or whose it was."

"Were they talking about that still?"

"Talking about some still."

"They were discussing the fact that Kate and Lou had turned it up?"

"No sir."

"What did you hear them say about it?"

"They were talking and I would catch a word once in a while."

"Just tell what you caught of it."

"I just heard them, I didn't hear them say who turned it up."

"When did you first hear that you were connected in this?"

"Saturday morning."

"Where?"

"Up there at the inquest."

"The Brownings then told it?"

"I didn't hear them, Mr. Sam Greenwell told me about it."

"He was a member of the coroner's jury?"

"Yes sir."

Carroll then asked, "What made you run so when the officers came out to your place?"

"I was going to meet them." was the defensive reply.

"Did you continue on up to meet them?"

"No sir, when they commenced to run, I run."

"Why did you run?"

"I didn't know what they were up to is the fact of the thing, and I thought that I had better get out of the way."

"Had you done anything that you should run?"

"No sir."

"What did you run for then?"

"I hadn't done anything for them to run after me for. I was going toward them and I didn't know who they were and when they commenced to run I thought it would be safer to get out of the way."

"You knew that you were being accused?"

"Yes sir."

"Did you know that they were officers?"

"I thought maybe they were."

"Did they shoot before they began to run?"

"No sir, I don't think they did, I didn't know it if they did."

"What did you have in your hand?"

"Nothing."

"Did you lay down or take away anything?"

"No sir."

"How far did you run?"

"I didn't run very far, I got over there in the woods and stopped; I didn't run very far."

"When you got over there in the woods did you come back to the officers?"

"No sir."

"Why didn't you?"

"I didn't know that there was any use of coming back." he admitted.

"You knew that the officers wanted you didn't you?"

"No sir."

"They came to your house?"

"They came to Leslie's where I was."

"Well you knew that they were looking for you?"

"I didn't know who they wanted."

"Then why did you run?"

"I started to go on up to them and would have if they hadn't started running toward me like they did."

"Isn't it a fact that you started up to these men and discovered that they were officers and ran?"

"I allow that they were officers when they pulled up in the car and stopped."

"When you got up to start to them you thought that they were officers?"

"Yes sir."

"Then you ran?"

"Yes sir."

When Mr. Carroll returned to his seat, Mr. Funk asked Selby, "The officers never did arrest you, did they?"

"No sir, not in my life. I never was in a court room before."

"You came in and gave up, didn't you?"

"Yes sir."

"That is when you found out that the officers wanted you, isn't it?"

"Yes sir."

Satisfied, Funk sat down, but Carroll stood and inquired, "That was after you had received information that most of the other defendants had already come in and given themselves up and your attorney had sent you word to do that?"

"Me and Arthur, my other brother."

"The officers had been trying to find you before that?"

"I don't know that they had been hunting for me."

"You had no information as to that?"

"No sir."

"You had no information that the officers had been looking for you?"

"No sir."

Mr. Carroll just shook his head sadly, and declared, "No more questions, your honor."

Golden & Leslie Hodge Testify

Two defendants remained to take the stand. First up was Golden Hodge who testified that he was twenty-seven years old, married, and lived in the Hobbs community which was about four miles from the Browning place as the crow flies.

Like the others before him, he denied being at the Browning place that night, denied shooting at anyone including specifically Bennie Browning, and denied being any part of the trouble.

Mr. Creal rose to begin questioning the witness, and asked "Weren't you over at your brother Les Hodge's that afternoon?"

Receiving an affirmative reply, he then asked, "And you and Les were over at your brother Frank's that evening?"

"Yes sir." Golden agreed.

"What time of the evening were you over there?"

"About five thirty."

"Was Frank home?"

"No sir."

"What did you go over there for?"

"To take a calf."

"Did you ask anything about Frank?"

"No sir."

"You or Les didn't see him or make any inquiries about him?"

"No sir."

"You didn't obtain any information about where he was or anything about him?"

"No sir."

"You and Les stayed all night together that night didn't you?"

"Yes sir, at my home."

"How come him to stay all night with you?"

"I don't know," he replied, and then offered "That me and my
wife always visited them and they did us."

"Did you and Les go out anywhere that night?"

"We went to Frank's."

"Then after you got back from over there, where did you go?"

"Went back to Les's."

"Then where did you go after that?"

"To my home."

"What time did you get back home?"

"About dark."

"Did you go out any more?"

"No sir, I never."

"Did Les?"

"No sir."

"He stayed there with you all night?"

"Yes sir."

"How far does he live from you?"

"About a mile and a half."

"Did you have any information about this still being raided?"

"I don't know that I heard anything about it until I was arrested
for murder."

Mr. Creal was finished with the witness, but Mr. Funk had a few
additional questions to ask.

"When were you first charged, or arrested on this charge?"

"Last Tuesday morning."

"When did you first know that you were wanted on this
charge?"

"Monday night."

"You weren't charged on the examining trial?"

"No sir."

"You weren't charged by the federal officers?"

"No sir."

"During that trial, your name was brought out, you got information of that didn't you?"

"Yes sir."

"You hadn't ever received any information up until the time you were arrested?"

"No sir."

Mr. Funk dismissed the witness and called Leslie Hodge to the stand where Mr. James would question him.

They established that he would be twenty-four in December, that he lived in the Lotus community which was about three and a half miles from the Browning place, and that he had not been at the Browning home the night of the fire.

He denied having any involvement in the shooting and denied helping or encouraging anyone else to do it.

When asked where he was that night, he indicated that he was with his brother Golden Hodge.

Then Mr. Creal approached the witness and asked "You were with Golden that afternoon?" to which he received an affirmative reply.

"Were you over at Frank's late that evening?"

"Yes sir."

"You were over there at five o'clock or after, weren't you?"

"Four or five, something like that."

"Did you get information over there about this still having been raided?"

"No sir. Cora Greenwell told us that they passed her house with one of these Crenshaw boys in a machine with some other man."

"Who was with you at the time she told you this?"

"Nobody. Golden had done gone on."

"Did she say who turned it up?"

"Said she saw Mandy and Lou Browning in the car with them."

"How long had it been since you spent the night with Golden?"

"Been about a week."

"Do you go to see all your brothers that often?"

"I go to see all my neighbors, and I guess I go less to Frank's than any other brother that I have."

"When was the last time that you were at Frank's?"

"About two months ago."

"What time in the day Friday did you decide to go down to Golden's for the night?"

"Early Friday morning I told Lizzie that I had to go down to Golden's to take this calf over to Frank's and told her that we would go over there and stay all night if she wanted to, and she said that it didn't make any difference with her, and we went over there that afternoon and stayed all night."

"Whose calf was this?"

"It was Golden's."

"How did you know before you went over to Golden's that he was going to take this calf over to Frank's?"

"I was down there a day or two before that and he wanted me to take it that day, and I told him that I would go down and look at it, and I went and looked at it and I figured that I couldn't take it by myself, and I went back over there on Friday to take it."

"What time of day was it that you got information that the officers passed with Crenshaw?"

"About four or five o'clock."

"You hadn't been to Frank's then?"

"No sir."

"What business are you in?"

"First one thing and then another."

"Did you have an interest in Elmer Crenshaw's still?"

"No sir." was his emphatic reply.

"When did you first learn that you were connected in this trouble?"

"Someone said there at the house on Sunday that they had the Hodge boys connected with it, and then my wife was up to Arthur's on Thursday and Mr. Monroe was up there and told her to tell me to come to town, they wanted me down here."

"On Sunday after the coroner's inquest, weren't you at home?"

"Yes sir."

"Someone then came down there looking for you, didn't they?"

"They came down there all right. I will tell you the reason I didn't stay. I had some liquor there in the house and I thought maybe that they was looking for that, and I didn't want to get caught with it, and I took it and left."

At this Mr. Creal concluded his questioning, but Mr. James spoke up and asked, "Are you related to Elmer Crenshaw?"

"No sir."

"No relation at all?"

"Not that I know of."

Quickly Mr. Creal was on his feet, and inquired, "You are a brother of Golden Hodge, Selby Hodge, Arthur Hodge, and Frank Hodge, aren't you?"

"Yes sir.

As both lawyers were finished with the witness, he was dismissed, and Judge Richardson called for the noontime recess, stating that court would reconvene at one o'clock.

Alibi & Character Witnesses Begin

When Judge Richardson called the court to order, Mr. James called Arthur Hodge as the next witness.

His inquiries elicited from Hodge that he lived about a mile and a half above Hobbs, which was three to four miles from the Browning place. When asked if he even knew where the Brownings lived, he said, "No sir, I didn't know where Lou Browning lived. I never was up there in my life."

James inquired, "You were charged at the examining trial of being there and were dismissed, weren't you?" and received a positive reply.

However, when he asked, "How many of the Brownings accused you of being there?" the prosecution objected to the question and was sustained.

That concluded Mr. James' questions, and Mr. Creal only had one question.

"You were dismissed on a motion of the Commonwealth Attorney, weren't you?"

"Yes sir."

The next witness for the defense was Walter Crenshaw.

In response to Mr. Bradbury's questions, he testified that he was twenty years old, a son of Clarence Crenshaw and brother to Elmer Crenshaw.

Bradbury then asked him if he was there the night of the fire and killing, or had anything to do with it, and his answer was an emphatic no.

"You were charged with this offense at the examining trial and dismissed?" asked Bradbury.

"Yes sir."

Then, through a series of questions, he reported that he had been at Shepherdsville that evening, first at the junior play at the school with a girlfriend, and after taking her home, he went to the pool hall, arriving there about ten thirty.

Bradbury then asked, "After you left the pool room where did you go?"

"Went home."

"Did you go directly home?"

"No sir."

"Did you stop somewhere on the road?"

"Yes sir, I stopped at Elmer's."

"Elmer Crenshaw, is that your brother?"

"Yes sir."

When the lawyer asked "Why did you stop?" Mr. Creal objected about the question's relevance, and was sustained.

Coming at it from a different direction, Bradbury asked, "Did you see Elmer at home that night?"

"Yes sir."

"What time were you at his house?"

"About twelve."

"Then from Elmer's, where did you go?"

"On home."

"When you got home, was your father at home?"

"Yes sir."

"When you were at Elmer's, was he in bed or not?"

"Yes sir, he was in bed."

"Did you call him?"

"Yes sir."

"Where did you go after leaving Elmer's?"

"Went home."

"What time did you get home?"

"About ten or fifteen minutes after twelve."

"Your father was at home?"

"Yes sir."

"Where was he?"

"In the bed."

"How do you know?"

"I was talking to him."

"You saw your father there in the bed and was talking to him when you came in?"

"Yes sir."

Satisfied that Walter's testimony helped with his father and brother's alibis, the lawyer turned him over to Mr. Creal whose first question was "How close was it to twelve when you left Shepherdsville that night?"

"About eleven thirty or a quarter of twelve."

"Where did you get that time?" he inquired, determined to punch a hole in the alibis if he could.

"Mr. Clark said that he closed the pool room between eleven thirty and a quarter of twelve that night."

"Before you could start home after you left the pool room, where did you have to go, where did you leave your machine?"

"It was sitting in front of the pool room."

"How long did you stop at Elmer's?"

"About five minutes."

"About how far do you live from here?"

"About seven miles."

"Do you think you could leave here a quarter of twelve and stop on the road and talk five minutes and get home at quarter after twelve?" Creal challenged.

"Sure." was Walter's assured reply.

"How far off the road does Elmer live?"

"About a hundred and fifty yards I suppose."

"Did you drive down there?"

"Yes sir."

"And talked with him about five minutes?"

"Yes sir."

"Then got in your car and went home?"

"I got a plow there that my father told me to stop by there and get as I come back by that night." By this he managed to get in why he had stopped at Elmer's.

"How is the road down to Elmer's?"

"Good."

"Is it a pike?"

"Yes sir."

"All the way?"

"Yes sir."

"How long had it been since you had seen any time piece?"

"I don't know what time it was."

"You have no idea about the time except your best judgment?"

"No sir."

Creal shook his head as if he found the testimony hard to believe, and dismissed the witness.

Aunt Susan Crenshaw, a spinster lady, was called to the stand next. She declared that she was seventy-two, and lived up in the Leaches precinct where she kept house for Jim Harris, the defendant.

She was asked where she was on the night of May 4th, the night Kate Browning was killed, and she said she was at home all night. She told the lawyer, "Yes sir, I went to bed before night, just as soon as I got the chickens fastened up."

Mr. Bradbury wanted to know, "Was Jim Harris at home?"

"He come home about a quarter after eight and eat his supper and went to bed and wasn't off the place any more that night."

"How do you know?"

"I could hear him snoring. I was awake several times that night and I heard him snoring every time I was awake."

In answer to the next question, she agreed that she knew Lou Browning and her family, and had known Lou thirty-five or forty years.

Then the lawyer asked a question that, in one form or another, would be repeated numerous times as the day wore on.

"Do you know their reputation in the community in which they live, and among those with whom they associate with for truth, veracity and morality, as to what people generally say of and about them?"

Aunt Susan shook her head, looked him in the eye, and declared, "Well they ain't very truthful, I can tell you that."

Wanting more than just her personal opinion, he asked, "Do you know what people say about them, not what you know yourself?"

"Yes sir, they don't say anything much good about them."

Trying again, he asked, "The question that I ask you is do you know their reputation from what the people say of or about them for truth and veracity and morality?"

"Yes sir."

"From what other people say, is that reputation good or bad?"

"Bad." She spat, and repeated, "Bad!"

With that, Mr. Bradbury turned the witness over to Mr. Creal whose first question was "Did you sleep any at all that night?"

"Yes sir."

"Did you hear Jim snoring while you were asleep?"

"No sir." she answered, thinking to herself that it was a pretty dumb question.

"Did you hear him snoring all night?"

"No sir."

"Did you hear him once or twice?"

"Yes sir."

Deciding it was useless to pursue this further, he said to the judge, "No more questions, your honor."

Mr. Bradbury announced that his next witness would be Claude Coleman, and Mr. Coleman was sworn in.

Bradbury asked, "Where do you live?"

"Dave Raser's place."

"Do you know Jim Harris?"

"Yes sir."

"How close do you live to him?"

"About two miles."

"Do you know the Brownings?"

"Yes sir."

"On the night that it is said that Kate Browning was killed, did you see Jim Harris?"

"Yes sir."

"What time was it when you saw him?"

"Around eight o'clock."

"Where did you see him?"

"Come up to my house and called me out."

"Which way did he come from?"

"From toward the store."

"When he left, which way did he go?"

"Went toward home."

"How long was he at your house?"

"About a minute I guess."

While the testimony was useful for Jim Harris' alibi, Bradbury now wanted to use Coleman as a character witness against the Brownings.

"Mr. Coleman, do you know the general reputation of the Brownings for truth and morality for what people generally say of and about them?"

"Yes sir."

"Is that reputation good or bad?"

"Bad."

Next Bradbury asked the second question that would be repeated again to other witnesses.

"From what the people generally say of or about them, are they entitled to credit under oath?"

"No sir."

"Thank you sir."

Mr. Creal walked toward the witness as he asked, "You weren't with Jim Harris any more that night after he left your house, were you?"

"No sir."

"What time did you go to bed?"

"I went to Louisville after eight o'clock that night."

"And you say that Jim Harris went on toward home about eight o'clock?"

"Yes sir."

Creal returned to his seat, and Bradbury announced his next witness as Lucile Bolton, the sixteen-year-old daughter of John Bolton.

"The night that this trouble occurred down at Browningtown when Lou Browning's house was burned down and Kate Browning was killed, where were you?"

"At home."

"Where do you sleep, upstairs or down?"

"Upstairs."

"Where does your father sleep?"

"Right below me."

"Between 11 and 12 o'clock that night do you know whether your father was at home or not?"

"Yes sir."

"Was he at home?"

"Yes sir."

"Tell the jury, if you know he was at home, just how you know it?"

"My little sister wanted to drink along about 11 o'clock and I got up and went down to get it for her and just as I got down the clock struck eleven, I was looking for a match to light a lamp and my father asked me what I wanted and I told him and he told me that I didn't need any light."

"You recognized your father's voice?"

"Yes sir."

"Did you have any other young lady visiting you that night?"

"Yes sir."

"Who was that?"

"Anna Mae Messer."

"Did your father go off any place after that that night?"

"Not that I know of and we were awake until about 11:30 for I heard the clock strike half past before we went back to sleep."

Mr. Creal declined to question the witness, but reserved the right to recall her to the stand, and Bradbury next called her sister Bertha Mae Bolton who was thirteen.

"The night that the trouble occurred down in Browningtown, were are you at home?"

"Yes sir."

"Where was your father if you know?"

"At home."

"Do you know whether he was there along about the middle part of the night or not?"

"Yes sir, my little sister cried for a drink and my big sister went down to get it for her and was looking for a match, and my father asked her what she wanted and she told him, and he told her she didn't need any match, and we never went back to sleep anymore until after the clock struck 11:30 and we could hear him snoring then."

Again Creal had no questions for the witness, and Bradbury next called Annie Mae Messer to the stand.

After identifying her, Bradbury asked, "Where do you live?"

"I live in Shepherdsville, but I am working in Louisville now."

"Are you employed in Louisville?"

"Yes sir."

"Who do you work for?"

"At the American cigar factory."

"On the night of May 4, were you out in the country and spent the night out there?"

"Yes sir."

"Where?"

"At John Bolton's."

"Was John Bolton at home that night?"

"Yes sir."

"How do you know?"

"Because he was sitting there reading the paper and talking to us."

"Was he at home during the middle of the night?"

"Yes sir."

"How do you know that he was?"

"He spoke to Bertha Mae and Lucille."

"Did you recognize his voice?"

"Yes sir."

"What did he say?"

"He asked the girls why they had come downstairs during the night."

"What time of night was it?"

"Eleven."

"Did you stay awake long that time?"

"We heard the clock strike 11:30."

"How much longer were you awake after that?"

"That is the last I heard it strike."

"During that time did Squire Bolton get up and go out of the house?"

"No sir."

"If he had, could you have heard him?"

"Yes sir."

This time Mr. Creal was ready with questions.

"Who do you live with?"

"My mother."

"How long have you been living in Shepherdsville?"

"Since the 9th day of June 1927."

"Do you still live in Shepherdsville?"

"My mother still lives here."

"How old do you say you are?"

"Sixteen."

"Had you been asleep when they went downstairs after a drink for the baby?"

"Yes sir, I had been asleep."

"You heard what he said to them?"

"Yes sir."

"Did you count the number of times the clock struck?"

"Yes sir."

"How many?"

"Eleven."

"How long had you been in bed at that time?"

"Since nine."

"Is that the only time you've heard it strike that night?"

"We heard it strike just before we went to sleep."

"Who did you first tell about knowing what time it was when they got up and got the drink of water for the baby?"

"The girls, that night I heard one of them say I guess it is striking eleven and I said yes it's struck eleven."

"Who else did you tell about that?"

"Mr. Bolton."

"When did you tell him?"

"Next morning."

"Was he asking you about what time it was when you heard him down there?"

"No sir."

"How come you to tell him?"

"I just said that the girls were down there at eleven."

"He was asking you about what time it was and reminded you of the time wasn't he?"

"No sir."

Satisfied he had created some doubt about her testimony, he concluded it.

The next witness was John Lane, Jr. He testified that he was twenty-eight, that he lived up above Cedar Grove Church, and that he knew Clarence Crenshaw and lived about a mile away from Crenshaw.

Bradbury then asked, "On the night that this trouble occurred down in Browningtown where were you?"

"At home."

"Did you go to Clarence Crenshaw's any time that night?"

"Yes sir."

"What time was it when you went there?"

"Twenty-five after eleven."

"What did you go down there for?"

"After Vicks salve for my baby."

"What was the matter with the baby?"

"Tonsillitis and earache."

"Was Mr. Crenshaw at home?"

"Yes sir, I was talking to him."

"Did you get the medicine that you went after?"

"Yes sir."

"What was he doing when you got there?"

"He was in the bed."

"How do you know that he was there?"

"Because I was hollering for him and he was right there and answered me."

When his turn came, Mr. Creal asked the witness, "Who is your nearest neighbor?"

"Judge Bolton."

When asked if Judge Bolton was related to John Bolton, the witness responded, "I don't think so."

Feinting curiosity, Creak asked "Why didn't you go to his place instead of Clarence Crenshaw's then?"

"Because it was off the road."

"You went double the distance down here to Clarence Crenshaw's to get the Vicks salve, why did you do that?" he asked, still sounding curious.

"Because I knew that they had babies and knew that these other folks didn't have any."

"How old are these babies at Clarence Crenshaw's?"

"Maybe six or seven years old something like that."

"Your idea was that you could find Vicks salve wherever there might be babies?"

"I had an idea that they had some."

Creal then asked a leading question.

"You and your other neighbors are on good terms aren't you?"

"Yes sir."

"About how far is it from your house to Clarence Crenshaw's?"

"About a mile I guess."

"How far is it to the other place?"

"Something like a half a mile."

"Then that is double the distance?"

"This other one is off the road though." the witness insisted.

Trying to establish some connection between the witness and the defendants, Creal asked, "What were you doing on Friday before the Brownings' home was burned on Friday night?"

"Cutting bushes."

"Whose land were you cutting these bushes on?"

"I was cutting them on my daddy's place to put out tobacco."

"Who do you work for?"

"Work for the county."

"Do you work for John Bolton any?"

"No sir."

"Do you work for Elmer Crenshaw any?"

"I helped him bale hay."

"Were you working for him anytime in April or May?"

"No sir."

"How long had this baby of yours had this tonsillitis and earache?"

"For a day or two."

"Why didn't you go get some Vicks salve before this?"

"Because I didn't think it was so bad."

Deciding he was getting no where with the witness, Creal ended his cross-examination.

Mr. Funk then called Annie Biven as their next witness.

They quickly established that she was Frank Hodge's mother-in-law, and that she lived about three-quarters of a mile from him.

Funk inquired, "Do you remember the night that this fire is alleged to have happened?"

"Yes sir."

"Where were you?"

"I was down at Frank Hodge's."

"What time did you go down there?"

"In the early part of the night."

"You don't know exactly what time it was?"

"No sir, it was early though. He came up there and I just had laid down and hardly went to sleep."

"Do you know what was the matter that he wanted you to come down to his house, where he wanted you to come?"

"Said his wife had the cramps and wanted me to come down there."

"How long did you stay?"

"I stayed all night."

"Was Frank Hodge there?"

"Yes sir."

"Did he go away any place that night."

"No sir."

"You were up at your son's along in the afternoon weren't you?"

"I don't remember whether I was or not."

Mr. Creal pounced on that final question by the defense, and inquired of her, "So you don't know whether you were up at your son-in-law's on that evening or not?"

"I don't remember whether I was or not." she replied.

"Didn't you testify on the examining trial that you were?"

"If I said I was, I was there."

"Were you up there?"

"I don't recall." She shook her head.

"How do you recall being up there that night?"

"They come after me."

"What were you doing up there that afternoon?"

"Just like I always do, up there to see Sally and the children."

"Did you know that she was sick that evening?"

"I knew she was grunting."

"How do you know she was grunting?"

"My child said she was."

"To refresh your recollection, didn't you state that you were there when they brought the calf?"

"Yes sir, I was there."

"That was the same evening before the house burned that night?"

"Yes sir."

"Was your daughter sick then?"

"Yes sir."

"What time did you leave that evening?"

"I left in time to get supper."

"Where was Frank that evening?"

"I don't know, I didn't see him."

"Who did you see there that evening?"

"Les Hodge and Golden Hodge."

"Did you see H. D. Perkins up there?"

"No sir."

"Did you see Bill Jackson there?"

"No sir."

"Didn't see either one of those men?"

"No sir."

"Do you remember whether or not it was milking time when you were there?"

"No sir, it wasn't."

"Who did you go up there with?"

"My daughter."

"Did she go back home with you?"

"No sir."

"What part of the evening or night did she come home?"

"Early part of the night."

"In your best judgment what time was it when Frank came up there after you?"

"About eight or a little after."

"Did you go with Frank?"

"No sir."

"Who did you go over there with?"

"My daughter."

"Did Frank go right back?"

"Yes sir."

"How was he over there?"

"Riding."

"How did you go down there?"

"Walked."

"Was Frank there when you got there?"

"Yes sir."

"What was your daughter doing when you got down there?"

"Grunting and going on."

"After you went up to Frank's did you go back to bed?"

"No sir."

"Did you have a clock there?"

"Yes sir, but I didn't pay no attention to it."

"You haven't heard anything to refresh your recollection about the time that this fire took place?"

"I have heard lots of people say, after that, that it was about twelve."

"Did you have any conversation that night with Frank about the fire that night?"

"We was out in the yard looking at the fire and I says to Frank that it must be up about town and he says 'no it ain't, it is too far to the right for that.'"

"Where are you out in the yard or in the house at the time?"

"Out in the yard."

"Had he been to bed at that time?"

"No sir."

"You had your clothes on?"

"Yes sir."

"After the fire, how long did you stay awake?"

"Might've been an hour or maybe longer."

"Did Frank go to bed?"

"When he went back in the house he laid down across the bed with his clothes on."

"Did he get up anymore that night?"

"Yes sir, his wife told him to get up so the bed could be fixed."

"Did you hear any shots up there on the road close to your home?"

"No sir."

"Charlie Biven is your son isn't he?"

"Yes sir."

"Did you hear any shots down there about his house?"

"No sir."

"Did you hear any shots down about Charlie Biven's?"

"No sir."

"After you heard those shots down there at that house you didn't hear anymore?"

"I heard some sounded like they were a long ways off and then I never heard anymore that night."

Unable to crack her story, Mr. Creal retired to his chair, and Mr. Funk then called Catherine Biven to the stand. Catherine was thirteen, a daughter of the previous witness.

After Catherine stated that they lived up on Ewing Crenshaw's place, Mr. Funk wanted to know where she was the night of the fire. At first she said she was at home, but not all night.

Funk questioned, "Where were you after you left home that night?"

"At Frank Hodge's."

"Did you stay up there all night?"

"Yes sir."

"Did you go to sleep?"

"Yes sir."

"Did you wake up any during the night?"

"Yes sir, I woke up and went to get me a drink, and I saw the smoke from the house."

"Who was there?"

"Frank Hodge and my mother and his wife."

"Did you see him any time any more that night?"

"No sir."

"Did he leave any time that night?"

"No sir."

In cross-examination, Mr. Creal wanted to know "How come you to wake up just at this particular time and want a drink?"

"I heard them saying something about a fire up there."

"Frank was there?"

"Yes sir."

"With all his clothes on?"

"Yes sir, I reckon he had them all on, I don't know about that."

Creal was always wary of questioning children too closely, fearful that it might turn a jury against him, so he ended his questioning there.

Mr. Bradbury next called Bertha Hodge to the stand and asked her first, "You are the wife of Golden Hodge?"

"Yes sir."

At this point, Judge Richardson interrupted, saying, "Gentlemen of the jury, as this woman is the wife of Golden Hodge, one of the defendants, it would not be competent for her to testify for or against her husband."

Bradbury then asked, "Mrs. Hodge, where do you live, if you please?"

"Up by the big trestle."

"Do you know Leslie Hodge?"

"Yes sir."

"The night that this trouble occurred up at Lou Browning's, were you at home?"

"Yes sir."

"Who was at your house that night?"

"Les Hodge and his wife."

In the next few moments, Mrs. Hodge testified that Les and his wife had come to her place right after the noon meal, that Les had taken a calf over to Frank Hodge's and returned about dark or a little after, that his wife had remained there during that time, that they had spent the night there and had not left until Saturday evening.

Bradbury's final question was "Did Les go anywhere that night?"

"No sir, he didn't." she replied.

Mr. Creal elected not to cross-examine the witness.

Having used Golden's wife to establish Les Hodge's alibi, Bradbury now called Les Hodge's wife to alibi Golden Hodge.

"Your honor, the defense calls Elizabeth Hodge to the stand."

As soon as she agreed that she was Leslie Hodge's wife, the judge once again reminded the jury that she could not testify for or against her own husband.

"On the night when the house was burned and Kate was killed, where were you that night?"

"I stayed at Golden Hodge's that night."

After that Bradbury's questions and her answers agreed in all relevant points with that of her sister-in-law before her.

The Witnesses Continue

Mr. Bradbury called Henry Crenshaw as the next witness. Henry was Clarence's brother, and Elmer's uncle. He testified that he was now living in Louisville, having moved there in early May. Before that he had lived up above Cedar Grove Church.

During questioning, Mr. Crenshaw testified that he and his wife had been at Elmer Crenshaw's home the night of May 4th, had arrived there about dark and stayed until after eleven.

Bradbury then asked, "Tell the jury whether or not Elmer was at home that night?"

"He was."

"Did he go away anywhere while you were there?"

"No sir."

Bradbury thanked the witness, and sat down.

The first thing Mr. Creal wanted to know was "What did you go down there for that night?"

"Just to talk with him."

"How far did you live from where he did?"

"About a mile and a half."

"Did you know at that time that he had been caught with a still?"

"I had heard it."

"Then for what business did you go?"

"I didn't have any business. I didn't go for any business, just a social call." the witness bristled.

"Then after that, you went back home?"

"Yes sir."

"Didn't you make the statement on the examining trial that you went done there to advise with him about the still?"

"No sir, I didn't go down there to advise with him."

"Did you make that statement?"

"No sir."

"Didn't you say that you went down there to console him?"

"I might have said that I went down there to talk with him."

"I will ask you whether or not you used this language, 'That when I heard he was caught I went down there to console him because I, myself had been caught'?"

"I might have said that I went down there to talk with him, but I didn't go down there to advise with him." It appeared that Mr. Creal and Mr. Crenshaw had different ideas about what "advise" meant.

During this exchange the counsel for the defense had repeatedly objected to the questions unsuccessfully.

" Did you make that statement?" insisted Mr. Creal.

"No sir, I don't think I did." declared the witness.

"What subject matter did you and he talk about?"

"Different things, not altogether about that."

"You didn't go down there to console him about that then?"

"It wouldn't take until eleven." Crenshaw declared to a smattering of laughter.

"Did you talk about that some?"

"Might have." he admitted.

"How did you know that Elmer was at home that night?"

"I had an idea that he was."

"Didn't you have information that the officers had carried him away that day?"

"Yes sir."

"How did you get that information?"

"Over the telephone."

"Who did you talk with that gave you this information?"

"I wasn't talking with anybody, my wife was talking to my brother's wife."

Creal asked a few more questions about when and why Crenshaw had moved to Louisville, and dismissed the witness.

Bradbury then called Molly Crenshaw, Henry's wife, to the stand.

He asked her "On the night of May the 4th of this year, where were you, if you please?"

"We were at Elmer Crenshaw's."

"What time did you get there?"

"Around eight o'clock. Just a little after dark."

"How long did you stay there?"

"About two hours and a half."

"Was Elmer at home when you got there?"

"Yes sir."

"Did he go away anywhere while you were there?"

"No sir, not that I know of."

"You would have known it if he had gone?"

"Yes sir."

"Was he there the whole time you were there?"

"Yes sir."

"Was he at home when you left?"

"Yes sir."

Bradbury turned to the prosecutor and said, "Your witness." When Creal had no questions, Bradbury called his next witness, William "Bill" Phillips.

Phillips testified that he was nineteen and worked for T. H. Miller.

When Bradbury asked, "The night that this trouble occurred up at Brownings' when Kate is said to have been killed, where were you that night?" Phillips said that he had been at John Lane's.

"What time did you leave?"

"About twenty minutes after ten."

"When you left there, was John Lane's baby sick?"

"Yes sir."

"Where did you stay the rest of the night?"

"Stayed at home."

"How did you get home?"

"Rode home in the machine with Mr. Henry Crenshaw."

"Who was with him?"

"His wife."

"What time did you leave John Lane's?"

"About twenty minutes after ten."

Mr. Creal had no questions for the witness.

Mr. Bradbury's next two witnesses were the sons of Frank Kinder. First was William Francis Kinder.

Bradbury asked him "Do you remember that night that this house is said to have been burned?"

"Yes sir."

"Were you at home that night?"

"Yes sir."

"Where was your father?"

"He was at home all night after eight o'clock."

"Tell the jury how you know that he was at home."

"Because I know he was there." the witness insisted.

"Where did he sleep? Did he sleep in the same room with you?"

"Yes sir."

"Did you see him go to bed?"

"Yes sir."

"Did he get up and leave that night?"

"No sir."

"Did he stay at home all night?"

"Yes sir."

Mr. Creal began his cross-examination by asking, "You have a two-story house don't you?"

"Yes sir."

"There are beds upstairs and down?"

"Yes sir."

The witness expected more questions, but Creal was finished.

Then Mr. Funk called Clarence Kinder to the stand and asked, "Do you remember the night that this house was burned?"

In a series of brief questions and answers, Mr. Funk elicited from the witness that he had been at home that night, that his father had been there as well all night, that they slept in the same room, and that Clarence had awakened and seen his father in bed about eleven o'clock.

Mr. Creal began by asking "How many members of your family?" and Clarence told him that there were seven.

Creal then asked, "Do you all sleep downstairs?"

"Yes sir."

"You hadn't been doing that before that night had you?"

"Yes sir, all that week we had."

"When you woke up, wasn't it dark in the room?"

"No sir."

"What kind of night was it?"

"The moon was shining on the bed."

"Do you know what time it was?"

"The clock struck eleven."

"Who did you first tell that you were awake at eleven o'clock, and your father was at home then?"

"I don't know."

"Did your father say anything to you about it next morning?"

"No sir."

"How did they know that you were awake at that time?"

"I told Mr. Bradbury."

"Was he the first fellow that you ever told about it?"

"Yes sir, when he was up home."

"What did you tell him?"

"I told him that I was awake and heard the clock strike eleven o'clock and my father was home then."

"Why didn't you tell your father before that?"

"I don't know, I just didn't."

The next three witnesses were the daughters of Arthur Hodge. Virginia was sixteen, Leona was fourteen, and Martha was twelve.

When Mr. Bradbury asked Virginia where she was on the night of the trouble at Browningtown, she indicated that she had been at home.

When asked about her father, she said he had been home all night, and had not left the house.

Creal had no questions for her, and Bradbury called Leona to the stand. Her testimony was essentially the same as her sister, and this time Mr. Creal inquired a bit sarcastically, "You heard the clock strike along about eleven didn't you?"

She shook her head, and replied "I don't remember whether I did or not."

"You don't remember?" He seemed surprised.

"I heard it strike four or five times."

"Do you remember what times you heard it strike?"

"I never did lay down until about nine or ten."

He smiled at her, shook his head, and returned to his seat.

Martha Hodge was up next. After she testified as had her sisters, and Mr. Creal, from his seat, inquired, "Did you hear the clock strike eleven that night?"

"No sir, I didn't." she smiled at him.

Mrs. Roy Shaw was the next witness interviewed by Mr. Bradbury. After determining her name and that she lived up at Solitude, he asked, "Do you know the Brownings, Bennie, Angie, Mandy, and Peachie, and Lou?"

"Yes sir." she replied crisply.

Then Bradbury asked his question about the general reputation of the Brownings for truth, veracity, and morality; whether it was good or bad, and her one-word reply was "Bad."

He asked, "From what people say of and about them, are they worthy of belief under oath?"

She replied quickly, "No sir."

Then Bradbury asked a new question.

"A short time previous to the time that this trouble is said to have occurred, the exact time I cannot fix, was Lou Browning in your house, and didn't she say there and then, nobody being present but you and her, in which conversation she said that Kate was getting so mean that she was going to have to get rid of her some way?"

"Yes sir."

Mr. Creal was quickly on his feet, asking "She didn't say anything about doing Kate any violence did she?"

"No sir, she just said that she was going to have to get rid of her."

When he next asked who she had heard discussing the Brownings' reputation, she answered, "I don't know exactly, just everybody."

Asked to name one, she said, "Smith Roby for one."

She responded negatively when he asked if she had ever heard John Bolton or Clarence Crenshaw discuss this reputation, and also when he asked if she was related to any of the defendants.

"Were they at your home when they made this statement that you testified about?"

"Yes sir."

"What did they come over there for?"

"Came over there to get me to write a letter to the home about the children, asking them to send them home to her."

"Was this Lou or Mandy?"

"Lou."

Mr. Creal then turned to the judge, and asked to have Lucile Bolton recalled to the stand. When she was seated, he inquired, "Lucille, who else was at your house the night that this trouble occurred down there except this young lady that was here?"

She looked puzzled, and he inquired further, "Was there a man working there?"

"Yes sir, Mr. Charlie Culver."

"Did he stay there all the time, including that night?"

"Yes sir."

"Where did he sleep?"

"Upstairs in the opposite room from us."

"When you went down to get a light to get a drink for the baby, what was it your father said to you about not lighting the lamp?"

"He said I didn't need any light."

"You didn't know whether he had on his clothes or not then did you?"

"No sir, I don't know."

"You didn't light any lamp in his room?"

"He sleeps with a light burning all the time."

"You didn't see your father when you were down there, did you?"

"Yes sir, in the bed."

"Did you go in his room?"

"Have to walk right through his rooms to get out."

With that, Mr. Creal dismissed her, and Mr. James called H. D. Perkins to the stand.

He testified that he lived with Selby Hodge and had for almost two months, and testified that he slept there the night of May 4th, and that Selby was there as well.

Mr. James wanted to know, "Did he stay at home all night?"

"Yes sir, I guess he did, because when I woke up he was still there."

He also testified that he woke up during the night and Selby was there then.

James inquired, "What time did he go to bed?"

"Along about eight o'clock."

"Did he go to bed before you did?"

"Yes sir."

Mr. Creal began his cross-examination by asking, "It was about eleven when you woke up, wasn't it?" It was becoming clear to everyone that Mr. Creal was finding it suspicious that so many people were awake at eleven o'clock.

"Between eleven and twelve. I looked over at the clock." he offered.

"Was there a lamp burning?"

"Yes sir."

"How long did you stay awake?"

"About fifteen or twenty minutes."

"Did you get up?"

"No sir."

"Just lay there in the bed and looked at the clock?"

"Yes sir."

"When did you remember waking up that night along about that time, after that?"

"Next morning I remembered it."

"Did you sleep in the same room with him?"

"Yes sir."

Changing tactics, he asked, "You were down at the Browning home on Saturday evening after the fire weren't you?"

"Yes sir."

"Did you find the axe there that had been burned the night before?"

"I don't know whether it had been burned or not; it looked like a new axe."

"It didn't look like it had been in any fire?"

"I never paid no attention; it was just black."

"You can tell the difference in an axe that had been through a fire and one that hadn't, can't you?"

"I never paid much attention to this one."

"Was it inside of where the fire was?"

"No sir. It was about four or five feet from the corner of the house."

"Who was with you when you found this axe?"

"Selby Hodge and Maude Hodge and Pauline."

"What did you do with this axe?"

"I gave it to Mr. Browning."

"Selby along with you?"

"Yes sir."

"Did he suggest that you pick the axe up?"

"No sir, he never said much about it."

"Did it have any handle in it?"

"No sir."

"Did you see anything of a chain around there anywhere?"

"If I did, I didn't pay any attention to it."

Now Mr. Creal went on kind of a fishing expedition, trolling the waters to see where Perkins might let something slip.

"When did you commence staying with Selby Hodge?"

"Before his wife got sick."

"When was that?"

"It has been right close to three months."

"Where did you come from when you came over there?"

"Leslie Hodge's."

"How long had you been living there?"

"About a year."

"Where did you stay before that?"

"At home."

"Where was that?"

"At my mother's."

"In this county?"

"Yes sir."

"What kind of work did you do for Selby Hodge?"

"Grubbed and fixed ground."

"Did you do anything else?"

"I worked for Hilary Hardy some."

"Had you ever been to Elmer Crenshaw's still?"

"No sir."

"You don't know where it was?"

"No sir."

"You don't know anything about it?"

"No sir."

With his hook still empty, Creal decided to pack it in, and dismissed the witness.

Mr. Bradbury then called Bill Jackson to the stand.

After verifying his name and that he lived up above Hobbs, about a mile and a half, Bradbury asked, "On Friday morning before this fire occurred on Friday night down at the Brownings', where were you?"

"I went to Selby Hodge's about sundown after a bucket of milk."

"What time did you leave?"

"I didn't look to see what time it was when I left, but I guess it was somewhere between eight and nine o'clock."

"Was Selby there?"

"Yes sir."

"What was he doing when you left?"

"Had his shoes off, fixing to go to bed, and was sitting there begging me to stay all night; he said that he was tired and wanted to lay down."

"Did he say he had been working that day?"

"Said he had been burning brush."

In cross-examination, Mr. Creal first asked, "Did you see H. D. Perkins there?"

"Yes sir."

"What was he doing?"

"He went out to milk with Selby."

"When you were over at Selby Hodge's, did you see Frank Kinder over there?"

"He came directly after I got there."

"Who else came?"

"Mrs. Vina Browning and Della Browning and some children came shortly after I got there."

"Was there anybody else there?"

"Frank Kinder's boy was over there."

"Did you receive any information that Elmer's still had been raided?"

"I remember hearing something about it." Jackson grinned.

"Did you receive any information as to who put the officers wise about it?"

"No sir." He was still grinning.

"Didn't you hear the Brownings discussed?"

"I have heard that talked."

"There that evening?"

"No sir, I don't remember when it was that I did hear that."

"Didn't you and Selby have a conversation about it there that evening?"

"No sir." He shook his head, not grinning as much now.

"Did you hear it there that same evening?"

"I don't remember."

"Which one of the Browning women did you hear turned it up?"

"I don't remember."

Mr. Bradbury stood and asked Mr. R. L. Simmons to take the stand. Mr. Simmons was both a farmer and the president of The Peoples Bank in Shepherdsville. He appeared uncomfortable at being a witness as he took his seat.

After the preliminary questions, Bradbury asked, "Do you know the Brownings?"

"Yes sir."

He carefully asked his, by now, familiar question. "Do you know their general reputation in the community in which they live and among those who know them best as to what the people say of and about them concerning their general reputation for truth and veracity and morality?"

"Yes sir." was the solemn reply.

"Is that reputation good or bad?"

Simmons hesitated, clearly uncomfortable at having to answer, before saying "Bad."

"From what the people say about them, are they worthy of credit under oath?"

"No sir." He answered.

Mr. Bradbury's questions might have been deferential in light of the banker's reputation, but Mr. Creal didn't hesitate to press the witness with his questions.

"Who have you heard discuss their reputation?" he challenged.

"Different ones." was Simmons' careful reply.

"You can't recall any one at all?"

"Just general talk."

"Can't you name a single one that you have heard say that their reputation was bad?"

"Well, I don't believe I can." Simmons apparently decided it would be better not to name names.

"How do you know you have heard it discussed?"

"I was on the grand jury several years ago when there were some Brownings indicted, and they bore an awfully bad reputation."

"That wasn't these Brownings that he asked you about, was it?"

"Not the same ones I don't suppose."

"Is that the reputation that you are talking about?"

"No sir, I have heard lots in the last two or three years."

"Did you ever hear of them telling anything but the truth?"

"Yes sir."

"Who did you hear discussing them?" insisted the prosecutor.

Relenting, the witness answered "I can name lots of names."

"Who?"

"Well, Mr. Swearingen for one said that they weren't very reliable."

"How long ago was that?"

"A year or two I guess."

"What did he mean by that, did he mean they wouldn't tell the truth?"

"Just bad characters I suppose."

"About their truthfulness and veracity, what about that?"

"People give them that name generally."

"Who did you hear give them that name?"

"It is such common talk that I just don't know."

"Can you name one?"

"I could if I could think about it a little bit." he answered evasively, unwilling to go any further.

Creal stared at the banker for a moment, and then returned to his seat.

Mr. Bradbury stood and asked a single question of the witness.

"You never talked with anybody about this case, did you Mr. Simmons?"

"No sir."

"Thank you sir, for your help in this matter." Bradbury ended, and then announced that Will Lanham would be the next witness.

After determining that Mr. Lanham lived about a mile from Browningtown, up near Cedar Grove Church, Mr. Bradbury asked, "Do you know Lou Browning, Angie Browning, Peachie Browning, Mandy Jones, and Bennie Browning?"

"Yes sir."

Bradbury paused a moment, and then asked the witness, "A short time before Christmas, Mr. Lanham, the exact date I cannot fix, didn't Lou Browning come to your house and make a statement to you that Kate and Bennie were beating Mandy to death and wanted you to call the officers for her?"

Mr. Creal was immediately on his feet. "Objection! This is both irrelevant and hear-say." He continued on, citing additional reasons why the question should not be answered, before the judge raised his hand to stop him, and sustained the objection.

Mr. Bradbury was satisfied that the jury had heard the question despite the objection, and he went on mildly, "What is your occupation?"

"Paper hanger."

Then Bradbury launched into his question about the Brownings' reputation for truth and veracity in the neighborhood, whether it was good or bad, and Mr. Lanham replied "Bad."

"From what the people generally say of them, are they worthy of credit on oath?"

"No sir."

With that he thanked the witness and turned him over to the prosecutor.

Like a bulldog, Mr. Creal bore down on the witness, asking "Who did you ever hear discuss their truthfulness?"

"Everybody around there."

"It has been more general since this trouble came up, hasn't it?"

"For the last six years."

"Who did you ever hear discuss their truthfulness, just the truthfulness alone?" By now the prosecutor had given up on the rest of the Browning reputation, and was hammering away at the truthfulness part.

"No one, I don't suppose." admitted the witness.

"Did you ever hear anyone say that they wouldn't tell the truth?"

"Lots of them!" he insisted.

"Who?"

"Every neighbor that they have down there."

"Name some of them?"

"Well, Bill Harris for one."

"Who is he?"

"A brother of Jim."

"Bill talked about it?"

"I haven't talked to him about it lately, but I have in time."

"You never knew of them telling you anything except the truth did you ?"

"I have talked to them but very little."

"These conversations that you have had about these Brownings, were they about them telling the truth or what?"

"Nothing in particular."

"They were just sorry folks?"

"Yes sir."

Satisfied he had done all he could do with the witness, Creal dismissed him, and Mr. Funk next called Bluford Clark, the owner of the Shepherdsville pool room, to the stand.

Clark testified that on the night of the fire, Walter Crenshaw had visited the pool room about ten thirty, and had left when the pool room closed at about eleven thirty.

Mr. Creal had no questions, and Mr. Funk called J. B. Berkholder to the stand.

Berkholder was the son of the local Baptist preacher. He testified that he had seen Walter Crenshaw at both the musical at the school, and later at the pool room Walter had been there until at least eleven fifteen or twenty when Berkholder left to go home.

Again Mr. Creal had no questions, and Judge Richardson called for a brief recess.

The Final Witnesses

As C. P. Bradbury sat waiting for the judge to return to the courtroom, he pondered how the case had gone thus far, and questioned in his own mind what his clients' chances were. With so many clients to defend, he had been forced to call a lot of different witnesses to support alibis. Now he was also attempting to convince the jury that the Brownings couldn't be trusted to tell the truth, and that there were reasonable doubts that things happened the way they had testified.

He had watched the jurors when other lawyers were leading the examinations, and his lawyer's gut instinct was that things were going the prosecution's way. There seemed little he could do except carry on with the plan to discredit the Brownings' testimony.

When court reconvened, Bradbury called Mrs. Bud Mann as a witness. After determining that she lived on the Shepherdsville side of Cedar Grove Church, he got right to the point.

"I will ask you if you know Lou Browning?"

"Yes sir."

"Didn't she make this statement to you in your home, nobody present but you and her, that Kate was getting so mean that she was getting jealous of her and her boys, and that they couldn't live there together, and that she was going to have to get rid of Kate?"

"Them very words."

At this point, Judge Richardson interrupted, and told the jury, "Gentlemen of the jury, you will not regard the statement of this witness relating to what Mrs. Browning did or said unless in your judgment it tends to affect the credibility of Mrs. Browning as a witness, and you will not regard it for any other purpose."

Bradbury next asked his question about the Brownings' reputation in the community for "truth and veracity and morality" and she answered, "It is bad the way I always heard it."

"From what people say of them, are they worthy of belief under oath?"

"No sir."

Mr. Creal, at his turn, asked, "Do you know Clarence Crenshaw?"

"Yes sir."

"He is on your husband's bond now for bootlegging, isn't he?"

Bradbury strongly objected to the question, and was sustained; but Creal knew the jury would remember it.

Mr. James then called Will Harris, Jim Harris' brother, to the stand, and asked "Do you know Lou Browning?"

"Yes sir."

"How long have you known her?"

"About twenty-five or thirty years."

"A short while ago, wasn't she at your house and you had a conversation with her in which she said that Kate was getting so mean that she would have to get rid of her?"

"Yes sir, some way or some how."

"Let me ask you this question. If upon the occasion that I asked you about, nobody being present but you, Lou and Mandy, if in substance she made these statements: that Kate Browning was getting so mean that she was getting so they couldn't live together and that she would have to get rid of her some way or some how, and that Bennie and Kate were trying to run her away, and if they did then that house would go up in smoke. Did she make that statement to you, or that in substance?"

"Yes sir, she said that."

Once again the judge cautioned the jury to not regard this testimony for any purpose except as it tended to affect Lou Browning's credibility as a witness.

"Mr. Harris, do you know the general reputation of these Brownings from what people say of and about them for truth and veracity and morality?"

"Yes sir."

"Is that reputation good or bad?"

"Bad."

"From what the people generally say of them, are they worthy of belief on oath?"

"No sir."

Mr. Creal began his cross-examination by asking, "You never heard their reputation for truthfulness discussed did you?"

"Yes sir."

"It was just their reputation for morality wasn't it?"

"It was a general thing all the way around."

"Was it since this trouble came up that you heard this?"

"No sir."

"In the last two or three years, who have you heard discuss their reputation for truthfulness?"

"I haven't heard anybody particularly, it is just in the mouths of everybody."

The next witness was Mrs. Bud Pugh. She testified that she lived about a half mile from the Browning place, and then Bradbury inquired, "Mrs. Pugh, on the night that this house is said to have been burned, was Peachie Browning at your house that night?"

"I never saw him if he was."

"Do you have a conversation with Lou Browning over at your house, nobody being present but you and her, in which she said to you that Kate was getting so mean, or in substance to this that, if she and Bennie kept on being so mean that there would be a killing in the family?"

"Yes sir."

"Mrs. Pugh, did you see this fire that night?"

"Yes sir."

Mr. Creal's first question was "You don't know whether or not Peachie and Ewing Browning were over at your place there by the corner of the yard talking that night, do you?"

"No sir."

"They didn't come in the house that night?"

"No sir, they haven't been in there for a right smart while."

When she testified that she had been over to where the fire had burned the Browning home the next day, Mr. Creal wanted to know if she had seen the axe. She told him no, but she had seen the wedge that was used to fasten a handle in. When he asked if she had seen Selby Hodge there, she said she hadn't.

His last questions was "Did you see any chain around there where the door is supposed to be?"

"No sir." she answered.

Bradbury next called Mrs. Gabe McCormick to the stand. Establishing her identity before the prosecution could make an issue of it, he asked, "You are the former Myrtle Crenshaw, daughter of Clarence Crenshaw, aren't you?"

"Yes sir."

"Did you, at any time, tell Lou Browning that your father told you to notify her to stay off his place?" Bradbury asked, getting ahead of the prosecutor.

"I did not."

"Some time ago did you have a conversation with Lou Browning, nobody being present but you and her, didn't she say to you that Kate was getting so mean that she couldn't live with her any longer, did she say that, or in substance that?"

"Yes sir."

Mr. Creal, in his turn, first asked, "At the same time and place did you inform her that you yourself had nothing against her, but that your father said that if he caught her on his place what he was going to do to her?"

"No sir." she denied.

"At some other time or place, did you do that?"

"No sir, I didn't."

The witness parade continued when Tom Watts was called to the stand. Tom, who lived at Samuels in Nelson County, testified that he was at the graveyard the day that Kate Browning was buried, and when Peachie Browning came by there.

Bradbury asked, "Did you hear Peachie Browning, on that occasion in your presence and in the presence of Charlie Biven, Hugo Maraman and Charlie Browning, make this statement: on the previous night that he shot some person and that when he shot him he threw up his hands and that he hollered 'Oh Lordy' and he threw his gun in the ditch and run?"

"Yes sir." was the witness's reply.

Then Mr. Creal wanted to know, "Didn't he also say that that fellow was about the size of Frank Kinder?"

"Yes sir."

"What else did he say about him?"

"Not much more."

"Did they stop digging when Peachie told about killing that man?"

"I couldn't say."

"Did any of you go to look for that man?"

"No sir."

"You don't know anything about his truth and veracity do you?"

"No sir, I don't know nothing about that, I didn't know whether to believe it or not when he told it. He just volunteered to tell it."

"Nobody ever asked him any more about it?"

"No sir."

The next witness was Hugo Maraman, an adopted son of Ewing Crenshaw who was a distant cousin to Clarence Crenshaw. He testified that he lived about a mile from the Browning place. He further testified that he knew Peachie Browning, and had been present when Peachie came by while they were burying Kate Browning.

Bradbury ask him, "Did you hear him make this statement when he came up to where you were digging the grave, that the night before on the night that the house was burned that he shot a fellow out there in the thicket, and that he threw up his hands and hollered 'Oh Lordy' and fell backwards, and that he threw his gun away and ran?"

"That is exactly what he said." Hugo declared without hesitation.

"Do you know the general reputation of the Brownings for truth and veracity and morality in the community in which they live, and among those who know them best as to what people generally say of and about them?"

"Yes sir."

"Is that reputation good or bad?"

"Bad."

"From what the people generally say of and about them, are they worthy of belief under oath?"

"No sir."

Mr. Creal asked the witness, "You say their reputation for truthfulness is bad?"

"Yes sir."

"Who did you ever hear say that?"

"I know them well enough to know that."

"Did you ever know of them not telling the truth?"

"I have worked with them and I know they won't."

"Who did you ever hear discuss their truthfulness?"

"People that I have worked with and who have worked with them."

"Who?"

"Jim Harris and Willie Swearingen."

"Is that all?"

"Yes sir."

Charlie Browning was the next witness called. Mr. Bradbury knew that Browning was a first cousin to Lou Browning, so he handled him carefully.

After several inconsequential questions, he asked "How near do you live to Lou's house down there?"

"Pretty close."

"Is your house in sight of hers?"

"Might near."

"Do you have a shotgun?"

"Yes sir."

"What became of it?"

The purpose of the question was to help establish that Charlie's shotgun had gone missing for a time just when this trouble took place. But before he could answer, the prosecutor objected to the question on relevancy and was sustained.

Bradbury tried again, "Was your shotgun stolen?" and was halted by a sustained objection.

He then asked, "Do you know where your shotgun was?" and Judge Richardson sustained the prosecution's objection once more.

Bradbury was determined to get this testimony into the record, and asked, "Your honor, may we approach the bench?"

Out of the hearing of the jury, Mr. Bradbury said that if permitted to answer the witness would say that his shotgun, a number twelve gauge, was stolen on the day that the fire occurred, and the day after the fire and killing it was found on or near the ground where this killing took place and near the house. This avowal was duly entered into the court record.

An avowal is a sworn statement made before the court. Usually an avowal is made by a witness after a court rules that his/her testimony cannot be admitted in trial. Avowal forms part of the court record, and a higher court can consider it in an appeal against a denial to accept the testimony.

Mr. Bradbury then picked up a shotgun off the table, and asked, "Is this your shotgun?" Once again the question was objected to, and the objection sustained. With that, Mr. Bradbury again approached the bench and made the avowal, "The witness if permitted to answer would state that it is his shotgun."

Bradbury then asked, "Charlie, were you at the graveyard when they were burying Kate?"

"Yes sir."

"Did you hear what Peachie said when he came over there, in the presence of you, Charlie Biven and Tom Watts, that on the night that this fire took place over there in the thicket he shot somebody and he threw up his hands and hollered 'Oh Lordy'?"

"I heard him say that he shot somebody." was the careful reply.

"What did he say; did he say that in substance?"

"Something like that." he agreed reluctantly.

"Did he say that he threw his gun in the ditch and ran?"

"He said that he throwed his gun away."

Mr. Bradbury then approached the bench and spoke to the judge and prosecutor out of the hearing of the jury.

"Your honor, we intend to call Vina Browning to the stand to testify about this shotgun."

At first Judge Richardson refused to permit the testimony until Mr. Bradbury declared that if she were allowed to testify, she would state that on the day following the day that Kate Browning was found dead down there, she found this gun. At this point the court permitted the witness to testify.

Mrs. Browning took the stand, and the lawyer asked, "What is your name?"

"Vina Browning."

"You are the mother of Ewing Browning?"

"Yes sir."

"A short time after the trouble and fire there at Kate Browning's, did you find a shotgun out there in a ditch close by?"

"I found a gun on Sunday."

"What time Sunday did you find it?"

"On Sunday morning, and I went back and got it Sunday evening late."

"What did you do with it?"

"Took it home."

"Who has the gun now?"

"Mr. Carroll."

"He is the County Attorney?"

"Yes sir."

"Whose gun is that, if you know?"

"I don't know."

Taking his turn, Mr. Creal inquired, "Did you hear the shots down there that night?"

"Yes sir."

"How many did you hear?"

"The best I know, seven or eight."

"At the time you heard those shots, where was Ewing Browning, your son?"

"In the bed."

On re-direct, Mr. Bradbury asked her, "Where is Ewing now?"

"They say he is in Louisville in jail." The jury was not told that Ewing had been arrested on a three-month-old warrant, accused of shooting his own father.

The Sheriff was then recalled to the stand, and Bradbury asked, "Do you have that gun in your possession Mr. Monroe?"

"Yes sir."

"Will you produce the gun?"

"If the court tells me to, I will."

At this point, Judge Richardson ordered that it be introduced.

Mr. Bradbury thanked the court and took his seat. Mr. Creal then asked the sheriff, "Mr. Monroe, have you had much or little experience in examining or handling firearms?"

"I have always handled firearms."

"Where did you get this gun?"

"Up at Mr. Henry Browning's."

"Who turned it over to you?"

"Mrs. Browning."

"Is it in the same condition now that it was then?"

"Yes sir."

"Since you have had that gun in your possession, have you made any examination of where the plunger hits the shell?"

"Yes sir."

"When did you make that test?"

"I think it was yesterday."

"Did you examine the shells that you found as to the place where the plunger struck on the ends?"

"Not on those that I found up there, no sir."

Going to the evidence table and picking up the shells, he asked, "Are these the shells that you found up there at the Browning home on the ground that day?"

"Yes sir."

"Where are the shells that you tested this gun with?"

"I turned them over to Mr. Carroll."

Creal picked up those shells and handed them to the witness. "I will ask you to take these shells and examine them and tell whether or not from the position where the plunger of the gun hit them whether or not the same gun fired both?"

Sheriff Monroe examined each shell carefully, and then declared, "No sir."

On re-direct, Bradbury asked, "Mr. Monroe, is that the same gun turned over to you by Vina Browning?"

"Yes sir."

"Mr. Monroe, you don't know what, if anything, had been done with that gun after it was found before you got it, do you?"

"I know that there hasn't been anything since I have had it."

"You don't know what condition the gun was in when it was found out there in the ditch?"

"No sir."

"You don't know whether there was anything done to it or not?"

"No sir."

"Mr. Monroe, I will get you to examine that gun and state to the jury whether or not one of those plungers is larger than the other?"

"Yes sir, a little bit." he agreed.

Now Mr. Creal wanted to know, "Mr. Monroe, will both barrels of that gun fire?"

"No sir."

"Which one of them is it that won't?"

"The right one."

"You don't know how long that gun has been in that condition?"

"No sir."

"What kind of shells did you have to try that gun with?"

"The same kind that I picked up down there."

It was Bradbury's turn to ask, "were those shells that you tried Winchester repeaters?"

"Those that I tried yesterday were."

"Did you try any Rangers?"

"No sir."

"Your honor, we recall Charlie Browning to the stand." announced Bradbury.

"Mr. Browning, I will get you to examine that gun and state to the jury whether or not it is the same gun that was stolen from your residence?"

"It is the same gun." he admitted.

Mr. Creal then asked, "When did you first see this gun after it was stolen?"

"I believe it was Monday or Tuesday my sister said that she had found it."

"I will ask you to examine the gun and see whether or not it is in the same condition that it was in then or whether or not there has been anything done to it?"

"I don't see a thing in the world, it looks exactly like it did when it went away."

Then Mr. Bradbury wanted to know, "Would both barrels shoot?"

"They did when it was at home."

After that, the witness was excused.

Miss Minnie K. McGruder was next called to the stand by Mr. James. He quickly identified her employment at Charlie Samuels' store in Deatsville, and that she was working there on May 2nd.

James then asked, "I have in my hand five shotgun shells. I will get you to examine them and state to the jury whether or not shells of that brand or that make were stolen from C. T. Samuel's store on the night of May 2nd of this year?"

When the prosecution successfully objected, Mr. James spoke to the judge, out of the jury's hearing, and made the following avowal: "The witness if permitted to answer would say that these are the same make of shells that were stolen from the store of C. T. Samuels on the night of May 2nd this year."

He then stepped back and asked the witness, "On this occasion on the night of May 2nd was Mr. Samuel's store broken into?"

Again the prosecution successfully objected, and Mr. James made the following avowal: "The witness if permitted to answer would say yes."

The court at this point ruled that the attorney for the defendant ask these questions out of the hearing of the jury, and let the record show that the questions were asked. After the jury left the room, Mr. James inquired of the witness, "What was stolen out of this store on that night?"

Once again the prosecution objected, and Mr. James was forced to make the following avowal: "The defendants avowal that if the witness were permitted to answer she would say, meat, overalls, shirts, shotgun shells, cigarettes and tobacco, and candy and they got some knives."

He then asked, "What brand of shotgun shells were stolen?"

The witness was finally able to answer for herself, saying "Defiance and Winchester."

"What size?"

"12."

"What size shot?"

"7 1/2."

"Both Winchester and Defiance for that size?"

"The Defiance were number five shot."

Having heard the witness, the judge announced that the prosecution's objections to this entire testimony were sustained, and the jury was returned to the courtroom.

Mr. Creal began his cross-examination by stating, "You are a niece of the defendant Jim Harris aren't you?"

"Yes sir."

"Your mother was the sister of Jim Harris?"

"Yes sir."

"That's all your honor."

The defense next called C. T. Samuels as a witness with little hope that he would be able to testify as to the theft.

Mr. James' questions led the witness to identify himself, and that he had been running a general store at Deatsville for nineteen years. But as soon as the questions began to deal with the theft on May 2nd, the prosecution objected, and once again the series of avows were entered into the record. Then the witness was dismissed.

Nellie Maraman was called next as a witness, and examined by Mr. Funk. She testified that she lived in Shepherdsville, and was the widow of Frank Maraman who had died the previous November.

Mr. Funk then asked, "Do you remember the night that the Browning home was burned up and Kate Browning was killed?"

"I heard about it."

"Where were you that night?"

"Coming from Bardstown."

"About what time was that?"

"About twelve o'clock."

"Did you pass by the place where this house burned?"

"Yes sir."

"Where were you going?"

"Coming home."

"What road were you on?"

"Cedar Grove Road."

"Is that the Deatsville Road?"

"Yes sir."

"Did you come by the home of Charlie Biven?"

"Yes sir."

"Did you come by about the time this fire happened and saw the fire?"

"Yes sir."

"Did you see anybody along the road?"

"Not a soul."

"About what time was it when you passed Charlie Browning's?"

"About a quarter past twelve."

"Who was with you?"

"Frank Lee."

"Were you in an automobile?"

"Yes sir."

As Mr. Creal began his cross-examination, it appeared that he had not anticipated this witness's testimony. He asked her first, "What is your occupation?"

"I don't have any."

"Where do you get your money to live on?"

"My son-in-law." She was referring to James Wallace who had married her daughter Arietta.

Creal, still searching for a way to approach this witness, asked her again where she lived and then who lived with her. To that she replied, "My children."

"Who did you say was with you that night?"

"Frank Lee."

"Is he any relation of yours?"

"No sir."

"What business did you have over at Bardstown?"

"I went over there to see my daughter."

"Where does Charlie Browning live?"

"On the Deatsville Road."

"What kind of a house does he live in?"

"Just a little frame house."

"How do you know that this was Charlie Browning's house when you passed there?"

"I know that Frank Lee said when we passed there that it was the place where one of those Brownings killed that man, and I knew that Charlie Browning lived there."

Quickly, before the jurors could think about her statement, Creal asked, "All you know about it is what this fellow told you?"

"Yes sir."

"Is that the best road from Bardstown here?"

"No sir, but it is the shortest way."

"That is a very rough road around that way in an automobile isn't it?"

"Yes sir."

"Did you have any other business in coming back around that way?"

"Not a bit."

"What other road could you have come?"

"Through the Preston Street Road."

"Why didn't you go this other road?"

"Didn't want to is all I can tell you."

Pleased with Mrs. Maraman's testimony, Mr. Bradbury next called Ed Holton to the stand as a character witness against the Brownings. Holton gave his name and indicated that he had formerly lived near Cedar Grove Church.

"Do you know Lou, Mandy, Peachie, Bennie, and Angie Browning?"

"Yes sir."

"Do you know their general reputation in the community in which they live and among those who know them best as to what the people generally say of and about them concerning their reputation for truth and veracity and morality?"

"Yes sir."

"Is that reputation good or bad?"

"Very bad."

"From what the people generally say of and about them, are they worthy of credit on oath?"

"No sir."

Mr. Creal, after asking the witness if the attorneys for the defense had discussed the case with him in front of other witnesses, to which he said no, then asked, "Who have you heard discuss these people's reputation for truthfulness?"

"Well I have heard Mr. Theo Middleton over there."

"Who else did you hear discuss it?"

"John Bolton."

"Mr. Middleton is a brother-in-law of Clarence Crenshaw isn't he?"

"Yes sir."

"And Mr. Bolton is one of the defendants?"

"Yes sir."

"When was it you heard this talk?"

"I think it was back in 1919."

"That was nine years ago?"

"Yes sir."

"Did you ever hear anybody else say anything about them recently?"

"Yes sir, Mr. Earl Deacon and Don Simmons."

"What did they say?"

"They said that these people wouldn't tell the truth and that they would steal anything that they could get their hands on."

"When was it that you heard Earl Deacon say anything about them?"

"Last summer when we were working together."

"Do you know of anybody else that said that these Brownings wouldn't tell the truth?" Creal noticeably avoided the question of stealing.

"One of them worked for me and I ain't never heard of him telling the truth."

The next witness was Ed Holton's wife, another character witness against the Brownings. She was asked "Do you know Bennie, Lou, Mandy, Angie and Peachie Browning?"

"Yes sir."

"Do you know their general reputation from what people generally say of and about them concerning their reputation for truth and veracity and morality?"

"Yes sir."

"Is that reputation good or bad?"

"Bad."

"From what people generally say of and about them, are they worthy of belief under oath?"

"No sir."

Then Mr. Creal wanted to know, "Did they work for you at any time?"

"Yes sir. Bennie worked for Mr. Holton and Lou washed for me."

"Did you ever know of them not telling the truth?"

"Yes sir."

"What did you ever hear of them not telling the truth about?"

"She had come to my house to get things or sent the children after things to eat and promised to work for me to pay for them and then not do it."

The parade of character witnesses continued with Bert Deacon who agreed that Lou, Angie, Mandy, Peachie and Bennie Browning had bad reputations, and weren't worthy of belief under oath.

Mr. Creal attempted to blunt his testimony, first by asking if he was related to any of the defendants. His answer of "Not closely" was followed by the inquiry, "Did you ever have any business dealings with the Brownings?" received a reply of "Not much."

Creal then asked, "This talk that you heard about them was just about their sorriness and failure to work, no account, wasn't it?"

"Some of it, yes sir." the witness admitted.

"That question about them telling the truth, you never heard of that did you?"

"Yes sir."

"Who did you ever hear discuss that?"

"Most everybody."

"Anybody in particular?"

"The neighbors all around there."

"How recently was this that you heard this talk?"

"Since this happened."

"All been since this happened?"

"No sir, not all of it."

"Then their reputation for truth before this?"

"I have known them all my life and it has always been that way."

"Can you name any special one that has discussed their truthfulness that you have heard?"

"No sir." he replied, tired of the prosecutor's badgering questions, and determined to avoid anymore of them if possible.

The next witness was J. W. Hardaway, cashier for the Peoples Bank. Like the ones before him, he testified that Lou Browning's family had a bad reputation, and couldn't be trusted to tell the truth.

Using the same tactic as before, Mr. Creal asked, "This talk that you have heard had been about their sorriness and no accountness and failure to work hasn't it?"

"Not altogether."

"Hasn't most of it been along that line?"

"Well I believe it has."

"You never heard it discussed about their not telling the truth until this case came up did you?"

"I have heard it before this." the witness disagreed.

"You had heard their truthfulness discussed before this?"

"Yes sir."

"Who did you hear discuss that?"

"Well Hugo Maraman for one."

"Who else have you heard discuss that reputation?"

"Billy Deacon."

"How recently had you heard their reputation for truthfulness discussed?"

"About two or three years ago."

"Have you heard anyone discuss the reputation of these Brownings except the kinfolks of these defendants?"

"Yes sir, I have heard lots of people discuss it."

"That was since they have become witnesses in this case?"

"I have heard lots of talk in the last month, and I have heard it before."

Earl Deacon was the next witness. He also declared that the Brownings had a bad reputation, and couldn't be trusted to tell the truth. Then Mr. Creal asked him, "Are you related to any of the defendants?"

"Clarence Crenshaw and Jim Harris are cousins of mine." he replied.

Will Shaw was next. Like the others, he had nothing good to say about the Brownings, indicating that their reputation was not very good, and they were not worthy of belief under oath. However, Mr. Creal quickly got him to admit that he was related to both John Bolton and Clarence Crenshaw.

James B. Crenshaw testified next, and admitted knowing Lou and her youngest child. He too considered their reputation bad, and their truthfulness unbelievable. As he had already declared that he was distantly related (his father was brother to Clarence's grandfather) to the Crenshaws on trial, Mr. Creal had no questions for him.

Next came Richard Johnson "Jonce" Clark to testify. Admitting he was related to Mr. Crenshaw, the defendant, Clark testified that the Brownings couldn't be trusted to tell the truth, and he had known them "Ever since I can remember."

Mr. Creal's cross-examination allowed Clark to identify Mr. E. C. Barger's boys and Mr. Bud Pugh as ones he had heard discuss the Browning reputation. In naming Pugh, he said, "He has lived right there with them all his life."

James B. Crenshaw's son Herman was the next witness. he agreed with his father's testimony that the Browning reputation was bad, and they were untrustworthy. Creal had no questions.

J. H. Lane, Sr. was next. After he essentially repeated the previous testimony, Mr. Creal wanted to know if he or his wife were related in any of the defendants, but he declared he wasn't.

Trying a different tactic, he asked, "Who did you buy the farm from that you now live on?"

"I live on my wife's farm."

"Do you own more than one farm?"

"I bought one here at the court house door."

"Did you get it through Clarence Crenshaw?"

"No sir."

"Does he own an interest in it?"

"No sir."

"Is Clarence Crenshaw on your bond for that?"

"No sir, I put up two thousand dollars of my own money and they took land notes for the balance." Mr. Lane declared, a bit angry that his business dealings were called into question.

Frank Ratliff came next. He indicated that he was born and reared in the same neighborhood as the Brownings, and knew them well. He declared they had a bad reputation and were not trustworthy.

Mr. Creal's only question was "Are you related to any of the nine defendants?"

"No sir, only by marriage." He indicated that his wife's mother was sister to Clarence's mother.

His brother Gus Ratliff followed, and had the same opinion of the Brownings as his brother. He declared that he was not related to the defendants in any way. Mr. Creal pressed him regarding the Brownings' truthfulness just being an issue since the fire and death, but Ratliff disagreed.

Evelyn Ratliff was next. She agreed that she was the wife of Frank Ratliff, and that she was related to Clarence Crenshaw. When asked, "Do you know Bennie, Peachie, Mandy, Angie, and Lou Browning?" she said she did, that she had known the family all her life.

Again, like the witnesses before her, she indicated the Brownings had a bad reputation and couldn't be trusted to tell the truth.

Mr. Creal pressed her on the timing of talk about their truthfulness, but she insisted it had been both before and after the fire and death of Kate Browning. When asked who she had heard express this opinion, she said, "Mr. Crenshaw and Mr. Magruder and in fact all the neighbors that I have."

The next witness was William H. Crepps of Deatsville. He indicated he had lived there three years, and that he knew Lou, Angie, Mandy, Peachie and Bennie Browning. He agreed with the others before him about their bad reputation and untrustworthiness.

Mr. Creal began his cross-examination by asking "You live over in Nelson County, about three miles from the Brownings?"

"Yes sir."

"You lived last in North Carolina before you moved where you live now?"

"Yes sir."

"You have been out there about three years?"

"Yes sir."

"What are you doing out there?"

"Farming."

"What farm do you live on?"

"The Bohannan farm."

"Did you ever see these Brownings before this trouble came up?"

"Yes sir."

"Is that talk about their truthfulness, or is it about them being no account, wouldn't work and anything about that?"

"Well now, the way I have heard it, wasn't any good for anything under any circumstances."

"Who did you ever hear say that they weren't truthful?"

"Stoner Wilcoxson and Will Shaw."

"Did they say that they weren't truthful?"

"Said that they wouldn't risk them to do anything, that they were no good."

"Who else did you hear say that?"

"Alf Crenshaw and L. E. Woodward."

"What did you hear Woodward say about them?"

"He said that he wouldn't credit them for anything in the store he runs."

"The question of truthfulness, did you ever hear anybody discuss that?"

"Yes sir, I have heard L. E. Woodward."

"He said they wouldn't pay their debts, didn't he?"

"Well I concede that to mean the same thing."

"Since they have become witnesses in this case, you have heard quite a good deal of talk, haven't you?"

"Yes sir, quite a bit."

"Is that all you have heard about them, that they wouldn't pay their debts?"

"Yes sir, that is about all; it all amounts to the same thing."

"Just about their truthfulness alone, what about that?"

"Well, if you promise a man to pay him a debt and you don't do it, you are not telling the truth are you."

Mr. Creal decided not to argue the point.

Next up was Estella Crenshaw, wife of Alf Crenshaw and sister-in-law to Clarence. She indicated that she and her husband lived in the neighborhood of the Brownings for nine years before moving into Shepherdsville in March.

Mr. Bradbury asked her, "How long have you known the Brownings?"

"I have known Lou for twenty-five years, and I have known the children all their lives."

"Do you know their general reputation for truth and veracity and morality in the community in which they live and among those who know them best for truth and veracity and morality as to what the people generally say of and about them?"

"Yes sir."

"Is that reputation good or bad?"

"Bad."

"From what the people generally say of them, are they worthy of belief under oath?"

"No sir."

Mr. Creal made sure the jury knew her husband was Clarence Crenshaw's brother before dismissing her.

Her husband was next on the stand, and he supported each bit of her testimony.

Mr. Bradbury next called William S. Rouse to the stand. Rouse testified that he lived in Louisville, having moved there from Bullitt County four years earlier.

Bradbury then asked, "Did you ever hold any office in this county?"

"Yes sir, sheriff."

"Where did you live when you lived here?"

"Up in the eastern part of the county."

"When you lived up there, did you live in the neighborhood of the Brownings?"

"About four miles east of them." he replied, indicating the Solitude area.

"Do you know Lou, Peachie, Angie, Mandy and Bennie Browning?"

"Yes sir."

"Do you know their general reputation for truth and veracity and morality in the community in which they live and among those who know them best as to what people generally say of and about them?"

"Yes sir."

"Is that reputation good or bad?"

"Bad."

"From what people generally say of them, are they worthy of belief under oath?"

"No sir."

In his turn, Mr. Creal wanted to know, "Are you related to any of the defendants in this case?"

"I might be fourth or fifth cousins." he guessed doubtfully.

Bradbury was nearing the end of his list of witnesses as he called Hugh Wilson Magruder to the stand. Magruder was 28, tall and slender, and the clerk looked up at him as he took the oath.

Bardbury asked, "Where do you live?"

"About a mile on the other side of Browningtown."

"Do you know Lou, Angie, Mandy, Peachie, and Bennie Browning?"

"Yes sir."

"How long have you known them?"

"Ever since I have known anybody."

"Do you know their general reputation for truth and veracity and morality in the community in which they live and among those who know them best as to what people generally say of and about them?"

"Yes sir."

"Is that reputation good or bad?"

"Bad."

"From what people generally say of them, are they worthy of belief under oath?"

"No sir."

Bradbury himself was getting tired of repeating the words "truth and veracity and morality" but thankfully it was almost over.

Henry Jones took the stand after being sworn in, and Mr. Bradbury asked him, "Where do you live?"

"Over in Leaches."

"Are you related to any of the defendants?"

"No sir, only by marriage."

"Do you know Lou Browning's family?"

"Yes sir."

"How long have you known her?"

"I have known some of them for thirty years and some of them all of their lives."

Bradbury repeated his "truth and veracity and morality" question and received the wished for answer of "Yes sir."

And in response to his question, "What is that reputation, good or bad?" the witness gave the negative response.

Jones allowed that none of the Brownings were worthy of credit on oath.

When Bradbury asked him if he had held any office in Bullitt County, he replied, "Yes sir, deputy sheriff one term."

"How long since?"

"Seven years."

With no questions from the prosecutor, H. W. Bowman was called as a witness for the defense. He had been a resident of Solitude for seven years. True to form, he knew the Brownings, and considered their reputation bad, and their worth under oath unacceptable.

Finally, Bradbury called Sheriff Monroe back to the stand.

"Mr. Monroe, you are the sheriff of Bullitt County?" he asked.

"Yes sir."

"Do you know these prosecution witnesses, Mandy, Lou, Angie, Peachie, and Bennie Browning?"

"Yes sir."

"Do you know their general reputation in the community in which they live, and among those who know them best as to what people generally say of and about them concerning their reputation for truth and veracity and morality?"

"Yes sir."

"Do you know that reputation from what people say?"

"Yes sir."

"What is that reputation?"

"Bad."

"From what the people say who know them, are they worthy of belief under oath?"

"No sir."

Mr. Creal was on his feet, asking "Mr. Monroe, you have heard these folks testify in the Court of Inquiry, at the examining trial, and in this trial. Do you know of any statement that they have made in any of these trials that was different from the ones made in the others?"

Bradbury objected to the question and was sustained. However, Creal had made his point.

Instructions & Closing Arguments

The defense rested at 3:30 that afternoon. After consulting with the attorneys, Judge Richardson delivered the following instructions to the jurors.

No. 1. - If you believe from the evidence beyond a reasonable doubt that the defendants, Clarence Crenshaw, Elmer Crenshaw, John H. Bolton, Frank Hodge, Selby Hodge, Les Hodge, Golden Hodge, Jim Harris, Frank Kinder, or any one or more of them, in this county and before the finding of the indictment herein, did unlawfully, willfully, feloniously and with malice aforethought shoot and wound Kate Browning with a shotgun, a deadly weapon, from which shooting and wounding she presently died; or if you shall believe from the evidence beyond a reasonable doubt that in this county and before the finding of the indictment herein, the defendants Clarence Crenshaw, Elmer Crenshaw, John H. Bolton, Frank Hodge, Selby Hodge, Les Hodge, Golden Hodge, Jim Harris and Frank Kinder, or any one or more of them, or any other person then and there present and acting in concert with any one or more of the defendants, aforesaid, and unknown to the Grand Jury, returning the indictment herein, did unlawfully, willfully, feloniously and with malice aforethought shoot and wound said Kate Browning with a shotgun, a deadly weapon, from which shooting and wounding she presently died; and if you further believe from the evidence beyond a reasonable doubt that, at the time any one or more of the defendants, or such unknown person so acting with then, or any of them, did so shoot and wound said Kate Browning, any one or more of the other defendants was then and there present and near enough to and did unlawfully, willfully, feloniously and with malice aforethought aid, assist and abet the one or more of the other defendants, or such unknown person, to so shoot and wound said Kate Browning as aforesaid; then you will find the defendants, or any one or more of the defendants guilty, whether the identity of the person who so shot and wounded Kate Browning is established or not, and fix the punishment of the defendants or any one or more of them at death or at confinement in the penitentiary for life in your discretion.

No. 2. - If you believe from the evidence, independent and aside from the acts and statements of any of the defendants done and said not in the presence of the other defendants, beyond a reasonable doubt that a conspiracy was formed by such defendant and some one or more of the other defendants to kill Kate Browning and that such conspiracy existed at the time of such acts and statements of such defendant was done or made by such defendant, then you may consider such acts and statements of such co-defendant as against any one or more of the other defendants.

But if you do not so believe beyond a reasonable doubt, independent of and aside from such acts and statements outside of the presence of the other defendants that such a conspiracy was so formed and existed at that time as aforesaid, you will not consider such acts and statements of such defendant as evidence against any other defendant for any purpose whatsoever.

The word, "conspiracy," as used in these instructions means a corrupt combination of two or more persons to do an unlawful act or to do a lawful act by unlawful means.

No. 3. - The testimony of Frank Mather and Lou and Mandy Browning Jones relative to a still and the presence thereat, and the connection therewith of Elmer Crenshaw, must not be considered by you for any purpose in this case, except you may consider same as evidence to show or, tending to show, if same in your judgment shows or tends to show, the identity or motive of Elmer Crenshaw in the commission of the crime charged in the indictment and you will not consider same for any other purpose as evidence against said Crenshaw or any of the other defendants.

No. 4. - The testimony of Lou Browning, Peachie Browning, Angie Browning and Mandy Browning Jones relating to the acts and statements of Frank Hodge and Selby Hodge, on the road near the house of Charles Biven must not be considered by you for any purpose in this case, as against any of the defendants, except you may consider same as evidence to show or tending to show, if in your judgment it does so, the identity with, and motive for the commission of the crime charged in the indictment by said Hodges unless you further believe from the evidence independent and aside from such acts and statements of said Hodges, beyond a reasonable doubt that a conspiracy by said Hodges and some one or more of the other defendants, as defined in these instructions was formed and existed at that time, and that at that time said Hodges were acting in pursuance of such conspiracy, if any, there was, then you may consider such acts and statements on the part of said Hodges as evidence of identity or motive of said Hodges as against any one or more of such other defendants.

But if you do not believe beyond a reasonable doubt, independent of such acts and statements of said Hodges, such conspiracy was so formed and existed at that time, then you will not consider such acts and statements of said Hodges as evidence against the other defendants for any purpose.

No. 5. - The testimony of Mandy Browning Jones relating to the defendant John Bolton having wagon and meal on a road, must not be considered by you for any purpose in this case, except you may consider same as evidence as to the defendant, John Bolton to show or tending to show, if it does so in your judgment, the identity at or motive of the defendant, John Bolton for, the commission of the crime in the indictment and you will not consider same for any other purpose as against said Bolton, nor as against any other defendants.

No. 6. - The testimony of Lou Browning as to information given her by Mrs. McCormick as to statements made by defendant, Clarence Crenshaw to her, Mrs. McCormick, concerning Mrs. Browning are now withdrawn from your consideration and you will not consider same for any purpose whatsoever.

No. 7. - You may find all or any one or more of the defendants guilty or you may find all or any one of them not guilty.

No. 8. - If you have a reasonable doubt of the defendants or either or any one of them having been proven guilty, you should find them or either or any one of them as to whom you have such doubt, not guilty.

He then declared that each side would have two hours for closing arguments.

Tot Carroll opened the prosecution's closing statements, and early on advised the jurors that the Commonwealth would not be seeking the death penalty in this case.

He spent most of his time before the jury revisiting the testimony of the five victims, pointing out its consistency in the face of harsh challenges by the defense lawyers. He noted that, despite the horror of finding themselves trapped in a locked burning building, and struggling to escape with shotguns blasting towards them, their testimonies as to who and what they saw and heard was remarkably similar.

According to Mary Chenoweth, who had been covering the trial for *The Courier-Journal,* Mr. Carroll closed by asking the Hardin County jurors to "help the good citizens of Bullitt County wipe the stain of this horrible atrocity from its fair name."

Commonwealth Attorney Edward W. Creal then took the floor. He too advised the jury that he would not be seeking the death penalty. Then he turned to the testimony of the defense witnesses, starting with those who had testified in support of the defendants supposed alibis.

He was quick to point out how most of them were related to one or more of the defendants, and would be expected to support their relatives. He marveled at how consistently the witnesses managed to be awake just when the trouble occurred, and how often they just happened to be looking at a clock to tell what time it was.

Then turning to the witnesses who had testified about the Brownings' reputation and truthfulness, he again pointed out how many of them were relatives of the defendants, and how few of them could testify who had told them that the Brownings were not trustworthy.

He was quoted telling the jurors, "They say the Brownings won't tell the truth, they told the same tale in the examining trial, the court of inquiry and the present trial."

As he was making this argument, one of the attorneys for the defendants privately, without interrupting him, said he objected to that argument. The judge privately responded to him "I was watching it, I don't think it is incompetent."

At least that was how the Court remembered it. The defense remembered a slightly different version that went like this. "They say the Brownings won't tell the truth and bring a bunch of witnesses here to testify to their bad reputation for truthfulness, but they told the truth about that still and have been here three times in this case, the Court of Inquiry, Examining Trial, and in the present trial and they have told the same story each time."

Finally, turning to the penalty for this crime and the possibility that some jurors might be concerned about its length, Creal reminded the jurors that while the penalty was life in prison, "it is a matter of common knowledge men do not stay in the penitentiary longer than ten years because of weak-kneed governors and parole boards," to which defendant's lawyers objected and the Court admonished the Commonwealth Attorney to argue the fact in this case.

Hobson L. James, the Elizabethtown lawyer, began the closing arguments for the defense. He spent much of his time, pointing out the inconsistencies and contradictions in the Brownings' testimonies, but also challenged the prosecutor's assumption about them telling the same story repeatedly by pointing out that telling something over and again in much the same words doesn't make it true.

He dwelt for a time on the various testimonies as to the Brownings' bad reputation for "truth and veracity and morality," pointing out that in a rural community like the Leaches District, it was natural for families to be related, especially by marriage, and that who would know the Brownings better than their neighbors and the people who dealt with them on a regular basis.

C. P. Bradbury came last. He agreed with the prosecutor's contention that it was largely only relatives and close friends who supplied alibis for the defendants, and then made the point, why wouldn't it be like this. He challenged the jurors to consider who might come to their defense if they were falsely accused of a middle of the night crime; wouldn't it be their own relatives and close friends as well?

He then turned to the question of reasonable doubt. Pointing out the bad feelings among the Brownings themselves, testified to by several witnesses in which they quoted Lou Browning as saying she would have to get rid of Kate somehow, he offered that as a possible explanation for the death. He then described the testimony of witnesses to the claim by Peachie Browning that he had shot someone that night, and suggested it might have been Kate.

Reminding the jury that to convict they had to be certain "beyond a reasonable doubt" that the defendants were responsible for Kate's death, he encouraged them to weigh all these factors, and if they did, he was certain they could return no other verdict than "not guilty."

Both sides had now presented their best case; it was the jurors' turn to decide.

Verdicts Reached

According to his watch, it was ten o'clock that evening when the judge dismissed the jury to begin deliberations. It had been a long two days for everyone, and no one was surprised when the jury sent word less than two hours later that they would not be reaching a verdict that evening.

Judge Richardson directed Sheriff Monroe to take them to the Griffin Hotel for the night, and return Wednesday morning to continue considering the case.

Almost no one had left the courtroom that evening while the jury deliberated. Kinsmen and friends had gathered around the defendants, encouraging them and wishing them well.

The rain continued to fall as everyone departed into the night. Those defendants who had not been released on bail had the shortest journey, returning the the stone jail behind the courthouse. Never comfortable, the cold, damp stones would chill both body and soul of its occupants until the morning sunlight reached it.

The jury of twelve Hardin County citizens resumed deliberations at eight on Wednesday morning. As they returned to their room, the courtroom continued to fill with men and women, many with babies in arm, to await the verdict.

The town was clearly divided on what that verdict should be, and feelings were running high.

Prohibitionists and members of the Anti-Saloon League were naturally outraged that bootleggers and moonshiners had killed poor defenseless Kate Browning and attacked her kin. On the other side were friends and neighbors of the defendants angered that they were accused on such testimony as that given by the no-account Brownings.

There were even some who whispered behind their hands that it was a shame the attackers hadn't completed the job and gotten rid of that pack of thieves and liars.

The jurors deliberated all day, sending word to the judge on several occasions that they had not reached a verdict.

Then at 5:30 they returned to the courtroom, still undecided, unable to reach a verdict. Judge Richardson reminded them that the case was very important, one that many witnesses had been heard on both sides, and in his opinion it would require a lengthy deliberation to be fair with themselves and the defendants.

Following a meal, the jury continued to deliberate until 8:15 that evening, when they again reported that they were deadlocked, and asked permission to retire for the night which was granted.

Speculation was rampant with many convinced that the case would result in a hung jury. One newspaper even reported that it had learned the vote was split nine to convict and three to acquit.

Thursday morning arrived, and at ten o'clock the jury sent word to Judge Richardson that it had reached a verdict. When all had returned to the courtroom, the judge asked jury foreman Ben Ailes if they had reached a verdict. The room as deathly silent as he stood to speak.

"Yes your honor, we have." There were gasps heard throughout the courtroom. He then announced that all the defendants were found guilty and sentenced to life imprisonment.

Because the verdict had not named each defendant, the jury was instructed to return to the jury room and rewrite the verdict.

Frank Hodge's sister was in Mr. Carroll's office when she learned the jury was reporting. She seized her three-year-old daughter's hand and rushed into the courtroom.

While the jury was rewriting the verdict, the little girl walked to the steps at the foot of the bench of Judge Richardson and, looking up at him, appealingly asked, "Are you going to let my Uncle Frank go home with me?"

Judge Richardson, obviously touched, but unable to offer the child any comfort, turned away, and the child's mother came forward to get her.

When the jury returned, Mr. Ailes again stood, and this time read the following verdict: "We, the jury find the defendants Clarence Crenshaw, Elmer Crenshaw, John H. Bolton, Frank Hodge, Selby Hodge, Les Hodge, Golden Hodge, Jim Harris, and Frank Kinder, each guilty as charged in this indictment and fix the punishment of each to confinement in the penitentiary for life."

Judge Richardson had Mrs. O. H. Roby, Circuit Court Clerk, poll the jury. Each member of the jury answered, "That is my verdict."

Later, members of the panel would tell reporters that, during the fourteen hours they deliberated, there had never been any thought of dismissing any of the defendants, but that they desired to consider the evidence and court's instructions thoroughly before reaching a verdict, and that time was consumed in deciding upon the penalty for each of the defendants.

Meanwhile, defense lawyers announced "We have just started to fight. We will ask for a new trial, and if it is denied we will file an appeal, and make a motion for bond for our clients pending the disposition of the appeal."

The nine defendants were escorted to the local jail to spend the night. Meanwhile their lawyers worked deep into the night, preparing their motion and grounds for a new trial to be presented the next morning.

All returned to the now nearly empty courtroom the next morning where Judge Richardson examined the documents. Their motion had included twenty-nine grounds to set aside the verdict and grant them a new trial. It appeared obvious to the judge that no more than a handful of the grounds listed had any possibility of merit.

Believing that none of those had any bearing on four of the defendants, he overruled the motion for a new trial for the defendants Elmer Crenshaw, Frank Hodge, Selby Hodge, and Frank Kinder, each of whom then requested an appeal to the Court of Appeals which was granted.

He passed on the same motion for the remaining five defendants and continued it until the third day of the regular July Term, giving himself time to examine them more carefully.

Because of overcrowding in the local jail, six of the defendants, including Frank Kinder, Elmer Crenshaw, and the four Hodges, were transferred by Sheriff Monroe to the jail in Louisville on Sunday following the trial.

On July 28, 1928, Judge Richardson entered an order overruling the motion and grounds for a new trial for Clarence Crenshaw and John Bolton. An appeal to the Court of Appeals was granted to each of them.

In the same order, Judge Richardson wrote, "As to Golden Hodge, Les Hodge and Jim Harris, their presence and participation in the crime charged, not appearing from the testimony, of any other witness, and except Bennie Browning and Peachie Browning, and each of these three defendants being identified by only one of these witnesses, the said three defendants ... are each given a new trial."

Clarence Crenshaw and John Bolton remained in the Bullitt County jail pending their appeal. The other three was granted bail with their bonds set each at $500, and tentative trial dates set for November.

Court of Appeals

The summer wore on into autumn. The lawyers were busy presenting motions and counter-motions in their brief before the Court of Appeals. In November, the circuit court continued the trials of Golden Hodge, Les Hodge and Jim Harris to the April 1929 term, and they remained out on bail.

Then in December the Court of Appeals heard the case against Clarence and Elmer Crenshaw, John Bolton, Frank and Selby Hodge, and Frank Kinder.

After eliminating a number of the grounds given for a new trial, deeming them either repetitious or immaterial or non-prejudicial, the court examined first the issue of whether or not it had been lawful to call a special term of the circuit court to hear the case by posting notice at the courthouse door. After a lengthly examination, the Appeals Court ruled that proper procedures had been followed and overruled this ground.

The court then considered four alleged general errors including "(1) that the verdict is flagrantly against the evidence, and is not sustained by it; (2) error of the court in the admission and rejection of testimony; (3) misconduct of the commonwealth's attorney in his argument to the jury and the latter's misconduct, as well as that of the officer having it in charge; and (4) erroneous instructions and refusal of the court to give to the jury the whole law of the case."

The first error was rejected by the court after reviewing the transcript of the original trial. Essentially they did not believe the alibi testimony given by the defendants, but did believe that of the prosecution witnesses.

The second error, that of admission and rejection of testimony referred to the admission of testimony regarding the capture of the still, to the conversation Kinder had with Lou Browning, and to John Bolton being seen with a load of meal going in the direction of the still. The court ruled that these were admissible as they went to the matter of motive in a conspiracy. It also referred to the rejection of testimony regarding the theft of shotgun shells at the Deatsville store, and the apparent theft of a shotgun from a neighbor. The defense contended that this testimony would have supported the idea that the death of Kate Browning was the result of a family feud. This too was rejected by the court.

The third error contained two parts. The first part argued that, in his closing statement to the jury, the Commonwealth's attorney improperly referenced the likelihood that, if convicted, the defendants would not serve more than ten years due to governor's pardons. The Appeals Court ruled that "although the remark may not have been altogether proper" it was not sufficient to authorize a reversal of the verdict.

The second part referred to a charge that the jury had not been properly supervised, especially while on daily visits to the barber shop for shaves or haircuts. Both sides had presented affidavits to support their position. The defense had affidavits from both barbers that contended the jurors had been unsupervised at multiple times. However, the sheriff and all of the jurors had signed affidavits swearing they had faithfully followed the orders of the judge regarding their conduct while jurors.

There was also a question about how a Louisville newspaper had allegedly determined that the jury was supposedly deadlocked nine to three, with an implication that the sheriff might have been the source. The court found no evidence that this had occurred.

The final error, or grounds for reversal, was an argument that the judge's instructions to the jury had been flawed, hinging mostly on the question of conspiracy.

The Appeals Court reviewed this carefully and, after making the statement, "conspiracies from their very nature are most generally incapable of proof by direct testimony; hence the courts throughout the country permit the prosecution to take a wide range, and to establish the conspiracy, if possible, by circumstances corresponding to links in chains, and from all of which the jury are authorized to infer that a conspiracy existed," ruled that this ground was also rejected.

The Appeals Court ruling ended with the following statements.

"In conclusion, we deem it proper to say that this crime, as has been hereinbefore intimated is one that staggers credulity. It is inconceivable that in this day of civilized enlightenment people could be found who for a moment would entertain, much less undertake to execute, the thought of engaging in such savagery as this record portrays, but which testimony in this record strongly supports the conclusion *was* entertained and partly executed by the appealing defendants, who attempt to overthrow all the guilty evidence against them with their weak alibis, and by proving the pitiable standing in the community of their victims.

"We have concluded, from a painstaking study of this record, that defendants have had a fair trial, and that the record discloses no error prejudicial to their substantial right, and the judgment is affirmed."

With their appeal denied, Clarence and Elmer Crenshaw, John Bolton, Frank and Selby Hodge, and Frank Kinder would spend this Christmas in jail.

The Tide Begins To Turn

The case was back in the news in early February when several newspapers reported that the defendant Frank Hodge had made a confession to the authorities shortly after the Appeals Court had rendered its verdict.

The story broke when Sheriff Monroe removed John Bolton and Clarence Crenshaw from the Nelson County jail where they were being held and transported them to the Frankfort Reformatory. The other four, Frank Kinder, Elmer Crenshaw, Selby Hodge, and Frank Hodge were being held in the Louisville jail.

According to Sheriff Monroe, Frank Hodge had implicated three additional men in the crime, but had indicated that two of the three men still awaiting new trials were not members of the mob.

He was to be held in the Louisville jail the next day when the other three were transported to Frankfort, and would be given an opportunity to testify before the upcoming April grand jury at Shepherdsville.

Neither Mr. Carroll nor Mr. Creal would make any statement regarding the confession except that Creal was quoted saying, "to give any details of any statement that Frank Hodge may have made would be to let the cat out of the bag."

Sheriff Monroe indicated that the only comment by Bolton and Crenshaw on the way to the prison was, "it seems bad that we have to go to prison for life for something somebody else did."

Then in the first days of April, the papers reported that Frank Hodge, in his confession, said he had nothing to do with the shooting or firing of the cabin. He said "they tried to get me to do something, but I begged off."

The papers also reported that the three defendants still awaiting new trials had elected to ask for separate trials, and Jim Harris would be tried first.

Frank Hodge testified before the grand jury, and then was called as a prosecution witness in Jim Harris' trial. There, according to an Owensboro newspaper, he detailed how the mob, wearing black robes and carrying black masks, set fire to the cabin and shot down the fleeing occupants in a plot to "wipe out the Browning family."

As he was testifying against Jim Harris, it became clear that he was declaring that his two brothers, Leslie and Golden Hodge, were not part of the mob.

The names of the three additional men named by Hodge as participants were Claude Coleman, Calvin Good, and Henry Crenshaw.

However, the grand jury reported having heard no evidence corroborating these charges, and adjourned without returning any new indictments in the case.

It took the jury of twelve Jefferson County men less than fifteen minutes to return a guilty verdict and sentence Jim Harris to life in prison. After Judge Richardson denied his motion for a new trial, Harris decided not to appeal his conviction, and a few days later he and Frank Hodge were taken from the Bullitt County jail to Frankfort to begin serving their sentences.

New trials for the two remaining Hodges were scheduled for the July term at Shepherdsville. Then in July they were continued to November. It was beginning to appear that they might not come to trial again.

Two things on the national level were also beginning to affect this situation. The first was the stock market crash that occurred in late October 1929, which signaled the beginning of twelve years of depression. As we earlier noted, difficult times for farmers had begun much earlier in the decade, and now the panic was spreading across the entire economy.

Second, prohibition was not working. History tells us that more liquor was being consumed than ever, and prohibition had not only failed, but had created a new level of crime led by gangsters who became rich on illegal liquor.

The battle over prohibition was far from over, but the tide was turning. And the economic woes facing the nation as the century's fourth decade began would change a lot of minds about a lot of things.

Some people were beginning to question if the nine defendants had received a fair trial. But Maude Greenwell had never had any doubt but that they hadn't, and had always said so.

Maude Hodge had married James Greenwell in 1918, and they were living in Louisville with their daughter Dorothy when James was killed in a fall down an elevator shaft in the warehouse where he worked in November 1929. His death, and her sense of the injustice she believed her brother Selby Hodge had received, led her to lead the drive to petition for a pardon for him.

In May 1930, newspapers reported that Governor Fleming D. Sampson had received the petition to grant an immediate pardon or parole for the twenty-two year old Selby Hodge.

The petition was based of the claim that Selby had no part in, or knowledge of the crime. Interestingly, the petition was signed by Commonwealth's Attorney E. W. Creal, and former County Attorney T. C. Carroll who had prosecuted the case. Further it was signed by Judge Richardson as well as members of the jury that had convicted him.

The newspaper reported that Mrs. Greenwell stated, "Selby was convicted on the testimony of Mrs. Lou Browning that he was with Frank on the road when the Brownings fled from the burning house and were fired upon. It is true Frank was on the road, but he had begged off of taking any part in the attack. The person who ran away with Frank and called after him was his wife, Stella, who was trying to get him away so he would not be involved in the trouble in any way. Frank wanted to tell the truth at the first trial, but was persuaded by others not to, as they all thought they could beat the case."

The paper also reported that Bullitt County officials expressed doubt whether two of Selby's brothers, Golden and Leslie Hodge, would be tried again.

It would take several more months, but records show that Selby Hodge was released in September 1930, by Governor Sampson on a pardon.

An Almost Final Chapter

By the end of 1935, all of the remaining defendants would be freed, but Selby Hodge would not be there to greet them. A Sunday picnic in early August 1932 was the scene of a gun battle that saw Selby fatally wounded.

His cousin, Owen Hodge who was also shot multiple times, reported from his hospital bed, "there were lots of people at the picnic. Selby Hodge and his wife have been separated about a week and were standing to one side talking. I was talking to James Fox. Fox thought Selby was talking about him and I told him it wasn't true. He kept on saying Selby was talking about him, and said he was going to 'fix' him. He pulled his pistol and shot. I don't think Selby had a chance to get his pistol.

"Then the other Fox boy got into the trouble and I got my pistol and started shooting at the Fox brothers. Several others got mixed up in it, but I don't know just who. I know I hit one fellow over the head with my pistol."

Selby Hodge died a few minutes after falling with five bullet wounds. In December, Jim Fox was convicted of killing him, although he pleaded self-defense at his trial. Selby's sister Maude had rescued him from prison only to lose him to the violence fostered by the prohibition era.

The next year, when Governor Rudy Laffoon left the state to attend Franklin Roosevelt's inauguration in early March, the state constitution made Lt. Governor A. B. Chandler Acting Governor of the state. Chandler took this opportunity to issue multiple pardons and commuted many more sentences, including that of Elmer Crenshaw.

On March 6th, Chandler commuted Crenshaw's sentence from life to nine years, making him eligible for parole. Crenshaw was released a day or two later, after serving four years and twenty-nine days.

Then at the end of June, Governor Laffoon commuted Frank Hodge's sentence to eight years, making him eligible for parole, and he was almost immediately released.

The following March (1934) it was Clarence Crenshaw's turn. The governor, on March 29th, commuted his sentence to ten years, and he was released. *The Courier-Journal* reported that the governor said clemency was recommended by many outstanding citizens of the community in which the crime occurred.

"It appears from the record," the Governor said, "that the evidence upon which this conviction was had was almost, if not entirely all, circumstantial, and that it was given by the members of one family, whose mother [sic] was killed according to the charge in the indictment. It appears that the members of this family bore an unsavory reputation and were mental derelicts, some of whom had been committed to institutions of the State because of the commission of petty crimes. It is stated that the reputation of these witnesses for truth and veracity is not the best."

He continued, "The record discloses that the real intention of those charged with the commission of this crime was to rid the community of the presence of an undesirable family that had been giving it considerable trouble by the commission of petty offenses, which of course, was an unlawful act and should never have been engaged in, but when once begun was hard to control, and that the killing, while not at first contemplated, was in fact done."

He said he was informed Crenshaw had lost his life's savings as result of the trouble and that his wife died after his conviction, apparently of a broken heart, leaving a family of children.

It would be more than a year before the last three were released. In late August (1935) Governor Laffoon commuted the sentences of John Bolton, James Harris, and Frank Kinder to twelve years and they were paroled.

The newspaper reported the governor said that clemency for the three men was requested by (now) County Judge C. P. Bradbury and County Attorney Lindsey Ridgway. Also, Judge Basil Richardson had urged clemency for Bolton.

And now they were all free. But life would never be the same.

Frank Kinder returned to his family on their Bullitt County farm. By 1942, the family address was Star Route, Shepherdsville, and Frank was employed by Will Burns. The family put the terrible times behind them and moved on. When Frank died in September 1974, he was described as the devoted father of four sons and a daughter, and the beloved husband of his wife Fannie.

Jim Harris was a life-long bachelor. He may have wandered a bit after his release, but he returned to Bullitt County eventually. He was 76 when he died in 1950, leaving behind two sisters to mourn his passing.

Elmer Crenshaw does not seem to have returned immediately to Bullitt County. According to the 1940 census record, he was divorced and living in Louisville in the household of his sister-in-law, Ruby Crenshaw, widow of his brother Emmett. Elmer was working in a distillery at the time. Elmer and Ruby later married. When Elmer died in 1971 at the age of 70, he was living on Star Route, Shepherdsville, and was survived by three brothers and a stepdaughter.

Frank Hodge returned home to his family, and appears to have lived out his life in the area. According to his obituary, he died in January 1972 at the age of 75. By then it seems they had moved to the Cox's Creek area of Nelson County. He left his wife, Mary Stella, three daughters and two sons, a sister, and two brothers (Golden and Les) to mourn his loss.

As described above, Clarence Crenshaw's wife Lula died while he was in prison. Her death certificate indicates that she died of a cerebral hemorrhage; however Governor Laffoon may have been right when he said she died of a broken heart. For a time Clarence's sons Walter, Morris, Clarence, and Millard worked to keep the farm going; but debts soon put an end to that, and most of them ended up living and working in Louisville.

It appears that when Clarence was released he joined his son Morris who was living and working on a farm on Blue Lick Road in Jefferson County. He seems to have passed the remainder of his life in that area. His obituary indicates that he was living with his sister in Okolona on Preston Highway when he died in November 1949. He was 74, and survived by five sons and a daughter.

John Bolton was 52 and a relatively prosperous farmer when he went to prison. He was 59, and in poor health when he was released. He returned to his family in Bullitt County, but they soon moved to Jefferson County where he died in June 1941.

The Pioneer News wrote the following about him at that time. "John Bolton, 65, formerly of Shepherdsville, died at his home in Louisville. Mr. Bolton lived and reared a large family in Bullitt County in the Cedar Grove community. In recent years he made his home in Louisville. Failing health for several years has caused Mr. Bolton to be missed around his native county. Bad eyesight with other complications caused him to remain close to his home. Death was caused by a heart ailment."

And so came the end to the lives of these men who, but for one terrible night, might have lived much differently.

Lou Browning's Family

What became of Lou Browning's family?

They left a few traces that we can follow, some of which are speculative, based on records which we believe to be theirs, but might not be.

All five are listed in the 1930 census, living together in the Mt. Washington census district, although not necessarily in that town itself. However, both Ben and Peachie (Jerry) are also listed in the Franklin County census record for the Kentucky Feeble Minded Institute.

Both are listed in the institution's records as arriving in May 1919, and leaving in July 1930, and are listed as runaways. We speculate that they had run away prior to 1928, and that the institute removed them from their records in 1930 when it was clear they were not returning. However, it is possible that they returned there following the trial, and stayed a short time before deciding to leave on their own.

We know that at least part of the family was in Lexington, Kentucky by the end of 1934, as *The Lexington Leader* reported that Jerry Browning had assaulted Amanda Jones, fracturing her shoulder. This occurred on New Year's Eve. They were both living at the same address on Perry Street. He was charged with assault and battery, but that was amended later to breach of the peace, and he was given a 50 day jail sentence.

Then, in November 1935, the newspaper reported that Bennie Browning had been arrested for being drunk and for breach of the peace.

The 1940 census showed Lou, Ben and Mandy's son Elmer all living at the same address on Perry Street where Jerry had assaulted Mandy in 1934. Meanwhile, Jerry had apparently married Mittie Wilcher for they were living with Mittie's two grown sons nearby on Valley Street.

Neither Mandy nor her sister Angie (Susan Minnie Browning) were living at either location. However, we do find a Mandy Jones in the census as a patient at the Eastern State Hospital for Insane in Lexington.

It seems that the family members were all too frequently in trouble with the law. In early January 1942, *The Lexington Leader* listed Minnie Browning, Jerry Browning and Bennie Browning in Police Court, charged with breach of peace.

Then in November, Bennie was back before the Court charged with breach of peace, and this time the penalty was fifty days in jail. His name popped up again in 1944 with similar charges.

Then in February 1947, *The Lexington Herald* printed Bennie Browning's obituary. According to his death certificate, he had died of uremia, complicated by hemorrhagic hepatitis. In layman's terms, his drinking likely damaged his liver and brought on his death.

His obituary stated, "He is survived by his mother, Mrs. Lou Hilton Browning, Lexington; a brother, Jerry Browning, Lexington, two sisters, Mrs. Burt Hatchett, Lexington, and Mrs. Amanda Jones, Danville." The Mrs. Burt Hatchett apparently refers to Susan Browning, but we have no record of this marriage.

Except for two instances, in 1958 and then in 1962, when we find newspaper notices of a Mandy Jones having someone appointed to handle her affairs due to her incompetence, the family largely disappears from notice.

Then in June 1962, *The Lexington Herald* printed Lou Browning's obituary. It read, in part, "Mrs. Lou Browning, 71, of 944 Valley Avenue, died at 3 p.m. yesterday at her home after a long illness.

"Mrs. Browning was born in Bullitt County, a daughter of the late Joe and Liza Hilton Browning. She was a member of the Catholic Church.

"Mrs. Browning is survived by two daughters, Mrs. May Bowles, Covington, and Mrs. Mandy Jones, Lexington; a son Jerry Browning, Lexington, a half-brother Jim Hardy, Bullitt County, and five grandchildren."

Once again we have a different name attributed to Susan Browning. It does tell us that she was living in Covington, Kentucky then.

Jerry's wife Mittie died in August 1965.

After that we find little evidence of the remaining family until an article appeared in multiple newspapers around the state in September 1991, reporting that a lady named Ann Hamilton, living in Covington, had been arrested after police found a decomposed body thought to be her mother, who had been missing for several years.

Hamilton had been using her mother's name to obtain food stamps and Social Security benefits.

The police identified the mother as Susan Browning.

The landlord had become very suspicious when fellow tenants told him that a lawyer from Lexington had been at the house about a month ago. Browning's sister had died, and the lawyer was trying to find Browning.

There was no doubt but this Susan Browning was Lou Browning's daughter. Her Social Security records made that clear.

Hamilton said she had hidden the body and continued to collect the checks at her mother's orders; and later newspaper reports suggest that Miss Hamilton had been dominated by her mother from childhood.

Investigations led authorities to decide that Susan Browning had died in bed in January 1987, more than four years earlier.

From the report about the lawyer from Lexington seeking Susan due to the death of her sister, we think Mandy Jones may have died in July 1991, as there is a Mandy Jones of Lexington listed in Kentucky records as dying then.

Finally, in February 1996, a Jerry Browning died at the age of ninety. He was living in Lexington at the time. We have no way of know for certain that this is the same man, but we think it is.

Assuming these facts to be accurate, the lives of this Browning family were primarily blessed only with longevity. It seems that the highlight of their apparently desolate lives came in that courtroom back in 1928, when for perhaps the only time in their lives someone cared about them.

The Final Chapter

Who shot Kate Browning? For that matter, who decided it was time to teach those thieving Brownings a lesson? It must have begun there; a decision that blossomed into the idea of running them out of the community, once and for all.

It is unlikely that it began with the notion of killing anyone. Despite the fact that many of these men were engaged in moonshining, they were basically decent human beings who felt they were being pushed too far.

More questions come to mind. Who decided to wire the door shut and set fire to the house? Did everyone of them know the door had been wired shut, or was it the act of one particularly vengeful individual. Who decided to fire shotguns at the door? Did it begin as a way to scare the Brownings, and then escalate into something more deadly?

Who fired that final blast into the chest of Kate Browning? Was it by one who had taken too many swigs from the jug that night, clouding his judgment?

None of these questions will likely ever be answered. The men who knew what truly happened have taken that knowledge to the grave.

And this ends our story; a tragic story that shattered many lives, a story that has no happy ending.